# Muslim Women and the Politics of Participation

*Gender, Culture, and Politics in the Middle East*
Leila Ahmed, Miriam Cooke, *and* Simona Sharoni, *Series Editors*

# Muslim Women and the Politics of Participation

Edited by

## Mahnaz Afkhami and Erika Friedl

Syracuse University Press

First Edition 1997

14  15  16  17  18      7  6  5  4  3

∞ The paper used in this publication meets the minimum requirements
of the American National Standard for Information Sciences—Permanence
of Paper for Printed Library Materials, ANSI Z39.48-1992.

For a listing of books published and distributed by Syracuse University Press,
visit www.SyracuseUniversityPress.syr.edu.

ISBN: 978-0-8156-2760-9

**Library of Congress Cataloging-in-Publication Data**
Muslim women and the politics of participation : implementing the
     Beijing platform / edited by Mahnaz Afkhami and Erika Friedl.—
     1st ed.
               p.   cm.—(Gender, culture, and politics in the Middle East)
          "The book . . . is based on the philosophy of the Beijing Conference
     and the PFA without being doctrinaire"—CIP introd.
          Includes bibliographical references (p.      ) and index.
          ISBN 0-8156-2759-9 (alk. paper).—ISBN 0-8156-2760-2 (pbk. :
     alk. paper)
          1. Muslim women.  2. Women's rights—Islamic countries.
     3. Women's rights—Religious aspects—Islam.  I. Friedl, Erika.
     II. Series.
     HQ1170.M8473    1997
     305.48'6971—dc21          97-25582

*Manufactured in the United States of America*

# Contents

# Acknowledgments

This book is based in part on the proceedings of the conference "Beijing and Beyond: Implementing the Platform for Action in Muslim Societies," which was convened by the Sisterhood Is Global Institute 9–11 May 1996 at the George Washington University in Washington, D.C. Grants from several donors, including the Ford Foundation, the Shaler Adams Foundation, the Caritas Fund of the Tides Foundation, and the James R. Dougherty, Jr. Foundation, made the organization of the conference and production of the book possible. We are grateful for their generous assistance.

The conference and the book also benefited from the unfailing support and encouragement of a number of individuals who lent both efforts their energies, resources, and know-how. We are particularly grateful to Margaret Schink, president of the Shaler Adams Foundation, who gave us advice and guidance as well as moral support throughout the process of preparing for the conference. James Piscatori of the Council on Foreign Relations, Marjorie Leightman of the International League for Human Rights, and Patricia Ellis of the Women's Foreign Policy Group arranged for special events with conference participants and helped in various ways to make the conference a success. Margot Badran, Shahla Haeri, Deniz Kandiyoti, Ann Mayer, Fatima Mernissi, Robin Morgan, Gretta Hoffmann Nemiroff, and Farida Shaheed were most generous with their time and counsel. We are thankful for these friends and colleagues' advice and appreciate their ongoing cooperation with SIGI.

Diane Landino, SIGI's administrative assistant, took on much of the work of the organization of the conference and handled the task with efficiency, dedication, and good humor. Grace Ogden, who handled the media relations, did a great job to make an esoteric subject almost mainstream. SIGI program assistant Sonja Lichtenstein's punctuality and attention to detail were invaluable assets in getting the manuscript moving expeditiously between the authors and editors. We thank them for their expertise and hard work.

Above all, we owe our appreciation to the contributors to the book, whose diligence and timely responses to our requests made it possible to produce this collection in time for the second anniversary of the Beijing conference. We thank them for the wisdom, knowledge, and expertise they brought to the project and for making the work of compiling and editing the volume a pleasure. We are especially grateful to Cynthia Maude-Gembler of Syracuse University Press, whose faith in the project and constant support helped us cross with ease and equanimity the many hurdles that attend a work of this nature.

Clearly, what is good in this volume owes much to the organizations, colleagues, and friends we have mentioned, and to many others we cannot possibly name here. The shortcomings, of course, are ours only.

# Introduction
## Mahnaz Afkhami and Erika Friedl

### Background

The United Nations Fourth World Conference on Women in Beijing in 1995 was a threshold in women's struggles for women's rights; 189 national governments signed a document that explicitly states that women's rights are human rights and that all issues are women's issues. Ninety governments made commitments to take specific measures to implement the conference recommendations in their societies. For the first time in history women were situated at the center of global politics, associated with the concept and practice of power. The document in which this point is made most directly is the mission statement to the *Platform for Action* (PFA) of the Beijing conference.[1] The first and second articles read:

> 1. The Platform for Action is an agenda for women's empowerment. It aims at accelerating the implementation of the Nairobi Forward-looking Strategies for the Advancement of Women and at removing all the obstacles to women's active participation in all spheres of public and private life through a full and equal share in economic, social, cultural and political decision-making. This means that the principle of shared power and responsibility should be established between women and men at home, in the workplace and in the wider national and international communities. Equality between women and men is a matter of human rights and a condition for social justice and is also a necessary and fundamental prerequisite for equality, development and peace. A transformed partnership based on equality between women and men is a condition for people-centred sustainable development. A sustained and long-term commitment is essential, so that women and men can work together for themselves, for their children and for society to meet the challenges of the twenty-first century.
>
> 2. The Platform for Action reaffirms the fundamental principle set

forth in the Vienna Declaration and Programme of Action, adopted by the World Conference on Human Rights, that the human rights of women and of the girl child are an inalienable, integral and indivisible part of universal human rights. As an agenda for action, the Platform seeks to promote and protect the full enjoyment of all human rights and the fundamental freedoms of all women throughout their life cycle.

In December 1995 the U.N. General Assembly adopted a resolution fully supporting the Beijing recommendations.[2] It calls upon "states, the United Nations system and all other actors to implement the Platform for Action" by promoting a "policy of mainstreaming a gender perspective at all levels" (ART. 3) "to ensure that the gender dimension influences other areas such as poverty, housing, the environment and sustainable development."[3] In the resolution the General Assembly charges governments with "the primary responsibility for implementing the Platform for Action" (ART. 4) and with developing "comprehensive implementation strategies or plans of action" no later than 1996 (ART. 6), including "national machineries for the advancement of women" (ART. 7). It calls for monitoring by U.N. organizations (ARTS. 9, 10, 11) and for "the integration of a gender perspective in budgetary programmes" and for adequate financing of programs for securing equality between women and men (ARTS. 12, 13).

The point of the U.N. resolution and of the Platform for Action is to empower women, to promote social change in the direction of gender equality. In the platform are demands that debates by intellectuals, activists, and politicians about the status of women now be followed by concrete action on national, provincial, and grass-roots levels. The prospects of empowering women in Muslim societies, however, nowhere are as self-evident as the U.N. institutions and the U.N. resolutions suggest. In fact, in many predominantly Muslim countries, especially in North Africa and the Middle East, human rights conditions for women have deteriorated since the early 1970s. Economic conditions have worsened, democratic institutions are being challenged, religious radicalism with its androcentric political agendas has increased. Some of the governments that in 1975 had accepted the major international documents on human rights in principle now reject many of these rights on the grounds of a supposed conflict with specific local cultural practices. In the 1994 Cairo Conference on Population and Development, for example, Islamic and Christian fundamentalists, the higher leadership of the Catholic Church, and some Asian governments united in opposing women's universal human rights and jointly questioned the validity of women's rights on doctrinal or cultural grounds. They challenged the concept of universal human rights as a Western ploy, as cultural imperialism and intellectual colonialism. Muslim fundamentalists declared Islam as the only valid parameter of rights for Muslims.

Under these circumstances the implementation of the Platform for Action requires more than U.N. resolutions, signed documents, good will, and debates. Women need to study the specific historical and cultural contexts in which they are positioned, reconceptualize deeply rooted gender ideologies, question the so-called self-evident truths couched in various traditional interpretations of religious and legal texts, identify and dismantle patriarchal structures, and learn new strategies for managing social relations. All of this also requires large numbers of well-informed women of all walks of life who know how to debate, mobilize, and lobby at the regional and national levels, who are committed to the goals of the PFA, and who are ready to take great personal risks to realize them. Quite obviously, it is easier to talk about "women's empowerment" than to bring it about.

The first modern context for the promotion of women's rights in the Middle East was provided by the idea of progress defined as national economic and social development. A modern state had to educate women, for example, to spur economic development or, alternatively, to indicate to the world a commitment to building a progressive society based on equality. In most Muslim nations middle- and upper-class women demanded rights for women and were the main beneficiaries of new rights and opportunities. In the liberal-Left political dialogue women's rights and feminist issues were raised but within a class perspective subordinated to larger, utopian ideas of "liberation." Gender and gender relations as they pertained to everyday life within family and community were largely ignored. As a whole, therefore, women and their concerns were not seen as important enough to pose a threat to patriarchal social structures. Consequently, men treated women's human rights as a fiduciary function linked to such traditional concepts as "honor" and *harim*, rather than as a serious sociopolitical issue. It was, therefore, relatively easy for governmental delegates from Muslim nations to agree to the demands of the First World Conference on Women in Mexico City in 1975.

By the 1990s, however, conditions in Muslim regions had changed significantly. Socioeconomic development had helped many women to become educated, to become financially independent, and to reach positions of authority and responsibility. Women became visible. Even if only very few reached higher management ranks, their public presence could not be ignored but instead became emblematic of women's aspirations and potential achievements. During their "development" women became increasingly conscious of a gap between their human rights and social needs, on the one hand, and their objective conditions, on the other. They started to make public demands. Now "women's rights" became a serious issue; the patriarchy was faced with a challenge, and it began to react.

The most obvious strategy for those who felt threatened was to link women's rights to cultural imperialism, which made it easy to attack the very idea of women's rights. This strategy can be used by secular nationalists, who seek to achieve economic and social parity with the West, as well as by religious fundamentalists, who see in the West and its values a grave danger to the institutions they associate with Islam.

The Islamist argument is advanced on two levels: universalist and relativist. On the universalist level Islamists declare that the moral and legal principles of Islam are divinely willed and, therefore, apply to everybody, that they are superior to any man-made laws or principles, and that they will supersede the latter wherever Islam is practiced.

On the relativist level the argument is based on cultural relativism, which accords every society the right to practice its own customs and laws free of interference and judgment by others. No cultural practice is better or worse than any other. Using this argument, Islamists insist on honoring concepts and practices they present as authentic Muslim traditions, including what human rights activists see as unequal gender relations, and reject universal injunctions, such as those stated in the international documents of rights, if they contradict their preferences. In other words, an extreme relativist stance does not allow for universally binding norms in regard to human rights. This stance, which has the support of some Western intellectuals, at worst undermines any effort to advance women's rights over local objections as long as the objections are phrased in terms of cultural autonomy and cultural authenticity. At best, it promotes sensitivity toward local sensibilities, caution in suggesting courses of action that might seem nonindigenous, and change from within a culture with solutions to problems formulated by the respective people themselves.

Islamists insist that Islamic law ought to be universal law. To the extent that this law is claimed to be divinely ordained a set of paradoxes arises. The most obvious paradox is that protagonists belonging to different schools of Islamic jurisprudence in various Muslim societies adhere to different versions of a law all of them claim to be of divine origin and, therefore, immutable. A second paradox arises from the coupling of the law and culture in the sense of the proposition that at some golden period the Muslim *umma,* the community of believers, actually lived according to the proposed law. This contention forces the lawgiver to be in perpetual conflict with the forces of change, including those that assist women to achieve freedom and equality. A third paradox, resulting from the second, converts a demand whose legitimacy is claimed on religious grounds to a political confrontation increasingly sustained by the use of force. Thus, success actually diminishes religion by stripping it of its basic moral appeal. A fourth paradox, thus, is that Islamic fundamentalism must logically debilitate Islam as religion. Because Muslims, however, including Muslim women, need to believe as Muslims, it follows that Islam will have to be reclaimed against, or reimagined independently of, fundamentalism. This last point is materializing now within the civil society in most Muslim countries, including those that are governed by Islamist regimes.

Indeed, many Muslim women have begun to take an active interest in theological arguments regarding women. They claim the right to interpret laws and religious texts themselves and to learn the skills necessary for such interpretation; they challenge androcentric and misogynist interpretations of texts; and they are determined to find in Islam justifications for demanding individual freedom and women's rights. They have, in other words, joined the political struggle over the right to make their religion work for them.

Such an undertaking is by no means easy. It implies that women (and sympathetic men) must challenge not only political and religious authorities who rule over them but also values that are deeply rooted in their cultures and, therefore, instrumental to their identity. They must question the commonsense truths by which their communities function: the family, the village, the workplace, the city, male-female relations. They must dare to displease those who are near them emotionally and on whom they depend in times of need. They need to acquire the skills to identify and use resources to which they have little access. Nowhere is this more difficult than in Muslim countries where religious authorities, anti-Western and anti-modernist sentiments, Islamist agendas, and weak economies form very strong barriers to women's realization of their rights.

Discussing such issues women are hampered by the limitations and essentialist connotations of the terms *Muslim, Islam,* and *Muslim women.* These terms are problematic because they easily make people think in stereotypes that conceal a rich variety of different beliefs, practices, life-styles, and philosophies in Muslim societies. Many of these are diametrically opposed to others; all are enmeshed with local cultural traditions that historically cannot be justified with reference to Islam. Yet they frequently are used to deny women rights in the name of Islam. They are used as political tools to retain, forcibly where necessary, a status quo that favors certain classes of people over others or male interests over female rights. For activists working for the advancement of women's rights in these various Muslim societies skills in separating cultural conditions that impede women's rights from "Islam" often are crucial to success; one can argue that people are more likely to let go of mere "customs" than of their religion. Any attempt, however, to separate culture from religion will meet resistance. Those whom customs privilege will seek to legitimize them by linking them firmly to theology or religiously inspired law.

Although interference from outside, including the United Nations, may be resisted frequently for those reasons, international agreements on certain minimal standards for the treatment of women nevertheless are crucially important for the advancement of women's rights. These documents provide women everywhere with models they can use to compare and assess their situations. They also provide international standards by which every nation signatory to them must measure its performance.

Experience suggests that state intervention on behalf of women can enhance women's rights and improve women's conditions significantly, particularly in the fields of law, economics, and education. In the Beijing Platform for Action governments are made responsible for establishing the organizational structures, that is, the national machineries, necessary for the platform's implementation. The prevailing sociopolitical conditions in Muslim societies, however, make it unlikely that governments seriously will promote women's rights and expand services for women without some pressure. Few Muslim states have women's rights–related agencies. In some, even nongovernmental organizations devoted to women's affairs have little official support or have been co-opted by governments. It then falls on the international community to accelerate the human rights–women's rights momentum generated during and after the Beijing Conference, to give support to local activists, and to monitor the fulfillment of promises by individual governments.

Although many Muslim governments are reluctant to implement the Platform for Action, grass-roots movements concerned with women's issues are growing just about everywhere in Muslim countries. Women and men sympathetic to women's rights realize that women cannot change their society without the cooperation of those in power positions, mostly men, and without exercising political leadership themselves. Such leadership starts in the family and community and extends from there. Activist women also realize that awareness of rights is the first step in gaining a political voice and the political power to gain rights. Traditional power structures raise intellectual, emotional, and social obstacles against the attainment of such knowledge and awareness and integrate women into these barriers: for example, as "good" mothers, women socialize their children into unequal gender relations; as "good" wives and managers of their households, they are rewarded for their cooperation in the "patriarchal bargain";[4] as "good" sisters they selflessly advance their brothers' aspirations. But by playing the games of those in power women undermine their own positions and those of other women. By listening to fundamentalist sermons and reactionary political slogans that are designed to make apparent sense of their subordinated positions and restricted lives they miss opportunities to envision alternatives. By obeying decisions by others about their lives they perpetuate the myth of their social immaturity. Clearly, any advocacy of human rights has to start with education that deals with the politics of knowledge and power and with raising critical awareness of the limitations the women's own cultures impose on them.

It is encouraging that many women in Muslim societies (e.g., in Jordan, Morocco, Egypt, Pakistan, Turkey, Bangladesh, Iran) have taken the lead in studying, developing, and implementing strategies for women's empowerment. They do not necessarily study the Platform for Action itself, although many do, but they investigate possibilities that lead them in the direction of women's rights from within their cultural practices: they probe possibilities of interpreting the Quran and the *hadith* themselves, for example; they educate the political elite about specific women's concerns; they formulate and lobby for women-friendly legislation and policies; they establish dialogue among people of different backgrounds and experiences and national and international decision makers; they organize training sessions for literacy, legal literacy, marketable skills, health education; they disseminate information, organize local women's groups. For the time being, their goals seem moderate: they want to modify traditional customs and laws to accommodate women's needs, including the freedom of choice in their personal lives; they want equality with men before the law; they want to be heard and to be taken seriously; they want to get more rights, better education, more access to paid jobs, religious education. These are the prerequisites for the sweeping changes spelled out in the PFA. Given the prevailing religious and political trends in most Muslim countries, these efforts amount to an heroic undertaking that requires international awareness and support.

## The Book

After the Beijing conference, concern with women's rights and the advancement of women shifted from debating and formulating policies to finding practical ways to transform plans and commitments into action. To this end, in May 1996 Sisterhood Is Global Institute (SIGI) called a conference in Washington, D.C., Beijing and Beyond: Implementing the Platform for Action in Muslim Societies.[5] Women leaders from Asia, North Africa, and the Middle East and representatives of the United Nations, the World Bank, and international human rights organizations addressed an audience of 250 nongovernmental organization (NGO) activists, scholars, journalists, and policymakers.

Conference participants explored strategies for implementing the Beijing Platform for Action, focusing on political decision making and leadership. A necessary component of the search for ways of ensuring women's participation in political decision making and leadership is education in the broadest sense—from legal literacy to human rights awarenesss, from women's studies to the use of literature as a tool for creating civic awareness. Speakers presented case studies of projects underway in Muslim societies that serve as vehicles for implementing the Platform for Action.

The conference created lively interest among the participants but also in the media and in other institutions, organizations, and individuals concerned with human rights. Apparently, there is no lack of opinion and scholarship on the topic of women's rights in theory, but there is a dearth of knowledge on how to bring about those human rights in practice. The enthusiastic response to the conference and many inquiries about it prompted the creation of this book.

Some of the papers delivered at the Washington, D.C., conference are included in this book; others were elicited from experts and practitioners in the field. All speak to various aspects of implementation, and their different views, concerns, strategies, caveats, demands, and suggestions reflect the divergent experiences of women pioneers working in the complex and varied societies of the Muslim world. There is not as yet a solid body of knowledge of practices that work and pitfalls to avoid that activists can fall back on when they encounter difficulties in the field. There is not yet a well-defined common ground on which elite women and ordinary women living in quite different circumstances in the same country can meet easily. But there is a perception of the need for such common ground—for a body of knowledge that would articulate women's rights in ways that are not easily dismissable as "elitist," "Western," or "feminist" that could help activists to be proactive and to avoid being put on the defensive.

To the best of the authors' knowledge this is the first book devoted entirely to a discussion of these problems, of the ways, means, and possibilities for the implementation of the Platform for Action in Muslim societies. It reflects the current state of implementation studies: to define obstacles and devise ways to circumvent them; to agree on priorities; to channel divergent opinions into constructive dialogue; to lift the discussion of human rights implementation off the sticky ground of patriarchal squabbling over "right" and "wrong" interpretations of religious texts or laws and "authentic" versus "alien" ideas and practices onto a plane where Muslim women are able and willing to articulate freely their own concerns and then find ways to achieve redress.

The book, then, is based on the philosophy of the Beijing conference and the PFA without being doctrinaire: in the book, women from different Muslim countries and cultural backgrounds and with different agendas address topics they feel strongly about within the general theme of women's rights in the widest sense. Some of the contributors are optimistic, some pessimistic; some are adamant in their sweeping demands, others cautiously tread on slippery ground; some speak to general topics, whereas others describe the workings of very specific programs. All together, these women scholars' and activists' words amount to a loud and vigorous chorus that encourages women's hopes for the future of women's rights in the Muslim world.

The first part of the book is devoted to a theoretical assessment of some issues in the realization of the Platform for Action.

Deniz Kandiyoti explores what makes some Muslim women support measures of their own control in the discourse of "moral rectitude" and cultural authenticity and integrity of Islamist as well as reactionary secular groups. She suggests that the regulation of gender relations often is a site of struggle for contending power factions and easily elicits populist consensus, much to the detriment of women's rights. As a political ideology Islam is used to legitimize regimes and their practices of domination, which makes it difficult to establish democratic structures wherein women enjoy full human rights.

Boutheina Cheriet points out that the human rights discourse, which slowly developed out of a humanist tradition in the West, cannot be in tune with local cultural practices in the Muslim world immediately. The author explores various stages of Algeria's interactions with "the West," including the upsurge of anti-Western sentiments and political programs that problematize the acceptance of documents like the Platform for Action. Only by encouraging debates about human rights issues within Muslim countries and by making these issues a concern of the people rather than merely of politicians or outsiders can one hope to achieve social change benefiting women.

Azza M. Karam describes three main different "feminisms" operating in Egypt: the secular, Muslim, and Islamist ones. Of these, the rhetoric of Islamist groups has led to an Islamized political discourse that bolsters Islamic power and hegemonic knowledge to the detriment of women's rights. This hegemonic knowledge must be challenged by other feminists if women-friendly laws, the Platform for Action, and "Western-inspired" international treaties on human rights are to succeed.

Ann Elizabeth Mayer, reviewing some recent laws and legal cases involving women in Libya, Pakistan, Egypt, Sudan, and Iran, warns that Islamic rationales are being used by the courts to subordinate women and that human rights are violated with claims to compliance with religious law, the Shari'a. Yet the vigor of the women's rights discussion sparked in Beijing, and the widespread official acceptance of the *Convention on the Elimination of All Forms of Discrimination Against Women (CEDAW)* make it politically increasingly uncomfortable for governments openly to defend measures that harm women. Therefore, the pressure of these international movements indeed can counter and challenge successfully the politically reactionary use of Islam against women.

In the seven articles in the second part authors describe specific strategies, activities, or programs designed to bring about change in awareness, in skills, and in knowledge that enables women to take matters into their own hands.

Nimat Hafez Barazangi forcefully pleads for Muslim women's strong and direct participation in understanding Islam in all its dimensions. Otherwise, women not only are deprived of a fundamental human and Muslim right but will not be able to formulate their own goals, take responsibility for them, and attain freedom and dignity. Only "islamic higher learning" can challenge the misogynist patriarchal practices and interpretations of Islamic scriptures that pose as "Islamic" today and allow women to enjoy fully the rights and privileges of free human beings without having to substitute for their religion a Western, alien value system.

Azar Nafisi uses a famous story from *One Thousand and One Nights* to demonstrate how a critical reading of classical literature can change one's attitude toward adversarial circumstances in one's life and can, thus, make it possible to resist and to change creatively these circumstances. She shows how effective literature can be in shaping women's consciousness and in sharpening their abilities to influence their own situations in positive ways.

Fati Ziai addresses the problems that Islamism, or certain political uses of Islam, pose for governments and activists who wish to promote women's rights. She describes some effects of legal codes and their interpretations that are based on Islamic law on women and the family in Morocco, Algeria, and Tunisia. Because many of the provisions in the Shari'a perpetuate gender inequality and, thus, inhibit the full realization of human rights, strong women's advocacy groups such as the Collectif in the Maghreb, have to be vigilant, outspoken, and politically active to prevent the ascendance of discriminatory practices in the name of Islam.

Sharifah Tahir argues for the need to train young Muslim women to take on leadership positions within groups and organizations that advocate women's rights. All too often, she points out, young women in patriarchal societies lack self-confidence, role models, and opportunities to learn and to practice skills in articulating concerns, negotiating, debating and arguing, in the formulation of programs and agenda, and in working within organizations. Older, experienced women leaders and NGOs and other institutions as well need to mentor young women to maintain the momentum of the Platform for Action.

Eileen Kuttab and Laurie E. King-Irani both deal in their respective chapters with the possibilities of women's studies programs and institutes devoted to research on women. Kuttab describes the women's studies program at Birzeit University; King-Irani speaks of her experiences at the Lebanese American University. Women in such programs, working within universities or colleges, not only can be crucial for the raising of consciousness among students and the gathering of scholarly information on women's circumstances in a region but can use their links to a well-developed infrastructure for all kinds of activist purposes and for crisis intervention. Yet the close link to an often rigid administrative authority and lack of independent funding also make such programs vulnerable to political changes.

Mahnaz Afkhami introduces the first practical, detailed, step-by-step manual that can be used by anybody working with Muslim women to make them aware of their rights. The manual's goal is to enable Muslim women to think through and discuss their understanding of themselves, of their relationships within the family and the state, and of their rights and responsibilities as Muslim women. It is built on dialogue and participation and on indigenous values rather than on Western cultural assumptions. The introduction and two sessions serve as examples.

In the third part of the book five representatives of international organizations describe the work of their organizations in terms of benefits to women in Muslim societies.

Maryam Elahi assesses the organizational tools and the possibilities of bodies such as Amnesty International and the United Nations for promoting the rights of women after Beijing. She notes that the growth of the women's movement has resulted in increasing power to advocate and to monitor women's rights on all organizational levels especially after the rights of women as human rights had been affirmed at the Beijing conference. Human rights organizations such as Amnesty International now have become more gender-sensitive and more willing to be outspoken and active on behalf of women.

Mervat Tallawy brings her experience as a diplomat to the discussion of the importance of national machineries for the realization of the goals of the Platform for Action. She credits an increased participation of women in the formulation of goals for women's rights with recent successes but also points out that the international media's sensationalist attitude toward happenings in the region, fluctuating policies of donor-countries on issues such as population control, economic development, and human rights, and the use of religion as a political tool of oppression pose impediments to the full realization of women's rights.

Seema Kazi, taking up the issue of women's legal literacy, describes the work of Women Living under Muslim Laws (WLUML), a network of activists whose goal is to teach Muslim women to recognize and to fight discriminatory codes and laws and to be aware of existing laws they can use to their advantage. Making women aware of the fact that laws and legal interpretations vary widely among Muslim societies and that references to religion must be seen within the context of textual interpretations, gives women confidence to engage the legal process for their benefit.

Roslyn G. Hees explains how the World Bank can promote the goals of the Platform for Action in the region and that it has to be careful to fashion policies that are in tune with individual countries' cultural and political conditions to promote effectively the enhancement of gender equality. In several examples the author demonstrates that the awareness of local circumstances increases participation in the formulation of strategies and that supporting projects that target women directly and encourage their participation greatly benefits women's rights.

Noeleen Heyzer and Ilana Landsberg-Lewis together describe the work of the United Nations Development Fund for Women (UNIFEM), a U.N. organization that supports women's programs on all levels by advising governmental agencies, NGOs concerned with women's rights, and economic planners how to incorporate gender-sensitive plans and programs, how to involve women in setting national priorities, and how to translate the PFA into international, national, and local policies. With examples from some Muslim countries the authors illustrate how UNIFEM's funds and organizational expertise can help women in individual countries to devise their own PFA-related strategies.

# Contributors

**Mahnaz Afkhami** is the executive director of Sisterhood Is Global Institute (SIGI). She is the author of *Women in Exile* and editor of *Faith and Freedom: Women's Human Rights in the Muslim World.*

**Nimat Hafez Barazangi** currently is a Visiting Fellow in the Women's Studies Program at Cornell University. Her most recent publication is an edited volume, *Islam, Identity and the Struggle for Justice.* An activist for women's rights, she currently is working on self-identity and Islamic higher learning of Muslim women as a human right.

**Boutheina Cheriet** is a writer and professor of Comparative Education and the Sociology of Education at the University of Algiers. Presently she is a Visiting Fellow at the Brookings Institution, working on a book on comparative fundamentalism.

**Maryam Elahi** is the program officer for the Middle East, North Africa, and Europe at the Washington, D.C., office of Amnesty International. She has frequently testified before United States congressional committees and has met with U.S. administration officials to discuss human rights issues. She has been a mission delegate for the International Secretariat of Amnesty International to Turkey in 1991 and 1995, Northern Ireland in 1993, and Turkmenistan and Egypt in 1995.

**Erika Friedl** teaches anthropology at Western Michigan University. She has spent many years doing ethnographic research in Iran, mostly on women's and children's issues.

**Roslyn G. Hees** currently is chief of the Human Resources Division, Maghreb and Iran Department, of the Middle East and North Africa Region of the World Bank. Before joining the World Bank in 1979, she was coordinator of International Programs at the Population Reference Bureau, Washington, D.C., and assistant resident representative, U.N.

Development Programme in Haiti. She was a member of the World Bank delegation to the Beijing conference.

**Noeleen Heyzer** has been the director of the United Nations Development Fund for Women (UNIFEM) since October 1994. Under her direction, UNIFEM is implementing a comprehensive agenda for women's empowerment. She is the author and editor of numerous books, articles, and papers on development and women's issues.

**Seema Kazi** specializes in women and development. She worked for several women's NGOs before joining Women Living under Muslim Law (WLUML) in 1993, where she is engaged in the Women and Law Programme of the Women's Research and Action Group (WRAG) in Bombay, India.

**Azza M. Karam** is a Research Fellow at the Institute of Development Research, Amsterdam University, and program officer at the International Institute for Democracy and Electoral Assistance in Stockholm, Sweden.

**Laurie E. King-Irani,** an anthropologist, has lived and worked in Lebanon for four years. In 1995 and 1996, she served as editor-in-chief of the quarterly journal *al-Raida,* which is published by the Institute for Women's Studies in the Arab World at the Lebanese American University in Beirut.

**Eileen Kuttab** is a lecturer in Sociology and the Women Studies Program at Birzeit University in Palestine and the former coordinator of the Women Studies Program from 1994 to 1996. As a founding member of the women's cooperative organization Our Production Is Our Pride and president of the Board of Trustees of *al-Haq,* a Palestinian institution for human rights, she is working as an activist for women's rights.

**Ilana Landsberg-Lewis** is a human rights specialist at the United Nations Development Fund for Women (UNIFEM). She has worked extensively in the area of immigration and violence against women.

**Ann Elizabeth Mayer,** associate professor of Legal Studies at the Wharton School, University of Pennsylvania, is a historian and legal scholar, and a specialist on Islamic and Comparative Law, human rights, and women within legal systems.

**Azar Nafisi** is a writer and activist living in Iran, and a former professor of English Literature in Tehran, Iran. She has written extensively on the images of women in classical Persian literature. Currently, she is working on two books: *Tatary: Western Literature under Persian Eyes* and *Novel and Morality*.

**Sharifah Tahir** works for an international nongovernmental organization in Kuala Lumpur, Malaysia, in the area of reproductive health. Her interest in women's rights began while she was working on women's leadership and management development projects in Asia. Among her tasks is the exploration of opportunities to catalyze leadership training programs for young women.

**Mervat Tallawy** is ambassador of the Arab Republic of Egypt to Japan. She has served in the Ministry of Foreign Affairs for more than thirty years. Her posts include deputy assistant for International Political and Economic Affairs and chair of the main subcommittee on Health and Reproductive Rights at the Fourth World Conference on Women.

**Fati Ziai,** a lawyer, currently is a legal adviser to the United Nations Mission in Bosnia-Hercegovina after having served as counsel to Human Rights Watch/Middle East, where she concentrated on Morocco, the Western Sahara, Israel, the West Bank, and Gaza.

# PART ONE

## Assessing Women's Rights Issues in Muslim Societies after Beijing

# I

## Beyond Beijing

Obstacles and Prospects
for the Middle East
Deniz Kandiyoti

Compared to earlier United Nations events, the World Conference
on Women in Beijing can be argued to have displayed novel tendencies
in two important respects. First, it was the occasion for the emergence
of North-South alliances on matters concerning sexuality and family
relations such as the one led by the Vatican, which found support
among some Muslim participants.[1] Although Catholics concentrated
on abortion and Muslims on the dangers of premarital sex, the common thrust of their interventions was to define these issues as matters
not of individual choice but of doctrinal necessity. This position
pointed to the existence of distinct political platforms that cut across
religious persuasions and regions.

Second, the Beijing conference highlighted the increasingly complex outcomes of processes of globalization and post–cold war restructuring and a greater awareness of their gender effects. Whereas in
previous conferences discussions on world development tended to
revolve around North-South disparities, in Beijing a more complex
picture was emerging. Women of the South took stock of the effects of
structural adjustment programs; women from postcommunist states in
Eastern Europe and the former Soviet Union pondered the implications of the retreat of the state and the transitions to market economies;
and women of the North reflected upon the increasing curtailment of
the welfare state and growing unemployment. This complexity made
the expression of similar concerns over welfare provision and social
services possible across very different contexts and regions.

The customary equation of individualism and liberalism with the
West appeared problematic. In the very heartland of industrial me-
tropolises, movements now exist that seek to combat the atomization
and anomie of postmodernity by taking refuge in nostalgic familism

3

and conservatism. According to Agarwal, "romantic sisterhood"—whereby women, despite cultural divisions, are defined as a self-evident constituency united in their oppression—was giving way to "strategic sisterhood" built on a heightened awareness of divisions among women but also on a keener sense of the necessity for coalition building to confront global crises in the economy and polity.[2]

From the perspective of those working in different areas of the Muslim world these developments can be viewed as quite liberating. They allow a shift in the discussion of women's rights from Islam as a religion to Islam as used as an ideology or as the basis of regime legitimacy. This shift, in turn, may encourage a more informed evaluation of prospects for the development of civil societies in which women's interests are variously defined and adequately represented. Once one situates Islam in the realm of politics it becomes susceptible to inspection through criteria used to evaluate political ideologies and practices. To what extent do movements and regimes that claim legitimacy through association with Islam actually represent diverging interests in society, including those of women and ethnic or religious minorities? What sorts of popular mandates do such movements seek? Do they generate regimes open to change through elections? What kinds of social control mechanisms are needed to ensure compliance with the demands of such regimes? These empirical questions can be dealt with only through an examination of concrete cases. The scriptural texts of Islam, although they are invoked and subjected to different interpretations by political actors with different agendas, are in themselves of little relevance in answering these questions.

The basic question is whether Islamist parties, movements, and regimes have the potential to generate nonauthoritarian, pluralistic societal outcomes.[3] Judging by recent debates on democratization and the civil society in the Middle East, the discussion of this topic appears to be stuck in a quagmire.[4] One of the most contested issues is that of democratic pluralism. Is political Islam likely to generate pluralism? Or is it inevitably locked into a religious fundamentalism that "is based on the principle of denying the rights of the other"?[5] Opinions range from qualified optimism about Islamist movements' openness to integration into a liberal political system as components of an emerging civil society[6] to unqualified pessimism on the part of so-called neo-Orientalists.[7]

Women figure in all these debates. I explore some of the reasons why women are targeted primarily and explicitly as objects of social control by Islamist governments and movements and ask how women may become active and enthusiastic participants in such projects.

## Women and Citizenship

The imperfect nature of women's citizenship rights in Middle Eastern societies with secularist regimes has been widely acknowledged.[8] It results mostly from a built-in discrepancy between constitutions that award equal rights to men and women and shari'a-derived personal codes that undermine this equality and even more insidiously from secular codes that define women as wards of men and their families. Joseph quite rightly points out that the notions of citizenship and of rights in the Middle East may be quite at variance with the liberal construct of autonomous citizens/subjects entering social contracts with the state that endows them with individualized rights.[9] She argues, instead, that rights and entitlements are mediated via membership in families and communities that are animated by a patriarchal logic that privileges certain members (elder males) and disempowers others (juniors and women). Hence, "patriarchy weaves together civil society, state, market and the family in Middle Eastern societies, subverting the separations and boundaries that Western theorists argue are necessary for democracy."[10]

I would not generalize this statement to all Middle Eastern Societies without qualifications. Rugh attributes the attractiveness of resurgent Islam in Egypt precisely to the need for a reordering of personal lives on a different basis: "To meet everyday needs, Egyptians now must move beyond primarily kin-centered relationships to personal relationships of broader instrumentality. In steering individuals toward loyalty to the *umma*, or community of Muslim believers, fundamentalist ideology gives direction to this tendency, and ultimately encourages a reorganization of society integrated at the suprafamilial level."[11] The same can be said of Turkey where the idiom of kinship and community, although powerful and pervasive, does not retain exclusive influence on societal interactions. Interactions may be mediated by a wide variety of "interest" networks and associations. Nonetheless, Joseph's insistence on the pervasiveness of patriarchy leads to an important observation, namely, that the emancipatory measures directed at women (education, employment, legal reforms) by postcolonial states were never intended to lead to a renegotiation of men's existing privileges but merely to endow women with additional capabilities and responsibilities. It may be argued that these additional capabilities inevitably created constituencies of highly skilled, professional women with a stake in changing the balance of gendered power in their favor both in the home and in the public realm. Indeed, these women animate the secular women's movements in Turkey, Egypt, and Pakistan, to name but a few. In Pakistan it was the poorer women who bore the brunt of General Zia's Islamization laws while middle-class, professional women, who were least likely to suffer from them, led the protest.

There is, moreover, a powerful populist argument that contends that these measures only affected the members of a narrow elite and a small number of upwardly mobile women of humbler background and that these benefits opened the way to new forms of domination and control. This result left the vast majority of women (and men) to face the problem of living in an increasingly "modern" society where the mingling of unrelated men and women in public settings and new forms of consumerism created new tensions and uncertainty. Even women who did enter the public arena as professionals, civil servants, or politicians did so against a background of deep ambivalence concerning the legitimacy of their presence there. For many, an Islamic regime thus may provide a welcome relief from these stresses and strains by legislating unambiguously the boundaries of the permissible and even creating areas of legitimate latitude. For example, young women in Iran, who previously might have been denied access to education by conservative families who opposed their exposure to unrelated men, after the revolution gained access to education as veiled women. The same can be said about women adopting modest dress in Turkey and Egypt. Many women use their new attire as a means of mobility rather than seclusion.[12] If patriarchy is the order of the day, why not obtain whatever protection one may from the laws mandating men to honor their divinely prescribed obligations? And if men do not fulfill them, it might indeed be more effective to contest from within an Islamic discourse rather than to invoke dubious notions of civil rights in societies whose records demonstrate that these scarcely ever apply to men themselves anyway.

It is one thing to fight for an expansion of women's rights in countries under Islamic regimes where there is little space for a secularist opposition, such as in Iran, and quite a different matter to fight for women's rights in states such as Egypt, Turkey, or Tunisia where Islamist movements are contenders for state power within a pluralistic and diversified context. In the latter case, mobilization against the erosion of already existing rights for women may be regarded as a nontrivial priority. Some even may argue that any other type of engagement would be defeatist and diversionary. Nonetheless, for reasons described above, a significant female constituency may find not only solace and solidarity in Islamic militancy but a legitimate route to greater empowerment. Militant Islamists, however, often employ a powerful combination of revulsion against an allegedly morally corrupt and imperialistic West, class resentments vis-à-vis privileged local elites seen as aping the West, and a populist construction of the "local" and the "authentic" in opposition to the West and to elites. This rhetoric produces a discourse of moral rectitude and cultural integrity with authoritarian overtones.

This discourse is by no means either the exclusive province or the creation of Islamist movements. One only has to analyze political platforms such as those of the Bharatiya Janata Party (BJP) in India to discover striking similarities in the will to codify cultural authenticity and to condemn "the foreign," which, in this particular case, means the Muslims. But governments in the Middle East and North Africa have actually privileged Islamist opposition movements by design or as a side effect of the suppression of potential secular opposition.[13] They did so in the face of grave economic mismanagement, the necessity to implement unpalatable economic reforms, and the rapid decline of legitimacy. When governments press Islam into service as a means of enhancing their legitimacy, little political space is left for the notion of a nonsectarian, pluralistic, secular society. In Egypt, for example, in 1971 the constitution under Sadat referred to the Shari'a as *a* primary source of legislation; by 1980 it had become *the* principal source. The liberalizing law of personal status of 1979 was repealed and became the subject of protracted negotiations. Laws were proposed to imprison those who publicly broke the Ramadan fast. Religious authorities close to the government sanctioned the murder of a secularist author. The highest civil court ordered the separation of a Cairo University professor from his wife on the grounds of apostasy. Islamists in Egypt, thus, are not so much fighting a secular regime as making a bid for state power made more likely by the policies of the Egyptian state itself. In Turkey only an explicit onslaught upon the constitution and the secular laws could bring the Shari'a into play, and there are still effective constituencies who would try to block such a move. Nonetheless, the influence of Islamist parties and interest groups has grown even as these groups maintain a discourse of injury and marginalization vis-à-vis the purported hegemony of state secularism. In fact, significant sections of the government have come under their control through successive coalitions. What one often sees is not a contest between secularist governments and Islamist oppositions but an attempt by discredited regimes to gain a longer lease on life through recourse to populist Islamist mobilization. The proponents locked in struggle need each other to perpetuate their respective ideological fictions: the Islamists that of the ungodly secular state, and the secularists that of the threat of fundamentalism. Both proponents use their claims to justify repressive measures and practices. Against such a background women's rights become a stake in politics in quite distinct and specific ways that merit detailed investigation.

## The "Policing" of Women as Instruments of Social Control

One need not take at face value the view that women are the primary site of the expression of Islamic regimes or treat this as self-evident. A substantial literature now argues that women are often singled out as the bearers of their culture's authenticity and are made to serve as boundary markers.[14] Nonetheless, why should anyone witness such a high degree of politicization and codification of gender relations in Muslim societies? Is this the core, the irreducible kernel of the Islamic nature of movements and regimes, whatever their institutional variations may be?

I argue that, paradoxically, the emphasis on appropriate Islamic conduct for women may not be the result of Muslim doctrinal imperatives or fundamentalist impulses but of regimes' pragmatic needs to maintain social control. The pressures of accommodation of the demands of new macroeconomic and global policies and of conflicting demands of internal constituencies create an environment where social order may be experienced as chronically precarious. In an increasingly globalized world the areas of social life where an Islamic will and intent may be fully expressed and actualized have narrowed and have become more rigid. There are many reasons why the control of women and the regulation of gender relations may emerge as issues which generate broad political consensus. For example, the issue of Islamic modesty of women may activate cross-class alliances among men. In Pakistan since the late 1970s an Islamic idiom was favored by the landed and industrial classes to attract the political support of the urban lower middle classes. Generally, one of the pillars of populist consensus is to create the fiction of a harmonious and homogenous national community by projecting division and dissent to the "outside" and by labeling nonconformist conationals as dangerous aliens. The emotionally charged subject of domestic mores is regularly invoked to underscore national values.

The regulation of gender relations may become a site of struggle for contending factions even within the "Islamic" polity. I find it significant, for instance, that in Iran, where an Islamic regime has been in place for almost two decades, the debates between so-called pragmatist clerics, who recognize a need for economic reform and certain rapprochement with the West, and the hardliners are centered around social mores. Hardline policies often take the form of restrictions placed on the airwaves and on women's bodies. Where there is no longer either a secular state or a political opposition to combat, enforcement of Islamic law may be seen as an attempt at social control. It has little to do with religious dogma as such but follows the logic of realpolitik. This logic may induce not only cynicism and covert resistance (such as so-called bad veiling, where women adorn themselves inappropriately or allow locks of hair to appear from under the scarf), but also contestations from within an Islamic discourse aimed at enlarging the scope and interpretation of women's rights. Clearly, in a situation in which the only source of legitimacy derives from Islam feminist women and men are constrained to press their demands into a religious framework. Many also genuinely believe that this is the most appropriate way to enlarge women's rights. It is quite depressing, however, that it has taken Islamist feminists in Iran nearly twenty years to claw back bit by bit the ground lost by the abolishment of the Family Protection Law of 1975. This demolition resulted from only one speech by Khomeini.[15] After twenty years the task is yet incomplete, and hard-won concessions may be called into question again any time.

What should be clear from the foregoing is that the control of women is primarily a vehicle for social control where political repression may take the insidious form of "policing" the mores of the population. The most extreme example was witnessed in Afghanistan during the occupation of Kabul by the *taleban* militia who imposed a literal curfew on women. The restrictions were protested on grounds that they contradicted local mores, that they victimized female heads of households who needed to work for a living, and that they immobilized hospitals and international projects involving women. The protests were in vain because the restrictions were primarily part of a "law and order" package that was welcomed by those who thought a strong hand was needed. It seems that authoritarian measures appear both more legitimate and palatable when they are presented as a return to the full implementation of Shari'a law. It also seems that in societies with little or no democratic legacy authoritarianisms that are well grounded in local customs have a greater chance of eliciting consent than the surveillances of secular police states, which are generally the alternative. Such measures are even more popular when religiously sanctioned discipline is coupled with anticorruption rhetoric and welfare programs for the poorest to create an image of the Islamically "just" society. That this "justice" should be based on the curtailment of women's mobility, women's access to education and to paid work, and equity within marriage with respect to divorce, child custody, and rights to maintenance, may appear as a rather small and unimportant point in societies where these rights are by no means assured anyway.

## Conclusion

My relative pessimism concerning the possibility of pluralistic outcomes for women under Islamic regimes derives neither from the assumption of some implacable fundamentalist logic nor from what I see as the nature of religion per se. It is based, rather, on the recognition that in an increasingly interconnected world where accommodation and compromise in almost every area of social life are essential to survival, the area of gender relations and of women's conduct singles itself out as a prime terrain for social control. Furthermore, the control of women is a type of social control that may elicit a populist consensus from both male and female constituencies.

This dim prognosis may be tempered by the realities of economic restructuring and liberalization in the Middle East and North Africa. These factors may alter gender relations by mandating higher and different types of input by women into the labor force. Indeed, Karshenas argues cogently that the economies of the Middle East cannot become sustainable unless they break with the pattern that keeps women outside the paid labor force.[16] Yet I must counter that many countries in the region have demonstrated remarkable resourcefulness to ensure the stability of gendered divisions of labor. Turkey, for example, was able to embark on a vigorous path of export-oriented industrialization without a significant shift in the gender composition of manufacturing employment.[17] This feat is at variance with the statistics for many other regions. In Turkey women swelled the ranks of home-based workers doing industrial piecework for low pay and unfavorable social security. And it took nothing less than the Gulf War to place women's electoral rights on the agenda in Kuwait. One, however, may draw solace from the knowledge that no ruling ideology can freeze social relations but that it is subject to challenges and contestation. The dynamism and sophistication of societies often prove impossible to contain by state apparatuses and their will for authoritarian control. Women are an integral part of that dynamism and sophistication, and the growing gap between their rights and their actual contributions is likely to remain a tenacious source of tension that will find expression in new forms of struggle and organization.

# 2

# Fundamentalism and Women's Rights

Lessons from the City of Women

Boutheina Cheriet

## World Conferences Between
## Idealism and Inductivism

In the late twentieth century many international conferences around
the world have marked the emergence of the "world community" with
a "new world order." This order is based on a democratic model of the
polity and on human rights as defined in the *Universal Declaration of
Human Rights* adopted by the first fifty-one members of the United
Nations in 1948. Although the intrinsic good intentions of such norms
seem beyond question, the very historical process by which they have
been expanded geographically poses the fundamental conceptual and
methodological problems of the universality of any humanly devised
norms.

The popularity of such gatherings coincides by and large with the
end of colonial dependencies and the emergence of postcolonial social
dynamics in about three-quarters of world societies. Although the colonies had been established and managed by Europeans whose humanist tradition and Industrial Revolution experiences included
democratic ideas and human rights, for them the colonial experience
was one of confrontation and destruction rather than of civilization
and liberation. Africa and the Middle East are still grappling with the
immense discrepancies between the institutional and the normative
dynamics that developed in the aftermath of national liberations.

Recalling colonial history is not meant here as yet another rant
against colonialism or imperialism but is meant to situate historically
the emergence of concepts such as "world community" and "universal
human rights" and to identify the conditions that surround reactions
today to universal programs by various social groups. It is necessary
to emphasize that in the West these norms were the result of centuries

of often painful transformations and debates. It took the Inquisition, the theological rifts within Christianity, the Enlightenment, the French and American revolutions, colonialism, and two world wars for the concepts of human dignity and human rights to emerge as a universal enfranchisement. Only late and reluctantly did this enfranchisement encompass Western women, colonized peoples, African Americans, and South Africans. The Western powers who advocated human rights were themselves ambiguous about their application—the same powers that today are urging world societies to adopt this normative system without delay.

The long and painful process of thinking and discussion that produced humanist norms in the West is denied to other societies. The universalization of modernization processes did not provide opportunities for local civil bodies to debate, formulate, and implement their own notions of modernity. This inductivist stance has produced resistance and questions in Muslim societies as elsewhere. Indeed, the adoption of a discourse as complex and comprehensive as that of human rights should not be taken lightly. The export of human rights is carried on under conditions of post–cold war globalization, and this is as problematic as the model of economic and social development introduced by the newly independent states of the early 1960s. The procedures of the changes were not derived from local developments and were not coordinated with local cultural practices but obeyed the immediate demands for particular social relations within the unitarian nation-state and international business interests. Little was said then about the democratization of the polity and of society, let alone about human rights. It is not surprising that the developmental philosophy of these induced policies produced strong reactions.

### Lessons from *Dar al-Islam*

The ambiguities in applications of human rights by their original champions pose the problem of credibility. Why is it that the very powers that had shown so little concern with the rights of others to human dignity yesterday, today demand respect for human rights from everybody? How is one to reconcile the skepticism toward human rights as a political program with other elaborate discourses with universalist claims such as the Islamic one? How is one to do justice to the great variety of reactions to the introduction of the human rights discourse in culturally diverse Muslim societies?

The importance of the recognition of this diversity is emphasized in three prominent historical moments in the encounter between Muslim and Western ideas and their implication for the issue of human rights:

1. The Arab cultural Renaissance *(nahdha)* of the late nineteenth and early twentieth centuries.

2. The culturalist religious Awakening *(sahwa)* of the Islamic Brotherhood and related organizations since the 1950s.

3. The struggle for a culture of humanism within the "City of Islam" by Muslim women.

The reaction of the thinkers of the Arab-Islamic Renaissance to the import of European Christians' ideas was extremely favorable, for it was expected to bring liberating notions and strategies that could help to end the tyranny of the decadent, stifling Ottoman monarchy. Mohamed 'Abdu and al-Afghani, for example, visited various European cities, self-confident and rooted in their rich theological and intellectual tradition, to find out about the societies of the West that reportedly had successfully reconciled matter and mind by liberating the individual. Their writings exemplify the Muslim intellectual curiosity that started the Arab-Islamic enlightenment quest with hope and vigor. This quest was stifled by the military and administrative colonial powers that soon occupied the region.

By the end of the colonial period not much was left of the lively encounters between intellectual equals that 'Abdu and al-Afghani had enjoyed in their travels. In their place among Arab intellectuals were a profound confusion, paradoxically created in the wake of the forceful expansion of the Western educational system, and a bitter feeling of loss and self-doubt. In this intellectual climate the newly established postcolonial civil societies generated various debates from within about human rights as citizens' rights (rather than as universal rights). This can be viewed as a second attempt to create a renaissance from within Muslim societies in the late 1950s and early 1960s. It, too, was crushed, this time by techno-military elites within the new states, posing as sole interpreters of the ideal society that they planned to establish. By then most regimes had signed various international conventions, including the *Universal Declaration of Human Rights*, although the majority of their populations never had heard about them and were far from benefiting from them.

The more recent culturalist claim of Islamic revivalism emerged from the confusion induced by unitarian nationalism. As the ideological eclecticism of the new states' elites legitimized the systematic violation of citizens' rights, salvation politics seemed the last resort for the increasingly younger, dissatisfied populations of Muslim societies. Their legitimation had to come from an authoritative, transcendental source. Unlike the earlier Renaissance thinkers who were trained in the classical traditions of Islamic institutions, the Awakening ideologues since the 1950s had a double education, that of state-run schools and the universities of the West, which alienated them from their own traditions. For example, Abbassi Madani, the leader of the main Islamist party, the Islamic Salvation Front (which had won the municipal election in 1990 and was expected to win the legislative elections in 1992), is himself a product of the secular educational system in the 1950s and London University in the late 1970s. He characterized what he saw as the basic principles of the Western epistemological tradition as doubt and chaos in human spirits. Atheist ideology has replaced faith in the West, leaving the individual in a quagmire of doubts. This idea indirectly expresses concern for the increasing blurring of gender roles and the increasing allegiance to the state as the regulator of society.

The adherents of the Awakening movement identify the West not only as a cultural invader bringing estrangement but as detrimental to the divine order, which relies on a clearly defined gender-based cosmology. In Algeria the emergence of the so-called Islamic fundamentalist movement as a primarily culturalist claim coincided with the access of thousands of Algerian households to European and American cable television programs. These were simultaneously watched and condemned strongly by Muslim youths, who criticized especially what they perceived as immodest behavior between men and women in films and the high profiles of female characters. Their opinion was formed without the mediation of the cultural commissars of the administration. It was heard and it created debates in all levels of the society.

Postulates of gender equality and individuation of women have triggered passionate debates and resistance to the implementation of laws and programs designed to achieve these goals. The implementation of the Beijing Platform for Action likely will meet with similar objections, especially so as the notion of human rights is rejected altogether; both "human" and "individual" in this humanist-universalist discourse are seen as faithless, non-Islamic concepts. But the discussion of this issue has not ended. It is shifting to the discussion of the rights of the human being as a believer *(huquq al-ansan wal-mu'min)* in the context of all kinds of global developments.

### Lessons from the City of Women

In Muslim societies women's rights as human rights constitute the single most important topic of debate and confrontation between state and civil society and among different groups within the civil society. Indeed, the problematic of rights is embedded in the debates over citizenry.

For example, the political riots of October 1988[1] started a period in the country when an active citizenry with highly divergent social ties and interests started to press its claims. Islamist fundamentalists, cultural Berberists, and secular feminists all voiced demands. The 1989 constitution recognized all claims but ambiguously declared the state to be both religious[2] and secular. The first officially recognized political parties were those with agendas to build an ideal Islamic society: the Islamic Salvation Front, with a program of establishing a pure Islamic social order, had mass appeal and attracted young men and women; Hamas, *Harakat al-mujtama' al-islami* (Movement of the Islamic Society), used a more moderate rhetoric about the gradual establishment of the Islamic society and was more popular with older professionals; Nahdha, a reformist group, was active only locally.

The culturalist Berberist movement, which demands the recognition of the native languages of Algeria as national languages, is divided into two groups: the Front of Socialist Forces, Front des Forces Socialistes (FFS), with a nationalist agenda; the Gathering for Culture and Democracy, Rassemblement Culture et Democracie (RCD), active locally in the northern Kabylia region and in some urban areas.

Of all groups it was the women's movement of the early 1980s that first drew attention to the contradictions within the state ideology which, on the one hand, granted enfranchisement since 1963 in various versions of the constitution to all citizens and, on the other hand, denied women decision power in matters of family and personal life. The early feminists were the first to practice civil disobedience when small groups of professional women and women war veterans publicly protested in front of the then National Assembly in 1981 and 1983. Their protests led to the adoption of the Family Code of 1984.

The reaction of the City of Women to family legislation based on extreme patriarchal injunctions remains the most radical expression of modernity in Algerian society. The unpublished literature produced by the various women's associations at that time very much is about human rights as citizen rights: the right to participate in all affairs of the society, to make decisions in the private and the public realms. The ideals of equal citizenry, free individual expression, allegiance to a national society are to be realized in a modern republic. Before the women's protests, these issues were blurred within the populist social contract of Algerian socialism.

The ambiguity was also debated by Islamists who contested the state's monopoly over the political life in the nation and advocated the establishment of an Islamic republic. This political program appealed to masses of young people between eighteen and twenty-four years of age (in a society where 70 percent of the population is younger than thirty), including many young women students, who found in this ideology a comforting affirmation of femininity that the emphasis on genderless citizenship of the feminists lacked.

However much traditional patriarchal ideals and practices are expressed in these agendas, they give young women the chance to exercise political choice, to transcend the confinement of close kin networks. Their participation in a political movement is an act of active citizenship. It enables them to become involved in the interpretation of the scriptural legacy and in more or less learned theology and encourages them to acquire skills in debates and argumentation. The cumulative effects of these activities and opportunities cannot be ignored. Eventually, these young women in Islamist movements will come to interpret scriptures and laws to their benefit and will become articulate in pressing for their advances.[3]

These activities are an exercise of human rights, including debates about women's rights, that come from within rather than from outside, from lived experience within certain ideological and political circumstances rather than from an Enlightenment that posited universal rights that ignored women and many other groups until those groups started to fight for their own rights.

After family laws and personal status laws in Algeria had been changed to conform to a particular version of Shari'a law in the early 1980s, feminists and Islamists alike were alarmed. Feminists criticized the de facto treatment of women as minors with no legal voice in decisions affecting marriage, divorce, or child custody, for example, while Islamists demanded that Shari'a law replace all laws, not only those pertaining to the family. Even within the Islamist movements young women used their authority as members of religiously grounded groups to challenge restrictive paternal authority and to insist on their right to choose a political stance. Women found themselves the center of arguments and included in confrontations and debates. Thus, the struggle for humanism within the City of Islam was taken up by women. The opinions of young militants of religious parties, despite their backing by impressive religious ahistorical justifications, failed to impress a great many women. During the period between the general civil disobedience protests of October 1988 and the army intervention in January 1992 thriving debates took place and various political and ideological positions about women's issues and including women were formulated. Women war veterans and young, self-declared secularist feminists faced representatives of the Islamic parties, notably Abassi Madani, on television shows in heated debates on any and all subjects.

After the Arab Renaissance and the Awakening movements, this was the third most important moment in Algeria's modern history: social actors, facing each other directly, without the mediation of some myths of unifying nationalism, and fighting over their rights and responsibilities, that is, over human rights. These are painful debates, but they are necessary for the kind of liberation that can be sustained and can flourish within the cultural boundaries of a society. Only this way can contestations lead to new understandings of human rights of Muslims and can negotiations lead to compromises that will hold.

The Beijing conference, the NGO discussions, and the U.N. forum witnessed various groups with different programs come to terms with each other over the issue of the philosophy underlying women's emancipation. The total and comprehensive enfranchisement and empowerment of women are moral and structural imperatives in today's societies, but they cannot be demanded from outside. They must be demanded from within, forged in debates, in conflict and consensus in every Muslim society. Those seriously concerned with the implementation of the Beijing Platform for Action must encourage debates in Muslim countries over the issues raised in the platform to create the momentum of local engagement and activism without which social change benefiting women is difficult to achieve.

# 3

# Women, Islamisms, and State

Dynamics of Power and

Contemporary Feminisms in Egypt

Azza M. Karam

> *In so many hundred pages, the word* mother *is mentioned only six times
> and fathers are not mentioned at all!*
> —Egyptian Islamist woman activist
> referring to the Beijing Platform for Action

## Introduction

The implications of political Islam[1] on larger political dynamics have
come under diverse and extensive academic scrutiny.[2] It also has received its fair share of attention for its impact on women's issues from
many women activists.[3]

Much feminist analysis assumes that Islamisms are dangerous
forces of darkness that will take away hard-fought gains by women's
movements. Research that refers simultaneously to the role of the state
in the triangle of state-Islamisms-women is scarce and tends to give the
impression that women are powerless vis-à-vis both state and Islamist
discourses. By contrast, I look here at the dynamics of power relations
between the state, Islamisms, and feminisms in Egypt. I examine different feminisms, the analysis of the dynamics of power, and the possible implications of the different feminisms on the implementation of
the Beijing Platform for Action in Egypt.

## Contemporary Feminisms in Egypt

I understand and use *feminism* as an individual or collective awareness
that women have been and continue to be oppressed in diverse ways
and for diverse reasons because of their gender, including attempts to
eliminate this oppression and to evolve a more equitable society with

improved relations between women and men.[4] The women I refer to as feminists are either affiliated with political parties or have stated political aims in their organizational and group agendas. Even committed Islamist women do not condemn all that comes from the West. One such woman told me, "We must not reject everything Western simply because it is Western. There are some aspects worthy of emulation."[5] An investigative category of "women's activism" is ambiguous. By identifying and isolating certain forms of women's activism as feminisms, I am simultaneously highlighting differences and locating specificities while placing them within a broader frame of reference. The latter facilitates recognition and, thus, permits comparison and inquiry.

In the debates on *equity* versus *equality* during the preparatory meetings and during the Beijing conference in 1995 the main difference between equity and equality seemed to center around affirming women's access to rights that do not necessarily equal those of men and women's rights that differ from those of men without being subjected to any form of hierarchy. The supposedly alternative term of *equity* was accepted by and actually pushed for by Muslim countries, and it was propagated and discussed during the Beijing conference by Islamists and their "pro-family" religious colleagues from non-Muslim countries as well.

Apparently, the women's rights terminology is problematic, even where the actual efforts are not. Whereas the term *feminism* is refused widely, some of its meanings and agendas are, nevertheless, adapted by different actors within different historical and cultural contexts. The rejection of the term *feminism* does not mean the absence of a feminist consciousness and agenda. The Beijing Platform for Action (PFA) ought to be viewed in this context: women's rights are based on an agenda close to feminism in the sense defined above and, thus, constitute an important emancipatory tool for women worldwide.

Feminisms and feminist movements have been challenged on the grounds of cultural imperialism, have been accused of defining the meaning of gender in terms of middle-class, white experiences, and in terms of racism, classism, and homophobia.[6] All these factors combined to make feminism a suspect identity-definition and category of analysis. Western feminist discourse and political practice are neither singular nor homogeneous in aims or analysis. But, as Chandra T. Mohanty argues, there are

> various textual strategies used by particular writers that codify Others as non-Western and hence themselves as (implicitly) Western.
> . . . [Certain] analytic principles . . . serve to distort Western feminist

practices, and limit the possibility of coalitions among (usually white) Western feminists and working class feminists and feminists of color around the world. These limitations are evident in the construction of (implicitly consensual) priority of issues around which apparently *all* women are expected to organize.[7]

Mohanty criticizes certain Western feminists for their "monolithic notion of patriarchy or male dominance" which supposedly oppresses all Third World women in the same way. She argues that "it is in this process of homogenization and systematization of the oppression of women in the third world that power is exercised in much of recent Western feminist discourse, and this power needs to be defined and named.[8]

Taking these criticisms one step further, one can argue that insofar as some Western feminism has essentialized, homogenized, and universalized women's oppression, it has created a metadiscourse in need of legitimization. For example, in the beginning of the Iranian revolution some Western feminists rushed to show solidarity with their Iranian sisters who were supposedly "oppressed by the revolution." Received rather coolly by their Iranian sisters, this zeal for feminist solidarity was somewhat tempered. Clearly, a feminism devoid of hegemonic and universalizing characteristics is needed. Many women from developing countries engage with feminism even while they sometimes reject the label. Amrita Basu notes that despite widespread resistance to "bourgeois" or "Western" feminism, women identify indigenous alternatives to Western-style feminism within their own cultural and political contexts.[9]

Kumari Jayawardena, writing about feminist movements in Asia in the late nineteenth and early twentieth centuries, defines feminism as "embracing movements for equality within the current system and significant struggles that have attempted to change the system."[10] Jayawardena asserts that these feminist movements emerged in two formative contexts: the formulation and consolidation of national identities during periods of anti-imperialist struggles and the recreation of precapitalist religious and feudal structures in attempts to "modernize" Third World societies.

Different forms of feminist activism correspond to the types of oppression women perceive in different parts of the world. I agree with certain postmodern conceptualizations of feminism, which advocate a theoretical outlook that "is attuned to the cultural specificity of different societies and periods and to that of different groups within societies and periods."[11] But most importantly, in rejecting a single feminist epistemology space is created for feminist political practices that earlier would have been regarded as unorthodox. Different feminisms, encompassing diverse priorities, fields of power and influence, and consequent activisms, are bound to have an impact on the development and implementation of local and international laws or covenants on women's rights. Hence, the need to take these specificities into account when looking at the ramifications of the Platform for Action and its implementation.

Three main types of feminist thought and praxis operate in Egypt today: secular feminism, Muslim feminism, and Islamist feminism.[12] These feminisms cover a broad political and sociocultural spectrum. Although on certain issues they may converge and act together (e.g., appealing to the ruling National Democratic Party to lobby for the lifting of sanctions against Iraq), they remain, in general, separated on many points along the lines of social classes and urban-rural backgrounds of the various feminists.

I use the term *Islamist feminists* because many of the Islamist women I interviewed are indeed aware of an oppression of women and actively seek to rectify it by recourse to Islamic principles. Nevertheless, most of the Islamist women I interviewed shy away from the term *feminist* if they do not outrightly criticize it as an irrelevant Western term. Although many still feel that feminism at best is ambiguous and at worst is disrespectful of religion, what several women Islamists uphold is difficult to separate from what feminism connotes. I intentionally refer to these Islamist activists as *feminists* not to homogenize them but to distinguish them from their male and other women counterparts who think differently, because not all Islamists are feminists by any means. Later the term is useful to indicate possible points of intersection with other women activists.

In the opinion of Islamist feminists women are oppressed precisely because they try to be "equal" to men and are, therefore, put in unnatural settings and unfair situations that denigrate them and take away their integrity and dignity as women. For example, women who are "forced" to go out and compete in the labor market will come into contact with men in a humiliating and unsuitable way.

In other words, for Islamist feminists it is the demands of a Western and culturally unauthentic ideology that oppress women. For them, Western feminism, with its emphasis on total equality of the sexes, results in women striving to be "superhuman" and in the process carrying more burdens. For Islamist women, a just Islamic society is one that strives for a recognition of and respect for compatibility between the sexes instead of competition between them.

Many of them, when directly queried, are reluctant to distinguish between women's oppression and social oppression in general. They see what is happening to women as part of a societal process wherein proper Islamic principles are absent or, at best, are misused by a morally bankrupt and corrupt state regime. Yet, they see their mission as a *structural jihad*[13] that is aimed at "change toward more Islamization," which, in turn, occurs through "active participation in all spheres of life."[14] This mission, then, is not merely a call for women to stay at home. It is a call to enhance and to credit traditional women's roles within the family with an Islamist feminist nuance that gives women a sense of value and political purpose in these gendered roles and a sense of confidence as well: women are not less than men but equally important in different ways.

Muslim feminists also use Islamic texts, but their aim is to show that the discourse of total equality between men and women is Islamically valid. Muslim feminists try to steer a middle course between interpretations of sociopolitical and cultural realities according to Islam and the human rights discourse. Some of these Muslim feminists make it their responsibility to analyze the different U.N. texts (e.g., *The Convention on the Elimination of All Forms of Discrimination Against Women [CEDAW]* and the PFA) and to explain their applicability within an Islamic cultural context.

Many of them are proud to be seen as feminists or, at least, have no problems with the term insofar as it describes their main aims. As far as these women are concerned, a feminism that does not justify itself within Islam is bound to be rejected by the rest of society and is, therefore, self-defeating. Moreover, Muslim feminists feel that attempts to separate Islamic discourses from other current ones (whether "Western" or not), can only lead to serious fragmentation within the society and are, thus, unrealistic options. Such a separation, many argue, will prevent mutual enlightenment between the two discourses and, in fact, will make the Islamic one more alienating and patriarchal and the sole domain of Islamists and/or the state.[15]

Muslim feminists look upon the issue of the veil, for example, as one that should be based on a woman's choice and conviction, whereas Islamist feminists take the veil as an indisputable religious obligation and as a symbol of the depth of religious conviction and solidarity with other Muslim—if not Islamist—women. For Islamist women the veil is a must; without it, women have not made the essential commitment to a particular ideal of authenticity of identity. In short, there are no unveiled Islamist women. More to the point, however, the veil is seen as a means by which to bridge the gap between the otherwise separate male and female domains. The veil becomes, therefore, not only a symbol of women's identity as Muslims but a holy, sanctioned, and acceptable means by which to broaden and to further women's political, social, and cultural space.

Muslim feminists see the present family laws in Egypt as in need of serious reform—a view with which their secular counterparts agree wholeheartedly. Muslim feminists, however, argue for the need to reinterpret the relevant Shari'a sections on which the law is based in light of modern exigencies, whereas secular feminists favor severing the Shari'a from the family laws altogether. Islamists, equally dissatisfied with these laws, argue that they represent the Shari'a only nominally and are not interpreted in the proper Islamic manner and, therefore, call for the Shari'a to become the basis of all laws, not just the family laws.

Both Islamist and Muslim feminists argue for *ijtihad*,[16] and many Islamist feminists agree with Muslim feminists that women are indeed capable of taking on tasks involving the interpretation of Islamic jurisprudence and providing social and political leadership that previously were thought to be the exclusive domains of men. In that sense both kinds of feminists are arguing against existing patriarchal religious hierarchies and the implications of their interpretations on gender, and both use very similar analyses and argumentation. Both are extensively studying, analyzing, and referring to traditional Islamic texts to validate and justify their arguments.

Although both sets of discourses challenge established forms of thinking, there is an important difference in relation to their political position and, hence, their share of discursive power. Islamist feminists are part of a political movement that actively attempts to raise support for its ultimate quest for state power and legislation. In their bid to combine the support of their organized and unorganized groupings, Islamists, particularly the moderates, cannot afford to lose the political, social, and economic backing of women in these Islamist movements. Simultaneously, Islamist women have successfully reversed traditional value judgments about women's spaces. Women's knowledge of the home and child raising have been given a higher esteem and more political significance. Moreover, within the boundaries supposedly imposed by their understanding of Islam women are still able to be active in the public arena.[17] Islamist movements resemble nationalist movements of an earlier epoch in their attempts to mobilize women for their causes. Thus, for the time being there are few attempts to curtail the public activities of these women, at least not by the moderate male Islamists, especially when many of these activities are like traditional charitable women's activities such as organizing (Islamic) literacy classes and instruction in sewing and household management. Moreover, as a discourse of resistance to state power and as creator of alternative social, political, and economic structures, Islamism has attained hegemonic power itself, and Islamist feminists—few as they are—share in this discursive power.

Muslim feminists, however, are more likely to be part of mainstream women's groups and as such lack comparable political backing and power. Moreover, just as for secular feminists, there is little support for these groups from the state. On the contrary, the state's ambiguity toward women complicates matters for all women activists. For example, much media time and space is given to conservative Muslim preachers who advocate women's return to the home as a cure for unemployment, crowded transportation, and a host of other societal ills at the same time as the official ruling party line condemns Islamists in general and identifies them with terrorists. Furthermore, given that many of the Muslim feminists are attempting to reconcile the discourses of Islam with human rights, they are facing the same accusations of cultural inauthenticity faced by other promoters of secular discourses.

Secular feminists admit to the necessity of maintaining at least a dialogue with Islamist women in theory but in practice disagree totally with their points of view and their teachings. Not surprisingly, secular feminists do not identify their Islamist counterparts as even remotely feminist. In turn, as promoters of a secular discourse, they are not held in high esteem by the Islamists, and any strategic—let alone ideological—arrangement, such as to agree or to disagree on an issue, is anathema to all concerned. They are, to be blunt, political enemies.

Secular feminists firmly believe in grounding their discourse outside the realm of any religion and place it instead within the international human rights discourse. They do not attempt to harmonize religious discourses with the concept and declarations pertinent to human rights. Religion is respected as a private matter but is totally rejected as a basis from which to formulate any agendas on women's emancipation. Thereby, secular feminists avoid endless discussions on the position and status of women in religion and challenges from religious conservatives to their (re)interpretations of religious texts as well. Nonetheless, against them the severest and potentially most debilitating criticisms are directed; they are called clones of the West, implementers of imperialist agendas, and nonbelievers.

Attempts to study the possibilities and the effects of implementing the PFA in Egypt are substantially influenced by several factors resulting from the dynamics described above. Internal conflicts among the different feminists indicate that a needed consensus in efforts to implement the platform is, as yet, lacking. Moreover, different perceptions of the PFA itself remain contested among Egyptian feminists. Ultimately, the power contestations surrounding women's issues worldwide must be addressed as part of the implementation of the PFA.

## Power Contests

The impact of the Islamist discourse on Egypt's political culture is already visible. Almost all political parties in Egypt now agree—at least verbally—that the Shari'a should be a principal source of legislation. As Moustapha Kamel el-Sayed observes, "The language of political discourse abounds with references to verses of the Quran and the traditions of the prophet as well as quotations from the writings of Muslim jurists and philosophers."[18]

Part of the reason for the Islamization of the political discourse lies in the awareness of all Egyptian political actors that Islam has the powerful popular appeal of authenticity in the face of uncontrolled Westernization that in itself results in social disorder and has a language that is understandable across all social boundaries. In other words, Islam is not merely a faith but a lived culture. As such, politicizing Islam, as Islamists from the time of Hassan al-Banna[19] have done, remains a logical step for mobilizing people and for capturing state power. To organize and mobilize, Islamists have resorted to their own techniques of disciplinary power. One such technique would do Enlightenment thinking proud: the use of dichotomies such as male/female, truth/untruth, Muslim/non-Muslim, Islamic/Western now has become an essential ingredient in Islamist attempts to distinguish themselves and their followers from the rest of society. Those who agree with their line of thought are "good" believers, whereas those who do not are enemies. Opponents of Islamist thought find their arguments delegitimized, ahistoricized, and placed out of context. For instance, secular feminist discourse is simply dismissed as being Western, at best unauthentic and at worst anti-Islamic.[20]

Thus Islamist discourse is gaining legitimacy as the only credible social, economic, and political alternative to the existing "corrupt," "undemocratic," and economically handicapped state. Successful social programs carried out by moderate Islamist groups help to reinforce the Islamist groups' assertion that "Islam is the solution." In other words, Islamisms gradually challenge an increasingly impotent state by creating alternative structures and ideologies that they legitimize through successes. It is becoming increasingly politically advantageous to adopt certain features of political Islam to gain popular support and political clout.

Not only opposition politicians but also governments capitalize on these aspects of political expediency. The Egyptian state has attempted to incorporate the "attractive" aspects of the Islamist political discourse such as the adoption of the Shari'a as the bases of legislation in the Egyptian Constitution, for example. Consecutive Egyptian presidents since Sadat have attempted to argue along the lines of a "holier than thou" attitude vis-à-vis Islamists in general.

As long as the discussion revolves around who is the better Muslim, one can expect a vicious circle wherein the more the state uses religious discourses to counter Islamist political hegemony, the more Islamists will rigidify their boundaries between good and bad or Muslim and unbeliever.

The state's attempts to manipulate the Islamic discourse and to use repression to maintain its structures, for example, by cracking down on "Islamist terrorists," illuminate the crisis of legitimacy the Egyptian government faces. Here the state's self-defeating strategies are underscored: in the power struggles, Islamist regimes are strengthening the discourses they themselves are inventing and of which they are masters. Effectively, discourses elaborated by formerly peripheral Islamist regimes are becoming centers, or focal power points, while, nevertheless, reacting to and with state forms of repressive power. The awareness of this centrality is an important focus of attention for feminists because it may well indicate which way the wind is blowing and, thus, enable effective and timely mobilization.

After this overview of the different feminisms operating in Egypt today and the analysis of the power dynamics involved between Islamisms and the state, the question arises how these are interconnected. I argued that the state-Islamist power dynamics center on the appropriation of the discourse of political Islam by the state for political legitimation and that both parties agree on the issue of women's roles in society. It is no coincidence that at around the same time Islamisms were becoming an important political force in the mid-1980s institutional Islam as exemplified by al-Azhar[21] also was proclaiming that women should be primarily mothers and wives. This is not to say that all Islamists argue for only these roles for women. On the contrary, the existence of Islamist feminists who argue for women's rights to participate fully in public life indicates that Islamist gender discourses are diverse. The point here, however, is that because the state is more concerned with issues of legitimation within the Islamist discourse, the political nuances of women's roles are suppressed in favor of broad, simple outlines.

Political Islam constitutes a productive power that takes into account that women's support is important for a movement of opposition. Agencies of the repressive state do not necessarily take into account the need for women's support. Subsequently, the state ends up reinforcing specific aspects of Islamist gender discourses. For example, while some Islamist feminists argue that motherhood is a political occupation and the family—and, consequently, the household—is a political unit,[22] religious spokesmen of the state urge women to be good housewives instead of taking men's jobs. The latter stance is indeed an aspect of certain Islamist ideas on gender but by no means the only one. Islamists argue for motherhood because mothers are instrumental in bringing up the next generation as good Muslims who will build up a Muslim society. Islamist feminists are appealing to mothers to imbue their children with a sense of self-worth and political purpose so that they may join the Islamist struggle and encourage members of their families to do so as well. By elaborating on a certain aspect of women's roles only the state takes some of the Islamist pronouncements on gender out of context, which leads to a strengthening of specific aspects of Islamist ideas, for example, sacred motherhood, and neglects the other important Islamist notion of motherhood as political involvement.

On some level the state must come to terms with the demands and suggestions of secular and Muslim feminists. Muslim feminists actively support international conventions such as CEDAW and the PFA to which the Egyptian state is signatory. On the surface the state appears to adopt a contradictory stance. The reservations of the Egyptian state toward such international documents reinforce patterns of cooptation of what is politically expedient and feasible. Although Egypt signed, government officials made sure that the state actually was not bound to honor all stipulations.[23]

Secular feminists (e.g., members of the New Woman Research Centre) perceive the Egyptian state's reservations about CEDAW and the PFA as expressions of the state's own contradictory and muddled position vis-à-vis women's equality.

Islamist feminists (e.g., some members of the Muslim Brotherhood) perceive CEDAW as unnecessary in view of Islamic values and teachings and as a manifestation of Western cultural dominance. As one Islamist activist said, "Who needs all these treaties when we have the Quran?"

Muslim feminists (e.g., members of the Women's Committee in the Opposition Nasserist Party) are in the unenviable position of having to argue for both CEDAW and the PFA as "Islamically harmonious" texts. They take on the important task of reinterpreting the Shari'a and its principles because otherwise the whole task would be left to the state and its supportive male clergy. If the task of interpretation (of the Shari'a, of international conventions, and of laws) consistently is left to the state and its supportive clergy, then these documents will be nothing more than tools for the state to bargain with in its internal and external politics. It is up to Muslim feminists, therefore, to present alternative discourses on women that can compete with state and Islamist ones. Muslim feminisms will need to seek several middle paths between Islamism and its binary formulations and the state's selective appropriation of Islamist concepts. Such alternatives must challenge the domination of an Islamic metanarrative by promoting the diversity of local narratives, which then can facilitate discussions on all laws and conventions relating to women. *CEDAW* and the Platform for Action then will not be seen solely as inspired by a hegemonic West but as versions of local truths. This would, in turn, have implications on power dynamics; as elaborators of an alternative perspective, Muslim feminists may be able to break the escalating mutual reinforcement of Islamists and the state by joining the power dance and changing its rhythm.

# 4

# Aberrant "Islams" and Errant Daughters

The Turbulent Legacy of Beijing
in Muslim Societies

Ann Elizabeth Mayer

When the Taliban militia seized Kabul in 1996, their extremist ideology and their cavalier disregard for international opinion created shock waves. The Taliban leaders initially offered no apology for their so-called Islamic policies of excluding girls from educational institutions, barring women from employment—including in crucial fields such as medicine—and beating up females not swathed in all-concealing *burqas*. They made no efforts to conceal the harsh and discriminatory features of their policies because they were not self-conscious about how their policies deviated from international human rights. The very unusualness of the Taliban's attitude shows how influential the principles of women's international human rights actually have become. By 1996 ideas emanating from the Beijing conference had spread to most parts of the Muslim world, albeit maybe not to Qandahar, the home base of the Taliban.

Although universal compliance with women's international human rights still seems an elusive goal, the impact of the Beijing conference more often than not has placed opponents to women's equality on the defensive. Muslim leaders now seem reluctant to state squarely that they believe women are precluded from enjoying equality in rights by reason of their sex. Indeed, already during preparatory stages of the Beijing conference governments showed an awareness of the inadvisability of appearing to block the path to equality for women. Thus, Saudi Arabia preferred not to appear at the Beijing conference at all rather than to have to declare publicly that women should be segregated and supervised by male guardians. Obviously, Saudi leaders calculated that any defense of their policies toward women would expose them to fierce challenges and to ridicule. Unlike the naïve Taliban, Saudi Arabia's leaders had learned enough about

29

the authority of women's international human rights to feel uneasy about admitting how they treated women.

After the Beijing conference, the clashes of diverging views on women's rights seem to have intensified, with Islam being appealed to both by Islamic feminists and by foes of women's rights. The sharp confrontations over how Islamic requirements affect women's rights reveal a religious tradition in turmoil as Muslims variously react with enthusiasm or with hostility to the message of Beijing. While some Muslims have reacted by stretching and straining Islamic rationales for the subjugation of women, others, who are equally opposed to women's human rights, seem to consider it unwise to invoke Islam as the reason for denying women's rights. I review relevant women's rights issues involving Libya, Pakistan, Egypt, Sudan, Iran, and Afghanistan to illustrate the repercussions of Beijing and the variety of "Islams" that have emerged in its turbulent wake.

Some regimes are backing away from the Islamic reservations to the *Convention on the Elimination of All Forms of Discrimination Against Women (CEDAW)*, reservations that have attracted much negative comment. In response to such reservations the Beijing Platform for Action called for all governments to "limit the extent of any reservations to *CEDAW*; formulate any such reservations as precisely and as narrowly as possible; ensure that no reservations are incompatible with the object and purpose of the Convention or otherwise incompatible with international treaty law and regularly review them with a view to withdrawing them."[1]

The revision of Libya's *CEDAW* reservation, timed to coincide with the Beijing conference, seems to have anticipated that sweeping reservations would be challenged. The original Libyan reservation had attracted criticism. It read: [Accession] "is subject to the general reservation that such accession cannot conflict with the laws on personal status derived from the Islamic Shariah."[2] The broad reservation placed compliance with Islamic law above Libya's commitments to *CEDAW* without specifying the consequences. On 5 September 1995 Libya notified the secretary-general of its revised reservation, which is worded to suggest that Libya aims to protect women's rights:

> 1. Article 2 of the Convention shall be implemented with due regard for the peremptory norms of the Islamic Shariah relating to determination of the inheritance portions of the estate of a deceased person, whether female or male.
> 2. The implementation of paragraph 16(c) and (d) of the Convention shall be without prejudice to any of the rights guaranteed to women by the Islamic Shariah.[3]

Instead of the original vague reference to Islamic personal status law, now there is a specific reference to inheritance rules with language that suggests that the rules apply equally to the estates of females and males. This is misleading because according to the Shari'a male heirs are entitled to two times the share of female heirs. The inherently discriminatory apportionment of estates in Islamic law is not likely to be obvious to the average reader of the Libyan reservation. With regard to *CEDAW* ART. 16(c) and (d), the new reservation implies that the application of *CEDAW* could compromise Libyan women's rights as if Libya's Islamic laws guaranteed women rights superior to those provided by *CEDAW* concerning marriage and divorce and parental rights and responsibilities.[4] The confusing formulation suggests that Libya had been embarrassed by the negative reception of its original broad reservation and was eager to put the best possible face on its policy of retaining Shari'a personal status rules.

After protracted debates over possible Islamic reservations, Pakistan finally ratified *CEDAW* on 12 March 1996, appending this "declaration": "The accession by [the] Government of the Islamic Republic of Pakistan to the [said convention] is subject to the provisions of the Constitution of the Islamic Republic of Pakistan."[5] The hidden meaning of this innocuous-sounding declaration will probably be obvious only to those familiar with U.S. RUDs (treaty reservations, understandings, and declarations) to human rights treaties. These consistently qualify U.S. obligations by upholding the supremacy of U.S. domestic constitutional standards over any contravening principles in international human rights conventions.[6] Pakistan may have taken its cue from the United States, which disguises what are, in fact, reservations to treaty provisions by placing them under milder-sounding rubrics such as "understandings" or "declarations."[7] U.S. "constitutional" reservations to international human rights treaties so far have not been subjected to the same degree of critical appraisal that Islamic reservations have provoked.[8] For Muslim countries, a "constitutional" reservation can serve the same purpose as an Islamic reservation because almost all constitutions of Muslim countries establish Islam as the state religion, and many contain references to Islam. Examination of the Pakistani Constitution reveals that in addition to the ART. 2 provision that makes Islam the state religion, other Islamic features provide ample grounds for treating Pakistan's alleged "constitutional" reservation as an Islamic reservation in disguise—one that can accommodate Pakistan's practice of allowing Islamic law to relegate women to subordinate status.[9] The recourse to such circumlocution suggests that Pakistan was becoming uneasy about advertising that its Islamic laws stood in the way of full implementation of *CEDAW*.

As Pakistan was playing down the Islamic factor, controversial court cases were using Islamic rationales to roll back women's rights. Several cases in 1996 involved adult Pakistani women who were legally entitled to contract marriages but found their marriages challenged on the grounds that their male guardians (usually their fathers) had not consented to them.[10] In past centuries Hanafi jurisprudence prevailed on the subcontinent, but Pakistan seems to have abandoned the old Hanafi rule of *kafa'a*, which said that a woman's marriage could be nullified by her guardian on the grounds that she had married beneath her. Behind this rule stood the idea that a woman was a marker for male prestige: her marriage to a man of lower status than her father's would humiliate her family, and, thus, her guardian could sue to terminate the marriage. The Lahore High Court proved quite ready not only to resurrect the prerogatives of the marriage guardian in Hanafi law but to expand them to permit the voiding of a valid marriage simply on the grounds that the woman's father had not been consulted.

In the most sensational of these cases, Saima Waheed, a university student from an affluent family in Lahore, found her marriage to a teacher nullified by the court at the behest of her father, Abdul Waheed Ropri, a leader of a conservative Islamic sect. Her father's suit was not based on claims that his son-in-law was of low status but on objections to his daughter having married without his consent. The father had his daughter locked up in the family home where she was beaten and starved. Saima Waheed finally escaped. Determined to fight to be reunited with her husband, she sought advice from Asma Jahangir, a prominent women's rights activist. Like other Muslim women, Waheed realized that women's human rights addressed her concerns and that they gave her alternatives. Jahangir sheltered Waheed while her father tried to have her returned to his custody.

Islam was appealed to but inconclusively so because Islamic authorities disagreed on which side was right under Islamic law.[11] The father's lawyer advised the court that it was "the father's obligation to restrain his wayward children"[12] and that, even though she was an adult, Saima "cannot be left to roam around the Mall Road (a major Lahore thoroughfare) at will."[13] The mentality revealed by one judge as he justified the dissolution of Saima Waheed's marriage was transparently reactive. Siding with the father, he saw himself as defending morality endangered by "the West": "Following the West blindly had caused many problems in our society, leading it to moral bankruptcy. The race to modernize and catch up with the West, apart from achieving its desired motives, also led to the import of bad values."[14] The ruling dissolving the marriage essentially endorsed the idea of general female incompetence and the need for male guardians to control female wards regardless of their maturity.

Interestingly, however, Abdul Waheed Ropri did not baldly assert that he was entitled to order his daughter around. Instead, he feigned solicitude for his daughter's free will. After having imprisoned and starved her, he insisted that his daughter had been coerced by others: she had been abducted by her husband and compelled to marry him and had then been "brainwashed" by Asma Jahangir.[15] Thus, he pretended that his aim was to save his daughter from those who had forced her to marry against her will. Even this dyed-in-the-wool reactionary had come to appreciate that it was inadvisable to acknowledge frankly that he considered his adult, educated daughter a delinquent child. Toward the end of 1996 the Supreme Court suspended the High Court ruling that had dissolved Saima Waheed's marriage, leaving the final outcome of this case uncertain, but it was clear that both supporters and foes of women's rights in Pakistan had been mobilized by the controversy.

Recent rulings by Egyptian courts show the potentially harmful, dismal consequences that constitutional provisions that accord special stature to Islam and Islamic law can have for women's rights. After adopting a constitutional amendment in 1980 that made Islamic law the main source of legislation, the government showed little enthusiasm for doing more than "studying" Islamization. This amendment, however, encouraged Islamic activists to use litigation to establish the supremacy of Islamic law.

Many observers seem to discount as trivial Islamic personal status rules such as the ban on Muslim women marrying non-Muslims. In the hands of reactionary fundamentalists and like-minded judges, however, such Shari'a rules can have devastating results for women's rights as the notorious case of Nasr Hamid Abu Zaid shows. Abu Zaid, a professor at Cairo University, became a target of fundamentalist ire after he presented a scholarly thesis in 1992 proposing innovative ways of approaching the Quran as a literary text. In 1995 Islamic activists persuaded a court to rule that Abu Zaid was an apostate. This decision was affirmed by the Cairo Court of Cassation in August 1996 in a ruling that sparked intense controversy. The plaintiffs claimed to follow *hisba*, the Quranic injunction to enjoin the good and forbid the evil. They brought their suit against Abu Zaid and his wife Ibtihal Yunis as a personal status case in order to exploit the provision in Egyptian personal status law that judges may turn to Hanafi jurisprudence for guidance in the absence of a code provision. Because nobody had anticipated a claim that hisba principles entitled litigants to sue to void the marriages of unrelated parties, there was no personal status code provision covering the issues raised by Abu Zaid's foes. Referring to Hanafi jurisprudence, the courts ruled that hisba could be invoked even by strangers to separate a married couple. The courts decreed that Abu Zaid's scholarship contained heretical ideas that entitled them to rule Abu Zaid an apostate.[16] Being declared an apostate meant the termination of his marriage to a Muslim woman.[17] Had the couple continued to live together in Egypt after this "divorce," they could have been prosecuted for illicit fornication.

Abu Zaid was punished for his dangerous suggestion that religion should be an open system rather than a means for upholding tradition and a rationale for censorship. Most attention has focused on the curtailment of freedom of expression and on the courts' use of Islam as a tool of censorship and intimidation.[18] The symbolic importance of this ruling for women's rights, however, can scarcely be overestimated. The case could just as well be named after Ibtihal Yunis, who also is a university professor. Neither the plaintiffs nor the courts accorded the slightest weight to Yunis's opinion about whether her marriage should continue. Just as in Pakistan, in Egypt the courts, in ostensibly "Islamic" rulings, terminated the marriage of an adult woman without regard for her views, thereby treating the woman like a mindless object.

Before this case, one hardly would have anticipated that Egypt would disregard an adult woman's consent to her marriage. In theory, marriages between Muslims are based on the consent of the spouses, and the medieval Hanafi jurists' rule that male guardians may nullify their female wards' marriages to men of lower status is no longer in force. For Egyptian women who thought that kafa'a principles were a thing of the past, however, the Abu Zaid case provided a rude awakening. It told them that Egyptian courts were ready to take unprecedented measures to shore up patriarchy. In expansive readings of Islamic law prerogatives once enjoyed by a woman's guardian were broadened. No longer was the issue the protection of a family from the shame of a daughter's mésalliance. Now the grounds for marital dissolution had been expanded to include strangers' disapproval of a Muslim husband's religious ideas, making any man's opinion that a certain husband was unfit to be in charge of his Muslim wife grounds for divorce. In the process wives were treated like incompetent minors subject to a general patriarchal tutelage.

That such a blow could befall Egyptian women in 1995–96 is striking evidence of how fragile are the gains that women have achieved and how the failure to modernize Egypt's personal status laws can render women's rights illusory. Significantly, the blow to Ibtihal Yunis was administered by Egypt's secularized court system. Even though the ability of private individuals to bring such hisba claims has been curbed by subsequent legislation, this will not reform the attitudes exhibited by the courts in the Abu Zaid case. As in Pakistan, there is disturbing evidence that in the post-Beijing world seemingly modernized judicial institutions are ready to endorse extremist ideas that inflate Islamic rationales for subordinating women. Both the Egyptian and Pakistani rulings are in flagrant violation of norms of modern jurisprudence and of women's international human rights, probably quite deliberately so, because the views of educated urban women were being overriden in both countries.

In making Islamic reservations when ratifying CEDAW, Egypt had pretended that the impact of the Shari'a on women's rights was benign.[19] What connection should one draw between the Abu Zaid ruling and Egypt's Islamic reservations to CEDAW? It would be an oversimplification to say that the dissolution of Ibtihal Yunis's marriage directly resulted from Egypt's reservations to CEDAW. The ruling, however, ties in with Egypt's adoption of the idea that women's human rights can be qualified by Shari'a principles and that married women are to be treated as dependents of their husbands. Yet nowhere had Egypt's Islamic reservations claimed that women had impaired contractual capacity. Dissolving Ibtihal Yunis's marriage contract was breaching a CEDAW principle to which Egypt had never made an Islamic reservation, that is, the principle of equality in contractual capacity in ART. 15.2, which provides that "States Parties shall accord to women, in civil matters, a legal capacity identical to that of men and the same opportunities to exercise that capacity. In particular, they shall give women equal rights to conclude contracts and to administer property and shall treat them equally in all stages of procedure in courts and tribunals."

The Egyptian courts had in fact ruled as if women were lacking in contractual capacity. Ibtihal Yunis's marriage, a civil contract under Egyptian law, was retroactively invalidated on the premise that this university professor did not have the capacity to determine that her husband's ideas rendered him unfit to be married to her, a Muslim woman. Male strangers of no standing in the field of Islamic jurisprudence were treated as having superior ability to grasp the relevant Islamic principles and, therefore, as being entitled to make this determination on her behalf as if she were their ward.

In what way is this Islamic? One of the traditions of which Muslims have been justifiably proud is that, contrary to the old Western traditions of denying women contractual capacity and legal personality, Islam from the beginning recognized women's legal personality and, with minor exceptions, has granted women the ability to enter into contracts on a par with men. It has upheld their lawful contracts, barring only unusual situations such as breaches of the rule of *kafa'a*. Thus, one would not have expected to hear that there were Islamic grounds for objections to *CEDAW* ART. 15.2. The courts' treatment of Ibtihal Yunis and Saima Waheed actually was a sharp deviation from Islamic standards and an endorsement of views prevalent in premodern European laws. Instead of moving toward embracing *CEDAW* standards, some Egyptian courts were moving in the opposite direction and in the process distorting Islamic precepts regarding women's contractual capacity. Reactionaries, so quick to decry any signs of Westernization when seeking to delegitimize women's human rights, are mimicking alien Western concepts where these compromise women's rights. As Islam is being twisted almost beyond recognition to serve retrograde agendas, opportunities for exposing the cynicism and political contingency of such aberrant "Islams" are growing fast.

Egyptians' disparate views regarding the role of Islam in practices affecting women's rights showed in the mixed responses to the practice of female genital mutilation (FGM). Historically, Muslims have differed widely in their views about whether FGM is required or even allowed by Islamic law.[20] The restricted geographical spread of FGM proves that is has no intrinsic connection with Islam. Christians and animists in northeastern Africa practice FGM, whereas Muslims in most regions of the world reject the idea that Islam approves, much less requires, genital mutilations that jeopardize women's lives, health, and psychological well-being. In Egypt disputes about the Islamicity of FGM intensified in the wake of strong condemnations of the practice at the 1994 Cairo population conference and later at the Beijing conference. After the head of al-Azhar, Sheikh Gad al-Haqq, ruled in 1994 that female "circumcision" was an Islamic obligation, a mere two years later his successor, Sheikh Muhammad Sayyid Tantawi, proclaimed that it was not. This was a remarkable turnaround by the head of the preeminent institution of Sunni Islam and indicative of the degree of doctrinal tumult with which al-Azhar was trying to cope. Ignoring Tantawi, other Egyptians insisted that Islam required FGM, including Sheikh Yusuf al-Badri, a member of the Higher Council for Islamic Affairs. A group sharing his opinion decided to sue Egypt's health minister for having banned FGM in public hospitals, claiming the ban violated Islamic law.[21] This was not a call for respecting a custom of a traditional community but for allowing professionals in the public hospitals of a modern metropolis to excise women's and girls' genitalia in operations that the physicians knew to be hazardous and potentially life threatening.[22]

As in the Abu Zaid case, members of the professional elite became involved in perpetrating a flagrant violation of women's international human rights. The issue, instead of being handled as a public health matter and a concern of women's human rights, was handled as if the central question were compliance with Islamic law. When Islam is exploited as the rationale for legitimizing otherwise inexcusable practices, it becomes a self-defeating strategy. "Islams" that offer pretexts for denying women rights and for disregarding their welfare will become so fraught with negative connotations that, like the Islamic reservations to CEDAW, they will eventually be viewed as embarrassments best hidden away.

However worrisome the plight of contemporary Egyptian women is, some Egyptians took comfort from being able to look down on their fundamentalist neighbor to the south.

The Sudan in October 1996 enacted a new law for the city of Khartoum, requiring segregation of men and women at social events and in schools; ordering that women's sporting events be held in private; barring women restaurant workers from wearing jewelry or using perfume; and requiring women to be escorted by male relatives when shopping at night. Furthermore, people were enjoined not to look at members of the opposite sex.[23] As tends to happen when Islamic fundamentalists are in the ascendant, women are treated as if they pose threats to the moral order, which, in turn, justifies segregation and the imposition of rigid controls on women's dress and behavior.

Egyptian criticism put the Sudan on the defensive. Despite its commitment to a repressive ideology, the Sudanese government had been sufficiently exposed to the politics of human rights to realize that criticism of its treatment of women harmed its national image. A Sudanese spokesman in the Cairo Embassy therefore complained that Egyptian reports regarding Sudan's new laws were exaggerated and aimed at "tarnishing Sudan's image and harming its government." He pointed out that women had not been ordered to veil and even argued that the new laws aimed to protect women. In addition, he said, men now were barred from serving as hairdressers—a measure that he apparently thought balanced the extensive limitations imposed on women's freedoms. The spokesman insisted that the regime's appreciation and respect for women was shown by the appointment of three women judges and two women as ministers of social affairs and of health.[24]

Just as some Egyptians seemed to feel that the contrast between Egypt's freedoms and the Sudan's restrictions made Egypt look relatively civilized, Iran's leaders seem to have felt that the fiercely reactionary Taliban in Afghanistan gave them a golden opportunity to pose as enlightened defenders of women's rights. Thus, Ayatollah Jannati denounced the Taliban and their "fossilized" policies of barring girls from attending school and women from working outside the home in the name of Islam. What could be worse, he asked rhetorically, than violence, narrow-mindedness, and limiting women's rights, which all defamed Islam?[25] This denunciation resulted in bitter recriminations from Kabul and in charges that Iran was interfering in Afghanistan's internal affairs.[26] Attempting to counter the bad publicity surrounding the Taliban's reactionary policies on women, Afghan radio reported on a Kabul demonstration that included women, ostensibly proving the popularity of the new policies.[27] Within weeks the regime started to try to bring its official rhetoric in line with post-Beijing expectations, denying emphatically that Islam was in conflict with human rights.[28]

Iran's attempts to pose as the defender of enlightened Islam and women's rights indicate that Iran realized that it was becoming increasingly awkward to have Islam, the pillar of its authority and legitimacy, associated with measures that curtailed women's rights and discriminated against women. Indeed, the regime made many statements in the 1990s indicating that it wanted to improve its image in the area of women's human rights, even though it did not go so far as to ratify CEDAW. In November 1996 President Rafsanjani's daughter was sent to London on a public relations mission during which she asserted that Islam put women on an equal footing with men and defended Iran's "modest dress" rules on the grounds that they reduced violence against women.[29] Moreover, discussions in Iran in October 1996 of whether women could serve as judges showed the influence of moderates who realized that the ban on women judges was an embarrassing sign of the inferior status of women in the Islamic Republic.[30]

Under the Shah, Iran had played a prominent role in the United Nations in advancing international human rights. This role seemed to have come to an end with the Islamic revolution. Rafsanjani's regime, however, was eager to assume a leadership role again as demonstrated by the international conference that Iran hosted on the Afghan crisis in October 1996. There, Iran issued a statement urging an end to "evident violations of human rights, especially women's rights," according to the U.N. Charter.[31]

In its ambivalence Iran often is caught in self-contradictions. In July 1996, only a few months before Ayatollah Jannati condemned the Taliban, Iran passed a new penal law that signalled that Iran would reinforce its unpopular rules of Islamic dress by adding prison sentences of up to two months and large fines for infractions.[32] The parliament even studied the establishment of an antivice ministry.[33] That is, at the same time as Iran was trying to reestablish credentials in the area of women's rights, the government was pushing restrictive measures that rested on the same philosophy as the Taliban's and the Sudan's, namely, that women needed to be firmly controlled to uphold morality. Nonetheless, certain lessons seem to have been learned. Pressures for readopting a policy of segregating the sexes at Iranian universities elicited a negative reaction from Ms. Rafsanjani, who pointed out that Iran had experimented with segregation before and had desegregated after seventeen years of trial and error. With skepticism bred of experience she asked: Why should Iran "tread a repetitive and unsuccessful path again?"[34]

The ideas voiced at Beijing have created enormous waves in the Muslim world. As one might expect in a transitional phase, paradoxes abound as currents and cross currents meet. Iran's male clerical leadership denounces "fossilized" Islamic rules that infringe women's rights while Pakistan's courts expand antiquated paternal prerogatives under a woman prime minister. A decision that is supported in Egypt as resting on the bedrock of the Islamic principle of commanding the good and forbidding the evil looks suspiciously like an appropriation of long-discredited Western notions of women's contractual incapacity. Harsh restrictions are imposed on the freedoms of urban women at the same time as the language of human rights is incorporated in official discourse. The overuse of conflicting "Islams" to justify divergent government policies affecting women contracts with simultaneous efforts to exonerate Islam from blame for discriminatory treatment of women.

Although "Islam" appears as the ostensible rationale for retrograde measures and in many *CEDAW* reservations, it is used so inconsistently and with such obvious opportunism that it cannot in all fairness be identified as actually driving the opposition to the Beijing program. What is advanced as Islam often resembles rationalizations for patriarchy. The propositions that women should be beaten when attired "improperly," that public hospitals should be sites for the excision of women's external genitalia, or that adult women should never be able to escape male guardianship seem manifestations of desperate resistance to potent and appealing new rights concepts. The emergence of these "Islams" is probably a symptom of enormous stress in the traditional social structures and testimony to a panic among conservatives determined to block change at all costs.

But, why the panic? It may come from conservatives' perception that the enemy is already within the gates. Instead of a culturally coherent traditional community of Muslims facing modern norms of women's human rights, today one sees Muslims eager to realize the promise of the Beijing program facing off against other Muslims ready to grasp at anything that might stem the erosion of patriarchal authority. Where two incompatible value systems contend for the same space, clashes will be unavoidable. Observing these clashes, one can extrapolate that the message of Beijing has been heard. It may be premature to expect the Taliban to become feminists, but one can imagine that they are now becoming aware that they are not in Qandahar any more.

# PART TWO

## Strategies for Change

# 5

# Muslim Women's Islamic Higher Learning as a Human Right

## The Action Plan

## Nimat Hafez Barazangi

The topic of Islamic higher learning as a human right[1] emerged from my work as a Muslim woman of Syrian descent with North American Muslim women.[2] I was able to integrate socially the two very different cultures I lived and worked in because I conceptually accommodated their assumptions not merely through my higher secular education but after I changed the paradigm for understanding my identification with Islam. Similarly, as I searched for three decades to bridge the dichotomy between the ideals and realities of Muslim women's education, on the one hand, and the polarized views of Muslim women's identity, on the other, I maintained the pedagogical dynamics of Islam only after I consciously adapted to the Quranic paradigm of seeing Islam in its simplest, most direct, form. I, therefore, expanded my long-term activist scholarship with North American Muslim women into Muslim women's education in general and the situation among Syrian women in particular, to understand the educational practices among Muslim women within the context of the historical interaction between Western secular and missionary systems of education and contemporary Muslim dogmatic ones. This understanding may shed light on the process that was responsible for Muslim women's inability to reflect on their beliefs and their actions and, hence, may lead to positive changes.

My earlier research findings suggest a more serious problem than merely women's limited access to secular or religious educational institutions. They suggest that deeper knowledge of the sacred may pave the road to reversing the historical process of disenfranchisement or, at least, to finding new and better ways to conceptualize and study Muslim women.

One of the primary tenets of the Islamic revelation is justice (*'adl*) as the basis of human interaction. Justice is established when an individual makes a conscious, informed choice to reject or to realize the divine will as expressed in the words of the Quran and to make it the basis of action. According to the Quran (2:30), God has entrusted (i.e., given *al-khilafah*, viceregency, trusteeship) all humans with the divine will (shari'a, moral guidelines) to act in a moral, just manner based on freedom of choice. Will is not moral unless it is exerted freely and acted upon by a free, informed agent. Justice in Islam is based on this ethical moment of choice that encompasses all human thought and actions. The belief in One God, trusteeship, and justice must be realized in action.[3] But before this can happen, the listener to or reader of the Quran must avoid preconceptions and see "in Islam the unfolding of something unique, which has to be understood in its own terms."[4]

As human rights advocacy means to realize women's "active participation in all spheres of public and private life,"[5] human rights among Muslims are established by recognizing that Muslim women, regardless of how they are defined or define themselves,[6] can actually participate only within a particular ideological context of choice. For Muslims the unique authority of the Quran, the position of the Prophet as the greatest man, and the strength of the Muslim family[7] constitute the enduring frame for the constancy and flexibility of Islam over time. Two prerequisites, therefore, are needed to fulfill the human rights declaration within the Islamic concept of justice. First, Muslim women's self-identity must be acknowledged by both Muslims and non-Muslims before one can expect women to be agents of change instead of receivers of change. Second, Muslim women must formulate their own choice before one can claim that a free identification with Islam is actualized.

To move the Beijing platform from a plan into strategies of action for Muslim women, every woman needs to understand the platform's ramifications within the context of her chosen identity before one can claim a "people-centered sustainable development"[8] that will alleviate the present conditions of injustice. Here is where I argue that full access to Islamic higher learning, that is, deeper knowledge of the Islamic primary sources beyond the ritual religious acts, is the basis for Muslim women to effect a change. The fact that many Muslim women rely solely on others' interpretations of the scriptures to guide their basic spiritual, intellectual, and physical needs is evidence that a Muslim woman's right to understand, to choose, and to act on her choice is being compromised. Full access means that women take part in the interpretation of Islamic teachings and in the interpretation of the Platform for Action to maintain the dynamics of Islam rather than being limited to procreation and maintaining the Muslim family structure or individual human rights as suggested by others. Human rights and Islamic identity are not given but are gained by the individual's conscious efforts toward self-realization.

To realize herself as a Muslim a woman first must understand that her basic human right is to reject or accept Islam in its fundamental combination of faith and action, both rooted in divine will. To know the divine will human beings are given two things: revelation—a direct disclosure of what God, the source of all values and knowledge, wants them to realize on earth (the law of nature, *al-minha/al-nizam*) —and rational ability necessary to discover the divine will unaided. Humans must exercise moral sense to discover God's will. A human being begins his or her life with *fitra*, "natural endowment" (Quran, 30:30), but individual destiny is what each person makes of it. If one relates fitra to the most frequently recited verses in the Quran (1:1–2: "In the name of Allah, Guardian of the World, the Merciful, the Magnificent; thanks be to Allah"), the method of objectifying the Quranic principles becomes clear without the need of others' interpretations.[9] Such a strategy can be applied by any woman regardless of her level of education. For example, it was employed by early Muslim women who realized that by accepting the Oneness of God they were able to question the social constraints that surrounded them, including some of the Prophet Muhammad's own earlier injunctions. This is expressed in Sura *al-mujadalah* (58:1) and in Asma Bint Yazid's and Hind Bint 'Utbah's questioning of the Prophet on the respective roles and rewards of men and women at the time when they were giving their own vote to the Prophet and accepted Islam.[10] These women had not been taught critical thinking by anybody. It was their conscious choice to relate to the meaning of the Oneness of God as the core of values that made them critical even of the Prophet's interpretation of the verse about women's voting (Quran, 60:10–12).

My findings among both North American and Syrian women and their families are illustrations of this point. They indicate that a higher level of formal, secular, or religious education does not correlate with Islamic higher learning as explained above. Instead, it correlates with a widening gap between males' and females' understanding of Islam. Men tend to see Islam as something that gives them superior power and knowledge over others despite their definition of Islam as "submission to the will of God," whereas women see Islam as a protective power that requires of them total submission to the will of God as interpreted mainly by men. In addition, higher education (both religious and secular) has not changed the problematic attitude toward the proper place of women in Muslim societies. Muslim women are still viewed and view themselves as mothers, daughters, sisters, and as wives but rarely as having an autonomous trusteeship in line with the Quranic intention of al-khilafah (2:30).

In the Islamic worldview deciphering the signs, *(ayat)* of the Quran is, as Schimmel and Rahman[11] assert, endowed in human existence: "And we should show them our signs in the horizons and in themselves" (Quran, 41:53). What prevented women from deciphering the Quran in the last few centuries is the introduction of the perception that the act of deciphering the sacred requires special preparation and is limited only to elite males. For example, when I was trying to derive the meaning of *taqwa* (consciousness of Allah, usually translated as piety) from my interviewees both in North America and Syria, I asked them to tell me how they could be both pious to God and to other humans at the same time. A twenty-one-year-old female college student said: "As women, our first role is to attend to the family and, hence, our piety to God is only possible when we pray and fast while our piety to others is shown by accepting and fulfilling our role." Clearly, she had accepted a view of piety that showed a heavy male bias and resulted in a gendered meaning of the term. This biased meaning, it seems, has led to the injustice of denying women trusteeship and full moral responsibility. *Taqwa* in Islam is the only distinction between individuals (Quran, 49:13). This is the divine criterion by which every individual is judged: how well balanced he or she has discharged the responsibilities toward God and those toward people.

Muslim women's emancipation needs to be approached from another direction besides education, namely, perceptual and attitudinal change. The implications of this statement are more far-reaching than a critique of a misleading interpretation of the Arabic word *taqwa*. They imply that this college student assumes that one can only be pious or conscious of God's presence when performing the religious rituals, whereas Islam intends the conscious realization that "the standard whereby [human] action is to be judged, lies outside of [the human]";[12] that to be pious is to be silent, whereas Islam affirms that to be silent when injustice is taking place means to be impious (Quran, 5:9); and that to be silent is a woman's sign of consent to a marriage or any other matter that a male in her household may insist on, whereas Islam explicitly affirms that a marriage contract is a condition for the consummation of the marriage (Quran, 4:24). Such a realization makes conscience as central to Islamic identity as love is to Christian identity.

Educational, historical, anthropological, and sociological studies of Muslim women rarely show interest in women's spiritual and intellectual development that has more far-reaching meaning in Muslim women's struggles for justice than has mere "gender equality." Even recent studies in human rights among Muslim women pay little attention to the women's own realization of their part in understanding Islam. Before introducing women to concepts from outside the sphere of Islamic beliefs, such a realization is critical to effecting real and participatory change. Without realizing that her own perception of her role is in contradiction with the system that she has come to know as "Islam," a Muslim woman's changes of her role will only be temporary.

## The Content of Islamic Higher Learning

The Quran, as Rahman[13] suggests, is a document that is squarely aimed at the human being. Originally, it was intended as a "guidance for humankind" (as in 'hudan li'l-nas,' 2:185 and elsewhere), for proper action. To fulfill the purpose of human existence as the trustee that Muslims see as a Quranic mandate (Quran, 2:30), a Muslim woman must at least be acquainted with the Islamic system and its methodologies[14] before she can turn the article of faith into action. This acquaintance is not limited to women who are literate nor to those who read Arabic nor to those who acquire higher degrees in secular or religious institutions. To the contrary, by relying mainly on the oral traditions transmitted in local languages understanding Islamic guidance and the Islamic worldview is as simple as the ability to recite and know the meaning of the article of faith stripped of the many layers of translations and meanings that over time have added class, ethnic, or other biases. This does not imply being cut off from previous knowledge and tradition but keeping that knowledge and the traditions in their correct place as secondary sources. Nor does it imply a denial of the centrality of Arabic to spiritual immersion in Islam; Arabic is the only language of prayer, even when the praying individual does not understand the Arabic text. The language of the scripture itself is not only a tool of expression but a means of uniting the individual with God, once the basic message of the scriptures was communicated in the individual's own language. The issue in Islamic higher learning, therefore, is not access to secular or religious higher education but allowing the Quran to speak for itself to the individual, to be a person's guide. Schimmel[15] asserts that by listening to the primordial sounds, one understands why sound can be regarded as creative power. This deep significance in the recitation of the divine words even if the listener does not know Arabic[16] has become almost unavailable to Muslim women in the last few centuries because women were largely deprived of attending and participating in recitations. This deprivation is the result of many layers of restrictive interpretation that have accumulated to the point where some contemporary extreme Muslim groups even consider a woman's voice in public an 'awra (lack of chastity). Once Islam took on an institutional structure in which women were viewed as dependent on men, a Muslim woman's experience of God became a vague belief mediated through her male household, an Imam, or saint. Without direct access to what the Quran has to say (50:33, 37) so that her belief in God's existence will become clear in her mind and in her heart, the proxy structure will remain standing in the way of her trusteeship, and the "functional existence of God"[17] that calls on every individual to reflect on the meaning of Allah in her own life will be denied.

Islam as a belief system and a worldview ought to permeate individuals' thoughts and actions. Higher learning in Islam is the direct, deep contact with Islam's basic principles, primarily in their oral form, and in interactions of the sacred word and text with daily life. A Muslim woman who, for example, recites the verses "In the name of Allah, Guardian of the World, the Merciful, the Magnificent" (Quran, 1:1–2) tens of times in daily prayers without relating to their significance as defining the human relationship to God and to others may not be able to realize herself as a Muslim. This phenomenon, it seems, is one of the main reasons that Muslims in the last three centuries have been missing the meaning of three main points of these verses: (1) that everything except God is contingent upon God; (2) that God's might is essentially a mercy; and (3) that both these aspects entail a proper relationship between God and humans and, consequently, also a proper relationship among humans.[18] I argue that because women were prevented from direct involvement in Quranic studies, beginning with the art of listening and recitation and ending with the science of interpretation, they in effect are not practicing Islam as a pedagogical system of the trusteeship. As a result, women do not realize themselves nor are they being realized as Muslims in the full meaning of the word.

The belief in the Prophet Muhammad is troubled by the fact that the Prophet is a man. The result of the difficulty in separating Muhammad the Prophet from Muhammad the man may result in cognitive dissonance. Although the confusion seems to exist in the minds of most contemporary Muslims because of the idealization of the Prophet over the centuries, it is a more acute problem for women because the suppression of their Muslim identity is the result of the claim of male superiority and guardianship. Idealization of male authority prevents living one's trusteeship fully.

The Quran itself in effect became marginalized by interpretations and by being recited only during certain rituals. It lost its purpose of being God's guidance of human behavior through direct contact. (See

Ibn Sad's account of the early Muslim women. He devoted an entire volume of his *Al-Tabaqat* to women.) As this aim receded in importance behind rituals, women's identification with Islam became particularly ritualistic, atomized, confusing, and ineffective. In addition, the interaction between European missionary systems of knowledge and the view of some Muslim philosophers resulted in "preaching orthodox religion to the masses and a kind of rationalist, natural law deism to the elite."[19] This historic change in teaching the Quran affected women's Islamic higher learning negatively. Such learning deteriorated further with the introduction of universal schooling with its separate curricula for males and females:[20] home economics and child care were the core for females' education in the Third World even beyond the 1960s.[21] Islamic education is referred to in the Quran (3:110) as the process of shaping character within the Islamic worldview, that is, to learn and to act as guided by the Book. Over time, Islamic education deteriorated from comprehensive training in the first Islamic community in Medina (c. 623) to a mere course of study on religion or its inculcation in social mores.

## Education and Islamic Higher Learning

After the introduction of secular and missionary educational systems in the Muslim world, women were largely prevented from participating in either of the educational systems because Muslims, largely men, feared cultural hegemony. Later, the curriculum in the few girls' schools was limited to memorization of some verses and *fiqh*, rules of jurisprudence of purity and prayer, and to home economics, whereas for males it included the study of *usul al-fiqh*, the foundations of jurisprudence, the art of recitation, and other Quranic and related sciences.

The introduction of universal schooling to Muslim societies could not change the attitudes about women's education nor about women's Islamic higher learning. Women in Western societies may have partially benefited from secular universal education because their minds had already been "sharpened" by medieval Christian theology.[22] Yet even where contemporary Western feminists have taken the interpretation of the scriptures in their hands, they could not change the concept that Eve was created of Adam's rib nor the perception of female morality resulting from Eve's fall as proclamations by the "new religious right" attest. Now, even when Western feminists discuss these spiritual and religious factors from within their own faith and with new conceptual tools, with very few exceptions (such as Fiorenza Schussler)[23] they do not contribute to the religious debate much because, in Rahman's words, secularism has destroyed the sanctity and universality of all moral values. Any reconstruction of these universal values within the secular framework will demand a grounding in a particular perspective and, consequently, relativism will continue to haunt any human rights standards no matter how just they may be. Muslim women, by contrast, may still benefit from the prevalent acceptance of Quranic moral values as the standards no matter how neglected they might be in practice at the moment. These standards may help Muslim women to interpret the specifics of the Islamic worldview without trapping the latter in secularism. Western feminists ignored the marginalization of women's "religious" higher learning early on in their own movements, and despite many failures they still largely do not recognize it as fundamental to social change when they reach out to women in societies where religio-moral worldviews prevail.

For example, in Muslim societies, universal secular schooling did not enable Muslim women to overcome any biased social construct of womanhood. Thus, contemporary female graduates of Shari'a schools such as al-Azhar, the oldest Islamic university in the world, are not members of Muslim councils (Majalis al-Shura) and other similar religious bodies. After two hundred years of secular education and about fifty years of UNESCO's war on illiteracy, most Muslim women still could not change the misconceptions surrounding their social roles. Had Western feminism been equipped to discuss Muslim values as part of the general paradigm of Islamic studies, of Muslim women's studies, and of area studies, women might have had more success in facilitating change, might have less-polarized views, and might have a paradigm for the study of Islam and of Muslim women different from the present static, dogmatic Muslim and the atomized, secular-based Western ones.

Without placing the Beijing Platform for Action within the framework of women's Islamic higher learning, I argue that women may be able to translate some of its articles into realistic gains for some Muslim women but may not be able to objectify the Islamic concepts as intended in the Quran away from their social and narrow ritualistic meanings nor enact the sustainable and effective participation that the platform recommendations suggest. Formal education and universal, secular schooling alone will not help bring about a profound change in the self-understanding of women. The recent reports on Syrian women's gains in third-level education support my argument. The U.N. World's Women 1995 reports that the number of Syrian females per one hundred males enrolled in third-level education was sixty-eight in 1990. The Syrian Arab Republic National Report to the Fourth World Conference on Women, September 1995, also indicates that female enrollment in Syrian universities in 1980 was 26.12 percent, increasing to

39.08 percent by 1993. Female university graduates rose from 27.33 percent in 1980 to 35.97 percent in 1993.[24] Although the statistics indicate a significant increase, when I probed deeply into the actual impact of these and other gains, my findings, confirmed by other studies conducted by Syrian women,[25] suggest that the same old hypocritical attitude toward women's liberation still exists at the individual, religious, and political levels, locally, nationally, and internationally: a woman's first role is to be a wife and mother.

This attitude becomes more consequential when the Syrian government, like other governments that claim secular administration, gives male graduates of Shari'a schools and other men prominent public exposure to preach a religious rhetoric against women's public participation under the disguise of protecting the social fabric. At the same time the state, claiming gender sensitivity, feminizes the teaching profession, and this reinforces traditional gender attitudes.[26] Meanwhile, none of the female graduates of the religious schools fill public preaching positions or serve in the Muslim councils that produce different *fatwas* (injunctions) against a woman's right to self-realization. This situation became worse when some of the extremist women's religious groups were allowed to develop their own study groups, preaching gender differences and segregation. Although some may argue that these extremist groups show increasing women's participation, their gender politics are endangering the real gains in women's human rights issues, nevertheless. The issue is not merely to let women participate in interpreting the divine will but to ask whose interest the interpretation serves and by what methodology, paradigm, and framework it was formulated.

What complicates the matter further among Muslims in Syria and in other places, including North America, is that Muslim and non-Muslim polarized groups continue to speak for essentialized Muslim women, reinforcing the misconception that a Muslim woman cannot self-identify her needs and course of action. As these groups speak at each other, the majority of Muslim women are caught in-between with no voice of their own and no solution of their problems in sight. Only a few of the universally schooled women, so far, are able to speak in their own voices, but fewer yet realize the prerequisite for identifying with Islam: self-identity through active participation in the interpretation process.

The Quranic chapter, al-Nisa', (the women) opens with the verse: "Oh, humankind, be conscious of Allah (your guardian) who created you of a single soul, *nafs wahidah*, and created of it her mate, *zawjaha*." About the understanding of the Islamic stance on women, this verse says that a Muslim woman who identifies with Islam is an essential part of the interpretation process of Islam. Human nature is distinguished by its soul, *nafs*, which realizes the existence of God through its relation with itself and nature.[27] The compelling richness of these meanings in the Quran, as Abd al-Rahman[28] wrote, is what has allowed generations of Muslims to find yet new interpretations. Yet, once a non-Quranic framework of interpretation was introduced and/or once a particular interpretation was enforced as the ultimate one, such as al-Ghazali's acceptance of the Greek, Christian, and Hindu concept of separating human nature into the mental and the physical,[29] the ability of Muslims to realize their direct relation to these meanings was lost.[30] One sees, for example, how the concept of Adam and Eve from the Judeo-Christian tradition has influenced the prevailing translations of Quranic verse 4:1 quoted above. The feminine marker of the word *nafs* was changed to imply both sexes and was translated as "person."[31] The feminine pronoun attached to 'zawjahah (her mate) was changed to a masculine one and translated as "his mate." Eventually, the order of creation was reversed to imply that Eve was created of Adam's rib[32] despite the fact that the concept of Eve does not exist in the Quran.

The question, therefore, is this: How is it possible for a Muslim society to provide identity when almost half of the society, the women, is paralyzed or not actively participating in realizing the Quranic meaning and following Quranic guidance? Because Islam is affirmed to be both a belief and a social structure that is not based on submission but on action,[33] being a Muslim requires active participation and not mere acceptance of teachings.

By the same logic, how can one assume that a Muslim woman has regained her human rights without her direct involvement in the interpretation and implementation of the Platform for Action? History indicates that she was stripped of these rights many times under the disguise of Muslim laws, of state sovereignty, but also of the many standards in interpreting human rights. The strategy, therefore, is to let Muslim women generate the meaning within the framework of self-identity with Islam themselves and for everyone else to recognize the necessity of generating meaning in this way as the operating principle for action.

## Islamic Higher Learning in Practice

By understanding the meaning of taqwa (of being conscious of Allah) when identifying with Islam, Muslim women can counter the claims of males to their spiritual and intellectual guardianship and the claims of superiority of certain classes, races, and national or cultural views. Mutual guardianship and equality in the decision-making process, particularly in religious and cultural matters, are more in harmony with the concept of developing individual autonomy and self-identity than is merely pushing for equality in access to resources, for example.

The strategy here is to ask Muslim societies to explain the claim of nonseparation of the religious and political domains that has prevented them from validating and implementing the platform in light of the fact that at least one-half of their population is expected to practice the religion by proxy instead of consciously exacting the divine will by choice and to explain this claim when some of them do not allow women to vote despite the fact that voting *(bay'ah)* is one of the fundamentals in rejecting or accepting Islam and the human trusteeship. Furthermore, one needs to ask how they can claim nonseparation when most of these societies exclude women from Islamic councils while women are members of parliament in some others.[34]

Human rights advocates need to choose among three options as they try to forge special strategies for Muslim societies. The first option is to change misguided, misogynist interpretations, such as that men are in charge of women's moral and intellectual well-being, (Sura 2:228, 4:34), and to modify the claim of the universality of human rights to include the specificity of self-realization and its full meaning in the Islamic sense. The second is to refute the claim that Muslim societies are acting within the Shari'a. The third is to change the Shari'a, that is, what commonly is translated as "Islamic law."

Because the third choice is neither acceptable nor possible for a Muslim woman who has chosen Islam, one is left with two choices. The simpler and more practical one for a lasting effect is the first choice. For example, the claim of men's moral guardianship of women mainly is based on the concepts of *qawamah* (responsibility toward) and *daraja* (a degree or an edge) (verses 4:34 and 2:228, respectively). To interpret them, one needs to put them in the contexts of their Suras and in the context of the Quranic concept of Viceregency, al-khilafah and the meaning of "God" in such verses as "In the name of Allah, Guardian of the World, the Merciful, the Magnificent" (1:1–2). Although these verses often are quoted in support of men's guardianship of women, qawamah (responsibility toward) in 4:34 only implies a man's domestic and financial obligations toward his wife's biologically essential role of procreation. Daraja in 2:228 only indicates an added responsibility for a husband when he initiates the divorce process. Elsewhere[35] I have suggested that the relationship between the meanings of verses 4:34 and 2:228 and Islamic justice and human viceregency is summarized in verse 4:32: "Do not enviously wish for that which God proffered on some and not on others. Men and women, to each belong the works they have personally accomplished." That is, although Islam regards men and women as created for different but complementary biological and domestic functions, it does not specify these functions, nor does it generalize them to cover other intellectual and social roles.

Nasr[36] argues that the sacred law, Shari'a, in Islam involves not only principles but also their application to daily life in the form of legal codifications. This argument is valid as long as one understands Shari'a as outlined in the Quran and explicated in the prophetic authentic tradition. The argument loses strength, however, once Shari'a is extended to include the different juridic and contemporary interpretations as part of the sacred. The Quranic principles affirm the unity of Islamic philosophy despite theological and historical diversity.[37] Each individual needs to be informed that "on no soul God places a burden greater than it could bear" (Quran, 2:286) before he or she can practice Islam. One must guard such transcendent principles from becoming limited or replaced by legal codifications, particularly when Muslim religious scholars try to impose one legal code in their attempt to guard the Shari'a from Western rationalized interpretations. One must insist that legal codifications are merely human interpretations in specific social and historical conditions and are not on the same level of sacredness as are the principles or the rules of interpretations that facilitated these codes. Moreover, to accept legal codifications as absolute contradicts the central dynamic of the Quran, that is, that it be understood in its simple pristine form and be open for interpretation at all times and places by capable females and males regardless of their backgrounds. Legalized codes cannot substitute for Muslim men and women's agency in the interpretation of the transcendent.

Neither, however, can a blind acceptance of Western scientific, rational interpretations of texts be made into universal principles. For example, the varied meanings of human dignity and human development do not support the universality of the basic human rights principles because they are culture-specific. Similarly, the claim that changes in the economic conditions by themselves will help women is limited and limiting.[38] Full agency is realized only when women have the opportunity to express their views and to share in all decision-making processes.

### Islamic Higher Learning in the Platform for Action

Islamic higher learning is fulfilled only when one has facilitated the development of the Islamic view of an autonomous spiritual and intellectual individual.

My "reading" of the Quran and the Hadith indicates that Islam established five basic principles to permeate the life of an autonomous individual who can make moral and intellectual choices in a just society:

1. The creation of male and female of a single soul (al-Nisa', "the women," 4:1).

2. The right and obligation to learn, to "be educated in the teaching/legislation," (al-alaq/iqra, "the clot/read," 96:1–4). Aisha, the Prophet's wife and major transmitter of his tradition, said, "Modesty did not prevent the women of Ansar from learning."

3. The right and responsibility to accept or reject Islam by voting, bay'ah (al-Mumtahana, 59:12). The Prophet Muhammad dedicated a special day for women to discuss Islam with him and to vote on his message and on accepting him as a Muslim community leader.

4. The right to receive and dispense inheritance and property (4:7).

5. Membership in the Islamic sisterhood and brotherhood with no distinction of sex, race, class, or ethnicity (al-hujurat, 49:10).

Within this Islamic perspective of social organization and of education as a means to approximate the ideals of a just society, one can specifically address the role of women and women's education for bringing about gender justice in Muslim societies. Islam's strongest argument in favor of tawhid (Oneness of God) is that the believer does not have to resort to the abandonment of logic to maintain her faith. The faith is compatible with any other form of knowledge. Allah created the universe in order to be known, and, therefore, "it is necessary that human beings be given the capacity to recognize and understand the Truth that brought about their existence." [39]

Similarly, the Platform for Action's strongest argument in favor of women's human rights is the individual's right to freedom of choice. Thus, as human rights advocates, women cannot insist on this right without recognizing the specificity of self-identification of Muslim women. Otherwise, "human rights implementation" may sound as if Muslim women were asked to abandon their agency or their beliefs to be able to achieve human dignity. Several studies show how external intervention without women's deep knowledge of what is "Islamic" has deprived women of the agency they had before the intervention. Badran suggests that such intervention could reinforce cultural resistance and promote the use of women as pawns in political manipulations of cultural "authenticity." [40] Thus, human rights advocates cannot assume that the implementation of the Platform in Muslim societies is just another "case study" within one large, uniform philosophical and methodological framework.

Muslim women must be reinstated as agents of their education. They must outline priorities themselves, beginning at home and ending at the mosque. This reinstatement can be facilitated by

1. Changing the paradigm of Islamic studies both in Muslim and Western societies and examining the widespread assumption that "Islam" is impeding women's development. Islamic simplicity dictates that each believer could and should be able to understand the teachings in order to perfect the practice of the system. The idea of ranking and restricting interpretations to certain gender, class, or ethnic groups contradicts the Islamic recognition that God is the only Guide and the All-Knowing. Thus, to think of Islamic studies exclusively in terms of scholarly and theological activities is as misleading as is the claim by secular human rights advocates that religion and religious interpretations per se are limiting women's freedom of choice.

2. The mosques not only have to be open to girls and women, but women and girls must be encouraged to frequent mosques and not only for special sermons. They must be told that the belief that Friday prayer is not obligatory for them is a misconception.[41] Schimmel writes that the Friday sermon and the Friday prayer are a duty for the community, and that women could be preachers, as was Maymuna al-Wa'iza, d. 1002, in Baghdad.[42]

3. One must focus on Muslim women's agency to counter the general misconception that Muslim women are passive and totally oppressed. From within their families Muslim women run kinship networks and neighborhood networks. They influence local politics. Singerman's story shows how powerful the Egyptian women who run such networks have become politically and economically.[43] Eickelman and Piscatori suggest that governments accord these networks de facto autonomy.[44] I argue that one ought to count on women to work for better control of their lives from within their families rather than to encourage them to revolt against their families and communities.

4. Membership in Islamic councils must be open to capable Muslim women who are learned in Islam. In the past Muslim women were narrators of Hadith, for example, that made them an important part of the isnad process, the ascription of an uninterrupted chain of authorities on which a tradition is based, and women were involved in the interpretation of the Quran.[45] It is, therefore, totally unjustified to bar women from Islamic councils today, especially if one keeps in mind that oral instruction was, and still is to a certain extent, the rule not only in teaching of Hadith but also in other Islamic sciences and arts and that this applies even more to the interpretation of Islamic philosophy. In Schimmel's view when one keeps in mind the Sufi insistence upon oral transmission of classical texts for "reading between the lines," one realizes the equal importance of such "reading" to the reading of the actual letters. This Sufi point of view also helps one understand why Shah Walliuldin of Delhi remarked that the books of Sufism are elixir for the elite but poison for the normal believer. Such

a remark could also be used to criticize Walliuldin's approach to the education of the believers. Instead of preventing the "normal believers" from reading Sufi books, Walliuldin should have made efforts to uplift the Islamic education of these normal people from less-valid and less-rational readings of Islam provided by the preachers and extremist Sufis to a higher learning of Islam. By extension, the only way to demystify Muslim women and to correct the wrong images of them as passive and helpless is by opening human rights agencies where Muslim women can speak for themselves even if their perspectives differ from the normative perspective of these agencies.

5. Muslim men and women must be coached to rethink Islam and to act within a balanced perspective of its first source, the Quran. This perspective must put in their proper place the many layers of *taqlids* (following of precedent) and interpretations and Western discussions of Islam as well. By dispelling the extremist mystics' and other elites' claims that there are hidden meanings that only a select few can know the Quran can become comprehensible[46] even to an illiterate person.[47] To educate the preachers women should attend the mosque regularly and should counter preachers' unfounded claims with clear arguments. Similarly, Muslim women must be involved in debates of the Islamic concept of justice in the face of outside influences. Such debates and encounters do not necessarily call for educated women theologians. After all, the woman who protested the second caliph's imposition of certain restrictions on women's visits to the mosque was acting from her simple understanding of the core of the Islamic message, that is, trusteeship to all.

6. Muslim women must be encouraged and given the means to educate themselves and others and to define their own identities as autonomous spiritual and intellectual beings. Such education must be facilitated by discussing alternative interpretations of themselves and their places in the community of believers.

In this enterprise community leaders must be involved to provide an environment for inquiry and learning and for building consensus around each step of the Platform. Community-based education that could be similar to already existing models, such as the *kuttab*, the school-like place where boys and girls were, and in many rural areas still are, taught the Quran and basic literary and math skills, and the *madrasah*, the collegelike place that provides higher Islamic education for male and female students.[48]

7. Human rights activists' programs must be interpreted within the Quranic understanding of a just human society. Educating human rights advocates in Islamic concepts of justice ought to be as important as educating local and state governments in human rights.

# 6

## Imagination as Subversion

### Narrative as a Tool of Civic Awareness

### Azar Nafisi

This is a story about the power of stories to shape reality and to teach what responsibility has to do with imagination.

Shahrzad's famous story goes like this: Once upon a time there were two brothers who each ruled over a different kingdom. One brother, Shahzaman, decided to visit his elder brother, Shahryar. On the way there Shahzaman realized that he had left behind his present for Shahryar, and turned around. Back at his palace Shahzaman found his queen making love to a slave. He killed both and with a heavy heart traveled to his brother's palace. There the brothers caught Shahryar's queen also making love to a slave in an orgy attended by other slaves. The two disappointed kings left their kingdoms and roamed the countryside.

One day, wandering by the Gulf of Oman, they noticed the sea part and a black column rise from it that turned into an *ifrit* (a demon). The *ifrit* opened an iron trunk out of which climbed a beautiful young woman whom he had abducted on her wedding night. Frightened, the two brothers tried to hide up in a tree. While the demon was sleeping with his head in the woman's lap, the young woman noticed them. She lifted her captor's head from her lap and under the threat of exposure and sure death forced the brothers to come down and have sex with her. Afterward, she added their two rings to the 570 she had already collected from her previous victims and explained that this was her revenge on the *ifrit*.

This incident had such an unsettling effect upon the two brothers that Shahzaman renounced the world and became a hermit while Shahryar had his wife, her lover, and the slaves killed, and then for three years married a virgin every night, only to have her killed in the morning. Soon the country ran out of virgins: they either had been killed or had fled with their families. In the end the vezir's wise and learned daughter, Shahrzad, offered herself as a bride. On the wedding night she got the king's permission to tell a story to her younger sister, Dunyazad. Shahryar himself, though, became curious about the tale and let Shahrzad live to hear the end. Cleverly, she strung him along with her stories until, after one thousand and one nights, the king, who by then had three sons with her, decided to stop the killings and to live with Shahrzad as his beloved queen. According to some accounts, his brother married Dunyazad. Obviously, they all lived happily ever after.

Like many others of my age and nationality, I do not remember when I first heard this tale. It is one of those stories one seems to have been born with. I do remember the last time I read it, though. It was for a literature class with six of my best and brightest women students. I used Shahrzad for a discussion of the relationship between fiction and reality before reading some of my favorite great novels with women as their central characters, such as *Pride and Prejudice* and *Loitering with Intent*.[1] Before we began reading the main texts we formulated questions that were on our minds, such as, how could these great works of imagination help us in our present trapped and helpless situation as women? Obviously, novels did not provide a blueprint for an easy solution, but just as obviously, the joy of reading them helped us to recreate our lives in the face of a seemingly unchanging and oppressive reality. The vezir's wise daughter's story seemed as good a place as any to begin an exploration of literature's power to change reality.

Shahrzad's own story contains a hidden theme, old and timeless —the theme of what can happen when reality closes all doors; when life seems uncontrollable and unchangeable; when life means death; when one's own life appears to be an insoluble puzzle and only one's own imagination can lead one out of a predicament. I could relate to this theme, and so I chose to use my own reality-puzzle as the frame for probing Shahrzad's tale. The connection between my puzzle and Shahrzad's is, perhaps, also a reason for my obsession with the tale. Over time Shahrzad had turned up in various cameo roles in my articles and talks, until I finally decided to ask her to play the major role in the present script.

I remember the morning we heard of Ayatollah Khomeini's death. Our family had gathered in the living room, lingering in that state of shock and bewilderment that death always brings with it. And this was no ordinary death. My daughter, who was five years old, was looking intently out of the window. Suddenly she turned around and shouted, "Mummy, Mummy, the Imam is not dead, women are still wearing their scarves." There was something in her words that has remained with me. It continues to come back every time I think about the so-called situation of women in Iran or about my own situation in my country. Why should one think somebody has to die for women to cast off the veil? What gives equal weight to both, Ayatollah Khomeini's death and veiling, matters that surely are not of equal magnitude? This question demonstrates how dependent political and social problems are upon the attitudes one takes toward private spaces and individual rights and how directly linked these rights are to what is commonly called the "woman question."

This episode always brings to mind another, seemingly unrelated, incident at the beginning of the revolution when I had first started teaching at the University of Tehran. At that time the university was torn by conflicts among various rival political groups. Very little was said about academic literary work and much about literature as an instrument to be used in the service of some "higher" political goal. The relative importance of goals and issues was debated. I remember a speech by a well-known leftist historian in which she declared her readiness to wear the veil for the sake of liberty. And I remember a photograph in a government-affiliated newspaper, *Jomhurie Islami*, which showed a group of women belonging to a Marxist-Leninist organization, all veiled from head to toe, and raising a flag with the hammer and sickle. Like the historian, these women sacrificed the "trivial" matter of the veil for larger, more important causes.

Ayatollah Khomeini's death was like a problem that, although influencing and changing my life in radical ways, was not really mine. I was obliged to make it my own because those whose problem it really was—politicians and their ideologues—disputed women's right to occupy private and imaginative spaces created by reading great works of literature and by taking seriously women's personal experiences as women. I could understand why the most serious threat to those who desired absolute power was the demand for such imaginative spaces. To give in to such a demand would be tantamount to the dangerous admission that reality could be viewed and lived differently and that the present state of affairs need not be a permanent one. Rather than left to contemplation and inspiration, reality was created and shaped according to the dictates of those who held the power to define things for others.

This, then, was my predicament: How is one to act under restrictive circumstances? How is one to be a woman? A scholar? A reader of works of art? The opposition provided no answer. The stance taken by those in opposition did not essentially differ from that of those in positions of power. For both, individual rights and private spaces were trivial when compared to the "larger" political issues. They both spoke and acted within the same framework; only their political positions differed. If I wanted to solve my predicament, I had to view it differently, had to frame my questions differently, had to step outside the rigidly defined reality.

I discovered that my dilemma, no matter how directly related to my daily life, could only be answered inadequately by that life. Reality can only be experienced and analyzed as it changes, and it cannot change without recreating itself through the mirror of imagination. This point is where Shahrzad enters.

It has been said with some justification that the most significant story in the *Thousand and One Nights*[2] is the frame story itself. Although it looks simple and is less fantastic than some of the stories told by Shahrzad, it is, in fact, the most magical of them all. Like all good tales it has the power to startle its readers with some miraculous discovery about their own lives. The listeners as well as the readers can elaborate and reinterpret the tale by relating it to some important aspect of their own life experiences. It is fantastic enough to seem not to have any relation to reality, but because it is so unreal, so truly fictional, it can expose and illuminate readers' experiences in unexpected ways.

Despite its simplicity the frame story in the *Thousand and One Nights* has a unified structure provided by repetition. The skillful use of variation through repetition creates the dynamic in characters and action. The use of repetition provides the frame story with the very spaces that allow the readers to reinterpret the story within their own experiences. Perhaps part of the excitement in reading Shahrzad's story is that through the links to readers' own lives they feel they are rubbing shoulders with the great lady herself as her story echoes in their memories.

The inner tempo of the tale is sustained by a series of different incidents, all repeating one act, betrayal. Betrayal is the central predicament of all the characters in the story. The individuals' actions are determined by the way each person perceives this problem and reacts to it. The first part of the tale, which I call the king's story, as opposed to the second part, which is Shahrzad's, mainly centers around how the kings deal with this dilemma. As the story progresses, one brother,

Shahzaman, gradually dissolves into the other brother until he just fades away from the scene. The same is true for all the main women, who are eliminated until only Shahrzad is left.

The king's story is divided into three almost identical discoveries: Shahzaman's discovery of his wife's betrayal; Shahryar's discovery of his wife's betrayal; the two brothers' discovery of the demon's betrayal by the woman he had abducted. The same action is repeated in relation to three different characters, but in each story the act of betrayal is magnified further. Shahzaman's queen betrays him with a slave; Shahryar's queen betrays him with a slave in an orgy, which implies that the king is cuckolded by many slaves; and the demon is betrayed for the five hundred and seventieth time. The two brothers' reactions to their discoveries of the betrayal of others are peculiar and remarkable: Shahzaman is relieved when he sees his brother's greater woe, and the two brothers resign themselves to their own fate when they see the demon's more horrible one. This means that the two kings learn about themselves through observing in others exaggerated versions of what had happened to them. The act of seeing, of observing others from a distance, leads to self-knowledge, to certain conclusions about oneself, which, in turn, lead to further action. The scenes of betrayal are like scenes enacted in a play for an exclusive audience wherein the audience's own lives are portrayed. This distancing becomes central to the actual frame story and to the role Shahrzad is to play in it.

But this is not the end of this story. The two kings are not only betrayed but humiliated in the worst possible manner: they are betrayed not by their equals but by persons of the lowest rank, two slaves. Later, they are forced to betray the demon who thus substitutes for the slaves. The kings now should feel even with their betrayers, yet somehow their revenge is more bitter than sweet. Their sexual encounter with the young woman is the reverse of the usual pattern in such cases: here it is the men who out of fear for their lives have to give in to a woman. To add insult to injury she informs them that they, as were hundreds of men before them, were chosen not because of their irresistible charms but as mere instruments of revenge. She leaves them no excuse to justify the matter as a conquest. The woman's revelations further lead the brothers to conclude that no man, not even a demon, is safe from the guile of a woman.

The kings realize their own plight not only by observing the demon's fate but also by enacting the role of the slaves, by becoming one with those they despise. One could ask—with justifiable irony—Which is more humiliating, to cuckold someone one despises or to be cuckolded by him? In any case, their experience is reason enough for the kings to condemn all women.

The incident with the demon and his young woman completes the turnaround of the two brothers' world. Once this world is completely reversed the kings find themselves unable to act as they had done before. Although now the brothers choose two diametrically opposed lifestyles—one withdraws from all worldly life while the other becomes a serial killer—the result of their actions is the same: they can no longer manage their lives as before; they are alienated and alone. At this point the two kings' lives and all they had taken for granted turns into a seemingly insoluble puzzle.

Before going any further, one must remind oneself that this is a tale and not a developed story. Its structure does not create the fullness and roundness that hide many inner complexities. Rather, it reveals the basic spine upon which the precarious lives of characters depend. This spine represents a strictly hierarchical society with the king at the very top. Each character is known through his or her position along it. Within such a structure there can be only little space for individual expression or interaction. Accordingly, most relations in the story are polarized with the king at one end and his subjects at the other, and the king has absolute power over the private and public lives of his subjects. He enforces his will through brute force if need be. Within this polarized framework differences are not resolved but simply eliminated.

In this world the private lives of citizens are dependent upon and subordinate to the citizens' public ones. In the world behind the walls a life unfolds that follows the same patterns and rules as the public one. Parallel to the use of brute force outside, inside the relation between the male master and his female victims is one of pure physicality. Their unions begin with his deflowering of the virgin bride, an act of violence, a conquest. A man's betrayal by a woman has only meaning within the sexual sphere and is punished by death as an act of disobedience. All three main male figures in the tale, who—not accidentally—represent authority, use force to gain their objectives in relation to their women. The demon does not think of negotiating with or wooing the girl but simply abducts her and imprisons her in an iron trunk. The two kings' judgment of their queens' infidelity needs no court or hearing. The acts themselves are presented as transparently sufficient for their condemnation.

Within any despotic mind-set the free use of words is very dangerous. The domain of words is the world of interpretation, ambiguity, and doubt. In the story the king cannot tolerate any dilemmas or questions. The virgin victims are silent. Nobody remonstrates or argues with the king. The possibility of a dilemma would immediately cast doubt upon the absoluteness of the king's power. Those who transgress his authority must be eliminated. Not only that, but those who have the potential to disobey, the virgins, must also be eliminated. What the two kings do not realize, but readers one hopes do, is that they themselves are also forced to obey when threatened by physical force. When the young woman forces them on the pain of death to copulate with her, the kings lose the courage befitting their rank and reputation. They, too, are defeated by force.

There is one more important point to be made. A hierarchical and polarized structure of society and of relations within it simplifies the use of force and, therefore, supports the power that rules society. Hence, tension and differences are suppressed and remain unresolved. The authoritarian relations make the king at once very powerful and very vulnerable. The unresolved tensions and differences ultimately create cracks in the social pyramid. When the bottom part of the pyramid starts shaking, the top most likely will fall first. So, ironically, the source of the king's power is also the main cause of the king's downfall.

To sum up the story so far, the king who defines himself only through his public role is undone by a most private affair. He has not yet allowed for differences, for interrelations between the public and the private spheres. Not knowing how to interact with others creatively, the only language he is prepared to use is that of force. What, then, has the king learned through his observations and his personal experiences? The answer can be found in the next part of the story in which the king and Shahrzad become indispensable to one another.

Before Shahrzad enters the scene, the women in the story are divided into those who betray and then are killed and those who are killed before they have a chance to betray. Although the woman abducted by the demon gets to tell her side of the story and survives, her role is mainly to emphasize the heinous nature of the two queens' crimes. The virgins who, unlike Shahrzad, have no voice in the story are mostly ignored by the critics. Their silence, however, is significant. They surrender their virginity and their lives as well without resistance or protest. Not asking, not conscious, incapable of influencing the king in any way, they can only surrender their physical bodies. They do not quite exist because they create no images, leave no traces in their anonymous deaths. They are the other side of the coin to the "naughty girls," the queens and the demon's woman. Both types of women tacitly accept the king's public rule by acting within the confines of his domain and its arbitrary laws. Had any of the virgins taken a knife with her to the king's bed one could laud her courage, but whether she killed the king or not, she would not have changed the relationship. Like the king she, too, would have tried to do away with her adversary in the simplest and speediest way, the act of elimination, which humiliates both the victim and the killer. To change the relationship imposed upon her she would have had to change the mentality that justifies violence as the way of settling differences.

Their story suggests that in relation to absolute power one has no choice but to obey completely and surrender one's identity or to cheat and lie. It seems that the two queens must be punished because their disloyalty challenges and threatens the brothers' potency as men and absolute power as kings. But the subsequent deflowering of the virgins does not restore to the king what one woman took away from him. Neither he nor they learn anything from their tragic fate. One cannot change a stagnated situation unless one can appraise it from a distance, can see it differently from the one who has created it, can see it reflectively and imaginatively to reveal possibilities hidden in the stalled reality. The women's infidelity does not take away the king's absolute authority, it takes away his balance. The demon's captive woman does not open his eyes to his own flaws; the king does not learn to see by killing his brides. As victims these women do not take the responsibility of trying to change the situation—they simply cheat or succumb. Only Shahrzad has the ability to contemplate her situation coolly and, thus, to rise above it. Like the king before her, Shahrzad has the chance to see herself through seeing others in her position. She is able to learn from the fates of other women, unlike the king, who never learns from the fates of other men. This distinguishes her not only from the king but from all the other characters in the story. Quite fittingly, she is the only woman who is described by her personal attributes and not just by her title and place in the social and gender hierarchy. The two kings are described as knowledgeable and courageous, but their knowledge does not help them in their crises nor solve their dilemmas, and it takes no courage at all to kill a hapless and helpless virgin every morning even by the standards of the day. Shahrzad alone is different.

What makes Shahrzad different? She is called knowledgeable (*dana*), with foreknowledge (*pishbin*). She knows about past poets, men of letters, men of wit, and kings. What is important here—not only in the narrator's choice of words but more importantly in Shahrzad's deeds—is the kind of knowledge she possesses, for knowledge is only revealed through the ways it is used. The word I have translated as foreknowledge in Persian literally is the ability to see ahead and also means cautious. Although the narrator and the translator of the *Thousand and One Nights* might not have been aware of the subtleties of the usage, both meanings make sense in the story not only because the story is open to many different interpretations but because the double connotation of the word fits Shahrzad's character and her actions so well. The ability to see ahead, cautiously, is one aspect of Shahrzad's knowledge; her ability to see the past, to know the people who had made the past what it was, is another. To understand the past and envision the future one needs the magical powers of imagination.

Shahrzad's imagination leads her to risk her life. One can claim that Shahrzad uses her tales to save herself. This claim is justified in the story itself. It is also the modern view of her character as a woman. In fact, the motif of the use of tales to save oneself or others from danger is common in the tradition of oriental story telling. It happens quite frequently in Shahrzad's own stories and is one element that links these tales to the frame story. I, however, look at the motif from a different, more literary, angle and base my arguments on the words in the text itself.

For three years the king has killed a girl each morning. The frustrated citizens have fled with their daughters. No virgins are left in the city but the vezir's daughters. The king orders the vezir to find him a suitable girl. There are no indications in the story that the vezir's daughters, who have the most privileged position among the women in the city, are in any danger of being chosen as the king's brides. When the vezir despairs of his search, he goes home sick with fear for his own life. Shahrzad learns the cause of his sorrow, advises him to forget his worry and to enjoy himself, and asks him to wed her to the king; she wants to try to save her people's daughters from this calamity.

Her father now uses a story to try to dissuade her from this dangerous task. He is afraid that what happened to the dehghan's wife in his story might also happen to her.

The vezir's story centers around a wealthy dehghan, a landowner who understands the language of animals. This is a secret that if divulged would cost the dehghan his life. One day the dehghan's wife becomes curious about his secret. She sulks and refuses to talk to him even when he informs her that the revelation of his secret would lead to his death. At last he decides to tell the secret and die. Preparing for his death, he overhears a conversation between his dog and rooster. The rooster boasts of his ability to keep his fifty wives in order while his master does not know how to beat sense into his one wife. The dehghan heeds the wise rooster's advice and beats his wife until she foreswears ever wanting to know any of her husband's secrets again.

Usually, at the end of such stories the listener learns from the moral implied by the narrator and acts accordingly. The vezir's moral of this particular tale is that women who persist in interfering in the affairs of men will come to grief. Shahrzad is no ordinary listener, though, just as later she is no ordinary teller of tales. She learns from the story the opposite of what her father intended her to learn. The unfortunate and foolish wife to her represents a caricature of all the other women in the main story: like the two queens she disobeys her master, and like the hapless virgins she can be controlled through physical force. In the same manner that she learns from reality Shahrzad learns from the story that which is hidden from others. She sees that to win she must not be like the others, definitely not like the dehghan's wife or the victimized virgins. To save the kingdom she will have to risk her life but not surrender it.

Shahrzad fashions her reality not through physical force as does the king but through imagination and reflection. This gives her the courage to risk her life, a courage that is spiritual rather than merely physical. What sets her apart from all the other characters in the tale is her attitude toward the predicament upon which so many people's lives depend. Shahrzad's imaginative knowledge gives her the power to treat this predicament in a very unusual manner, as a puzzle to be figured out. In fact, some of the best stories in the *Thousand and One Nights* are shaped around a riddle or a puzzle, the solution of which becomes a matter of life or death for the characters. I see this as the main reason for these old tales' ability to arouse interest and excitement in readers still today and as one reason for Shahrzad to seem so peculiarly contemporary to the modern reader. How does this quality in her create a link with readers so many centuries after she became a permanent part of literary reality?

Living at the end of the twentieth century, after so many tales have been told, I ask myself what sort of mentality, what type of attitude Shahrzad reminds me of in other fiction? Strangely enough, she reminds me of a type of character who did not make his or her way into what is called oriental fiction at all: the detective. Shahrzad reminds me of a sort of timeless female version of Sherlock Holmes. What connects these seemingly very dissimilar characters who belong to different times, different kingdoms, and different sexes is their mentality.

Sherlock is successful because he looks at crime as a riddle, meets it with emotional detachment, imagination, orderly thought, and takes a puzzling problem out of its domain and into his own personal private world. His mentality essentially is that of an artist. Time and again he defines himself as an artist and defines the tricks of his trade as artistic or in the terminology of a novelist. This is not unconscious on the part of his creator. Rather, Conan Doyle envisioned his detective as a kind of artist, even gave him an artistic genealogy. (In *The Greek Interpreter*, for example, Sherlock says that his grandmother was the sister of the artist Vernet and that "Art in the blood is liable to take the strangest forms.")[3]

Sherlock and Shahrzad have in common that they are artists in this sense. They confront reality through imagination, they do the job for its own sake, their ambition is grand, far greater than to save their own necks or to gain fame and wealth. They suggest that the only way to conquer the surrounding chaos, the pain and brutality that one cannot control, is to create alternative possibilities through detachment and imagination, through transcending given, seemingly unsurmountable limitations. Shahrzad and Sherlock succeed where others fail because they are artists who use art for its own sake.

To justify this analogy I need to redefine a key concept in Shahrzad's storytelling. What I call Shahrzad's imaginative power commonly has been called her "guile." On the one hand, it can be argued that to survive the weak have no choice but to become crafty and cunning and that, therefore, to women who are treated as the "weaker" sex, guile is a learned second nature. On the other hand, it can be argued that women are devious by nature. Shahrzad's use of guile can be defended or condemned according to one's perspective and bias.

Most ordinary mortals in fiction and in reality use guile to advance their own goals. But Shahrzad's artistry lies in the fact that she gives new meanings and possibilities to old concepts. In her stories are many women and men who use guile to defend themselves or to save themselves. They use guile the way witches in fairy tales use their magic sticks and brooms. Guile and craftiness distort and subvert reality and, perhaps, what one generally calls truth. The kind of guile Shahrzad uses so effectively is more akin to the way a good novelist uses the art of deception to create not just an illusion of reality but to provide some hidden truth, some hidden insight. These insights help readers sort out their puzzles and predicaments in real life. The illusionary reality in works of fiction does not offer a direct solution for one's riddles, but the insights they provide change attitudes, they let one look at life in new and subversive ways. Eventually, it becomes impossible to act as one did before in the face of all the new vistas, the new possibilities for thinking, feeling, and acting. Through them one becomes unstuck; kindled by new insights, imagination sets one free. Through her tales Shahrzad does not merely gain her life. She changes the king, she offers him a different view of himself and of reality, she brings him back to trust, hope, and life and, thus, frees herself and him.

It is interesting to note that what is called "genius" in Sherlock is called "guile" in Shahrzad. The attribute "guile" for Shahrzad's genius obviously reflects a despotic society dependent upon maintaining the hierarchy, which in doing so has to belittle its most potent subversive strategies. It is also indicative of the sort of possibilities that can open if one reminds oneself of how one weak woman through her ingenious refusal to play a despot's game gained what the strongest of men could never dream of achieving by force.

Now is an appropriate time to go back to the king as he listens to the tales night after night, becoming more and more involved, while attending to business as usual in the morning. He is seemingly un-aware of the changes wrought in him. By day the king only knows one domain, that of heavy-handed force. He is not aware of the different powers in his private world; he does not know how to connect his private nights to his public mornings. He lacks curiosity about women. As one who has the last word in everything, he does not probe; he does not see people as individuals, does not hear them. The tales teach him not to generalize but to see that the world is populated by differ-ent individuals, by women who betray, women who are loyal, women who are betrayed. His curiosity and his desire to know what happens next make him suspend the quick and unreflected judgment he passes in real life. Before the tales, his curiosity was not imaginative but was self-centered, blocked by his own limited vision. The tales teach him to come out of himself and become curious about the fate of others. Perhaps most important of all, the king learns to see the interrelation between his public and private life. His relation to women changes. What was simple sexual curiosity and domination now is infused with intellectual and imaginative curiosity. Only when the physical sexual act is accompanied by intellectual and emotional involvement does it turn into love and cure the king.

In fact, the king makes two different kinds of journeys: one at the beginning when he and his brother roam the country and meet the demon's young woman. Here it is reality that is illusory, that cheats the king and makes him believe in false truths or half-truths, that all women are disloyal by nature. His own eyes have cheated him. The second journey is the one Shahrzad takes him on, out of his narrow world and into another, that of fiction. It is here that his inner eye, the eye of imagination, leads him to the hidden pearl of truth.

At this point one discovers how the relation between the king and Shahrzad is reversed and how ironic this reversal is. When Shahrzad becomes the king's bride she, like the other virgins, is deflowered. She lets herself be conquered, "taken." But then she conquers the king by spinning her tales over the one thousand and one nights it had taken the king to spread his rule of terror by killing the young girls. She takes him to a world where his rule and his rules are alien and where he is so entranced by her tales that she can rule him, can teach him how to be a subject before he again becomes master of his own fate. It is quite logical that the king's relationship with Shahrzad is the only one that bears real fruits—three sons. Potency is much more than physical mastery over another sex.

Through Shahrzad the king learns to look at life and stories differently. Earlier, the king was watching the scenes of betrayal as an interested party, whereas now he listens to the tales for the pure joy of listening, that is, he participates in the tales as a disinterested listener. And he is rewarded for this kind of participation just as Shahrzad is rewarded through the king's cure. Both gain when they distance themselves from their own narrow goals.

In the tradition of Shahrzad's own tales one must now look for the moral, for a message. So once more I review the story, this time in the light of its message.

In the actions he takes Shahryar is limited by his position in society. As king he is the absolute ruler of the land. This entitles him to make and unmake both the private and public lives of his subjects. As the governing body the king does not need to differentiate his subjects, does not have to face relativity and ambiguity in his relationships. Yet, ironically, the king's very private feelings lead to the very public act of eliminating all women who enter into a private relationship with him.

It also seems that Shahryar's public role as an absolute monarch would ensure his rule in the private sphere, which seems less important than the public one, but it does not. Rather, one woman's infidelity throws the king off balance, and another's wisdom grants him a new balance. After all, his predicament was not caused by a threat from the outside, from a powerful political enemy, but from within the seemingly secure walls of his own palace. This reading of the text suggests that this story draws attention toward the interdependence of the public and private spheres as a metaphor of the most problematic relations in any society, that is, the relations between men and women, between those in power and those dependent on it.

This line of thought leads back to the beginning of this chapter and to the questions asked by my students and by me: What can one do when reality seems like a trap, when society offers no private or public spaces within which individuals can control and shape their lives? One answer can be provided by Shahrzad: many of one's rights in reality depend upon one's creation of those rights, on one's creation of free spaces in one's imagination, and upon the courage to fight for those rights and spaces. This is not easy. It is easier to abdicate responsibilities, to become mere victims, to place oneself outside blame and action, and, thus, to repeat the vicious circles. The choice is one's own—to be like those hundreds of nameless, faceless virgins, tasted but not tasting, transient without any traces, or to be like Shahrzad, who is waiting at unexpected corners of reality, redirecting life, subverting power, renaming relations, becoming immortal, loitering with intent.

This is Shahrzad's "message."

The story has ended. The ever-after is a happy one.

But there is one more point: it is said that after Shahrzad finished her stories she was pushed offstage again, for it was the king who ordered her stories to be written down. To me this matters as little as the fact that most probably her real creator and narrator was a man. It makes her image even more potent and powerful, and it does make a further point about the power and magic of imagination: good for the man who has the courage to imagine such a woman and for Shahrzad who allows the king to become so much part of her that he desires that her stories be recorded. He has forever become her work of art. Readers will always see him as she created him.

Now I return to my own frame story in the here and now, in another kingdom, another reality, and with a seemingly different predicament. I have learned that this reality is a puzzle, that upon its solution depend my life and the lives of my students and of others. Yet, having said all this, I somehow do not think that I need to go back and elaborate on my own reality. The ending of my story still needs to be created.

# 7

# Personal Status Codes and Women's Rights in the Maghreb

Fati Ziai

During the past several years, the regimes of Morocco, Algeria, and Tunisia (the Maghreb) have battled Islamism, either through the detention of Islamist leaders and suppression of free speech and association, as in Morocco and Tunisia, or through a near state of war, as in Algeria. Yet despite their opposition to Islamic rule these regimes have clung to the Shari'a, Islamic law, as the basis for their respective personal status codes. These laws, which govern the institution of the family and the legal and social status of women, have remained rooted in Islam even as the countries of the Maghreb have abandoned the Islamic framework in other areas of law. Moreover, reforms of the family codes in the Maghreb have scrupulously avoided challenging the premise that Islam, or one particular interpretation of it, should govern the rights of women; rather, painstaking efforts have been made to portray the codes and any modifications as consistent with the Shari'a.

Each country has codified the Shari'a's abundant and explicit provisions governing personal relationships and the status of women into legislation that can be applied in a contemporary legal system. Although the reliance of these laws on Islamic tenets is based on the belief that the Shari'a is sacred and immutable, when defining personal status, the provisions of the various family codes differ vastly, even among neighboring Morocco, Algeria, and Tunisia. But especially problematic is the premise in the Shari'a of male guardianship over women and a gender-based determination of rights and responsibilities. Thus, the codification of the principles in the Shari'a has created fundamental inequalities in the domains of marriage, divorce, filiation (parent-child ties), and inheritance. Many of these provisions, although purportedly protecting women, in fact perpetuate gender inequality.

As a result, the personal status codes of Morocco, Tunisia, and

Algeria are, in many key respects, at odds with the universal standards of equality and nondiscrimination embodied in international instruments such as the *Convention on the Elimination of Discrimination Against Women (CEDAW)*. Instead, these governments have sought to justify certain laws and practices that violate international human rights standards by arguing that universal standards fail to take into account religious and customary laws that may vary from country to country.

For example, although Tunisia has been a party to *CEDAW* since 1985 and Morocco since 1993, both have made significant reservations to the convention. Algeria did not even ratify *CEDAW* until May 1996. The basis for the reservations to *CEDAW* lies in the judgment that the manner in which the principle of equality is interpreted in the Convention conflicts with the Shari'a. In the case of Morocco the reservations to *CEDAW* are so extensive as to render its ratification meaningless. With respect to inheritance, for example, the government made reservations "especially to those [provisions] related to equality between men and women as far as their rights and responsibilities are concerned, which derives from the fact that this is contrary to Islamic Shari'a, which grants each of the spouses rights and responsibilities whose equilibrium and complementarity will preserve the sacred ties of marriage."[1]

With respect to the principle of consent to marriage, Morocco stated, "Marriages by proxy are a custom throughout the world. In Morocco, this custom is based on religion as well as on local and family traditions. . . . It is inadmissible that the Convention interfere with such traditions that are entirely compatible with the principles of free consent."[2]

Conscious of the danger of a religious backlash and the consequent loss in political capital or legitimacy, the governments of the Maghreb have gone to considerable lengths to demonstrate the compatibility of their laws and subsequent reforms with Islam. Modifications to the personal status codes have engendered highly politicized debates and resistance both in religious and secular circles, exposing the wide divide between "modernist" and "traditionalist" forces within these societies. The Majella (Tunisian Family Code), for example, makes no explicit reference to Islam, but its reforms have been presented as a "rereading" of the Shari'a. The Tunisian reforms nevertheless succeeded in bringing most aspects of the Family Code into compliance with international human rights standards, but poor enforcement of the code has undermined these advances. In contrast, modifications to the Moudawana (Moroccan Family Code) failed to address the most significant flaws in the code and, thus, made few concrete improvements in the status of women.

## The Personal Status Codes in
## Morocco, Tunisia, and Algeria

Both Morocco's 1959 Moudawana and Tunisia's 1956 Majella were adopted shortly after the independence of these countries, whereas Qanun al-usra (Algerian Family Code) was not adopted until 1984. In this section I focus on the Moroccan Code, which underwent reform in 1993, before briefly describing important aspects of the Tunisian and Algerian codes.

### Morocco

Despite recent progress in certain other aspects of the human rights situation in Morocco the impact upon women's rights has been slight. The activities of a group of women struggling for equality since independence led to the creation in the mid- to late 1980s of a number of nongovernmental organizations dedicated to protecting and increasing awareness of women's rights. One decade later, dozens of women's rights organizations are active in this effort.

The 1958 Moudawana is not only based on the Shari'a but is interpreted in the conservative Maliki Islamic legal tradition. The code contains many inequitable and discriminatory provisions and takes precedence over other basic laws such as the Moroccan Constitution, which provides that "all Moroccan citizens shall be equal before the law."[3]

The Moroccan government ratified *CEDAW* in 1993 but has failed to modify domestic laws in conformity with its obligations under the Convention. Moreover, it has yet to incorporate the Convention into domestic law by publishing it in the official government bulletin as required by Moroccan law.

In 1992 the Union de l'Action Féminine (Union of Women's Action [UAF]) launched a popular campaign for reform of the Moudawana. Faced with pressure and criticism from a range of women's groups and other activists, the king assembled a group of male *ulema* (Islamic legal scholars) to consult with women's groups and consider modifications to the Family Code. Women considered to be hardline feminists were excluded from this gathering, and others declined to participate. On 10 September 1993, a *dahir* (law) was passed announcing a series of amendments to the Family Code.

Although some of the reforms did introduce modest improvements, as described in greater detail below, they did not eliminate or even challenge the underlying discriminatory laws. Other important flaws in the Family Code were not addressed at all. Thus, although the reform served as an acknowledgment by the government and the king that the preexisting law had contained fundamental inequities, the limited scope of the modifications signaled that the government did not want to tread firmly in an area so inextricably linked to tradition and religion.

Although a thorough examination of the Moudawana is beyond the scope of this chapter, a few discriminatory provisions are examined here.

*Marriage.* With respect to marriage, the Moudawana sets forth different rights and standards for women than for men. In sharp contrast to the right in *CEDAW* "freely to choose a spouse and to enter into marriage only with their free and full consent"[4] Moroccan women must seek the permission of a male guardian before marrying. Rather than eliminate the institution of matrimonial tutelage for all women over the age of eighteen, as women's groups had urged, the new law merely removed the requirement that a fatherless woman over the age of eighteen obtain permission for marriage from a male relative, judge, or member of the religious community.[5] This change loses significance in light of the fact that women over eighteen whose fathers are living still require male permission for marriage, whereas men over the age of eighteen are not required to seek permission or approval before marrying.

Despite the requirement in *CEDAW* that men and women have "the same rights and responsibilities during marriage and at its dissolution"[6] the Moudawana retains numerous discriminatory characteristics with respect to marriage and divorce. For example, it sets different minimum ages for marriage for girls (fifteen years) and boys (eighteen years). In practice, even the low minimum age for girls is not respected because the Moudawana contains no sanction against those who arrange marriages for girls less than fifteen year of age as is customary in many parts of Morocco.[7] In divorce through repudiation *(talaq)*, the most common form of divorce, the law was amended so that repudiation could only take effect if both parties and a judge were present;[8] previously, a man could repudiate his wife in her absence. The article states, however, that a woman who is "summoned" and does not appear can still be repudiated but does not spell out the requirements and procedures for summoning the woman.[9] Women do not have the right to repudiation.

With respect to polygyny, the law was changed to require that both the new and the existing wife or wives be informed of the husband's decision to take a new wife, but the women's permission is still not required. The demand by women's groups that polygyny, which is not commonly practiced in Morocco, be outlawed altogether was not met.[10]

Another modification to the Moudawana permits a woman to stipulate in the marriage contract that her husband may not take another wife and that his failure to abide by this stipulation entitles her to a divorce.[11] According to women's rights activists, however, this right is rarely exercised in practice. Not only is the woman generally the weaker economic party and, therefore, reluctant to demand a right that she fears may result in the union not taking place, but even well-to-do families frown upon this requirement. Accordingly, many families, including well-to-do, educated ones, refuse even to consider this demand. This, although not a violation by the state, is a serious practical impediment.

The modified code also accords a widow both physical and legal guardianship over her children but restricts a divorced woman to physical guardianship.[12] The same article states that, even when she is the legal guardian, a woman may not transfer her children's legal property without a judge's authorization. There is no such restriction on men. Moreover, ARTICLE 105 removes legal guardianship over the children from the mother in the event that she remarries, whereas a man's right to legal guardianship is not affected by remarriage.

*Discrimination after Marriage.* One of the underlying premises of the Moudawana is the notion of "reciprocal obligations" in marriage. For example, the code specifies that the husband must provide support, including food, clothing, medical care, and housing, whereas the wife must provide fidelity and obedience.[13] The enumeration of these "rights" is incompatible with the requirement in *CEDAW* that men and women have equal rights and responsibilities in marriage.[14]

*Certification of Virginity.* Pursuant to the Moudawana, women, but not men, must provide information about their sexual history before they receive marriage certificates. This information is intended to establish either that a woman is a virgin or that she has been previously married. In practice, application of this provision is discretionary, and it is not uniformly followed by local officials. Nevertheless, this provision establishes a discriminatory basis for the state's ability to declare men and women eligible for marriage. It is also based on the presumption that female virginity is a legitimate interest of the family or the state and that such an interest overrides the right of a woman to bodily integrity and privacy.

*Lack of Enforcement of Women's Rights.* Even rights guaranteed to women by the Moudawana are not always enforced. For example, the code sets forth a series of conditions that permit a woman to seek divorce, including cruelty, lack of maintenance, and abandonment.[15] Nevertheless, despite the numerous bases for divorce in the code, Moroccan activists agree that the only factor that is always taken seriously by the courts is a husband's failure to provide economically for his wife or family; not even allegations of alcoholism or physical abuse are certain to achieve divorce.[16] The attitude of the courts has caused women to lose confidence in the legal system, and most do not even bother to file for divorce, fearing that they will be unsuccessful and only enrage their husbands.[17]

The lack of protection for women is also attributable to the fact that social and cultural norms serve to discourage women from seeking redress—such as bringing a law suit—when their legal rights are violated, particularly in smaller cities and rural areas. For example, despite provisions in the code for the payment of child support to women who have physical custody of their children, payment is often withheld. Thus, many women, particularly those living in rural areas, do not file for divorce because they are pessimistic about receiving financial support from their ex-husbands and are afraid that they will not be able to survive economically on their own.[18]

Finally, with a 68 percent female illiteracy rate, many women are not even aware of their legal rights.[19] The task of educating women about their rights has fallen largely to nongovernmental organizations, many of which have begun to establish programs aimed at increasing women's knowledge and awareness of their rights and the remedies available for abuse.

*The Significance of Reform.* Modest though they were, the fact that reforms in family law were undertaken at all in Morocco is noteworthy, considering how complex is the role of Islam in Moroccan society. Islam is the state religion, and the king is, according to the Constitution, the *Amir al-Muminin* (the commander of the faithful).[20] King Hassan bases the legitimacy of the monarchy and his own role as the political and religious leader of Morocco upon Islam, and claims that, as a direct descendant of the Prophet Muhammad, his religious authority ranks third after that of God and the Prophet.[21] Reform of the Moudawana—an area so closely associated with religion—was, thus, a sensitive undertaking for the king and could have provoked challenges to the monarchy's claims of legitimacy.

Equally significant is the fact that the impetus for change came from Moroccan women's organizations. These reforms, however, occurred at a time when Morocco was engaged in a large-scale effort to improve its image in the international community. Human rights suddenly appeared on the agenda as the monarchy sought to distance itself from its damaging record of torture and "disappearances." Viewed against the dramatic political changes and concessions made during this period, the reforms in the Personal Status Code appear insubstantial.

*Tunisia*

Tunisia's Family Code, which is considered the most progressive in the Maghreb, contains provisions that transformed traditional concept of the role of women in society. Most significant was the transfer of marriage and divorce from the religious to the civil realm. A 1958 law imposed the requirement of civil marriage, and ARTICLE 30 of the code abolished the practice of repudiation and introduced legal procedures for divorce. The minimum age of marriage for women was raised from fifteen to seventeen, and polygyny was explicitly prohibited.[22] Significantly, the code also eliminated the discriminatory institution of matrimonial tutelage.[23]

Numerous discriminatory provisions remained in place, however. The husband retained his position as head of the household, and the rights and duties of each spouse were also imbalanced: while the wife was bound to obedience and cohabitation, the husband had the duty to provide for his wife's needs.[24] Discrepancies in men's and women's status were also pervasive in the provisions related to child custody and inheritance.

In the early 1990s members of the Islamist movement in Tunisia began to question publicly the legitimacy of Tunisia's Family Code, which they felt deviated from the Shari'a. At the same time, women's groups and activists mobilized to pressure the government to implement reforms aimed at conforming the Tunisian Code to international standards. Resisting the demands of Islamists, the Tunisian government adopted a series of reforms to the Family Code in July 1993, introducing significant improvements with respect to child custody, male tutelage, and divorce.

In many respects the amended Tunisian Code is exemplary in its adherence to international standards. Yet there is a vast discrepancy between the written law and its application. Most at fault is the Tunisian judiciary, who have consistently resorted to traditional practices rather than enforced laws protecting women. The lack of equal standing in the social and economic status of men and women has also diluted the practical impact of this legislation on women's lives. As a result, the Tunisian Code serves, on paper, as a model toward which other North African countries can strive but also points to the irrelevance of good laws when an effective enforcement mechanism is lacking.

*Algeria*

In September 1981 the Algerian Council of Ministers made public a draft Family Code. The draft met with unprecedented opposition, including public demonstrations by women activists. Opponents focused on its codification of discriminatory practices in several areas, including marriage, divorce, and polygyny. The government consequently withdrew its proposal and later resubmitted a new draft that was adopted in June 1984. Ironically, the revised draft contained more restrictive provisions than the original version and, thus, proved to be an even greater setback to the status of women in Algeria.

The Algerian Code is not dissimilar to the Moroccan legislation. Some of its most blatantly discriminatory provisions are outlined below. Four provisions related to legal guardianship and tutelage relegate women to the status of minors regardless of their age. Specifically, responsibility for the contracting of marriage is removed from the woman through the institution of tutelage, which requires that a male relative agree to the marriage, thereby effectively nullifying the requirement of the woman's consent.[25] Although a woman's guardian may not force her to marry or prevent a marriage that is "to her benefit,"[26] he may oppose the marriage if it is not in the woman's "best interest."[27]

The husband is deemed head of the household, and the wife is bound to obey him.[28] Parental authority and guardianship are also generally granted to the husband. Divorce by repudiation is allowed, and the Code sets forth very limited grounds enabling a woman to seek a divorce.[29] Polygyny is permitted, and the wife's consent is not required although her husband must inform her of his decision to take a new wife.[30]

The code allows women to insert into the marriage contract clauses that would provide greater protection of their rights as long as they do not "contravene the terms of the Code."[31] Thus, in practice, women can only include language not intended to procure rights expressly denied them in the code.

## One Hundred Measures and Provisions

In October 1991 a group of women's organizations and activists from the Maghreb gathered in Rabat at the invitation of the Democratic Women's Association of Morocco (ADFM) to discuss the status of women in their societies and impediments to the attainment of sexual equality. The meeting led to the formation of the Collectif '95 Maghreb Egalité, which sought to devise strategies to counteract the invocation of religion and tradition as justifications for discriminatory laws. An additional element in the Collectif's goal was to ensure effective participation in the NGO forum that was held in conjunction with the Beijing conference.

One of the most significant achievements of the Collectif has been the drafting and publication of an alternative "egalitarian" personal status code entitled "One Hundred Measures and Provisions." The Egalitarian Code focuses on the goals of equality, freedom, and nondiscrimination, and its ultimate objective is to ensure the compliance of Shari'a-based laws that govern and control women's rights with the universal norms espoused in international human rights instruments.

The Egalitarian Code addresses equality in marriage, divorce, filiation (parent-child ties), and inheritance—the major areas encompassed by the personal status codes in the Maghreb. The provisions dealing with marriage are illustrative of the principles underlying the entire code. Unlike most Shari'a-based codes, for example, it sets eighteen years as the minimum legal age for marriage for both men and women.[32] The consent of both partners is required for marriage and is the sole consent needed.[33] Polygyny is expressly forbidden.[34]

The same grounds for divorce exist for men and women, including mutual consent and "fault."[35] Repudiation, although not explicitly prohibited, is not included as a means of dissolving a marriage, and the code specifies that only a judge can pronounce a divorce.[36] Further provisions require that legal guardianship of a child be shared by both parents as long as they remain married[37] and thereafter goes to the parent who is granted custody.[38]

The existing family codes in the Maghreb were essentially a codification of the Shari'a and traditional practices, and subsequent attempts at reform were often limited to improvements that would not pose a threat to traditional precepts. In contrast, the Egalitarian Code does not attempt to preserve or improve upon notions that are, at their core, discriminatory. Rather, its drafters have opted for an entirely new body of law premised upon equality and nondiscrimination.

### The Post-Beijing Struggle for Reform

After the Beijing conference, the Collectif '95 disbanded and reemerged as the Collectif 2000, whose mission is to seek adoption of the alternative Egalitarian Code. The group has continued to publicize the code through the media, conferences, and translation and publication of the text into different languages.

Responses to the Collectif's efforts have varied from country to country. In Morocco the Collectif '95 initially met with opposition, including from certain women's groups that declared its actions "counter to Islam." It had been anticipated that critics would point to the substantial social and economic problems facing the Moroccan population in general, and women in particular, and would argue that it was inappropriate for women to tackle the Family Code until important issues such as poverty, education, and employment rights had been addressed. Critical voices have not been raised against the Collectif, however—at least not publicly. Meanwhile, the official Moroccan response to the Collectif's activities has been more or less one of laissez faire. Nevertheless, the danger exists that the move toward secularization of the Moudawana could threaten, or be perceived as threatening, Moroccan stability by calling into question the king's commitment to Islamic principles.

In Algeria the debate over the Family Code has, in many ways, mirrored the nation's political divisions. Although the women's movement is far from homogeneous, its demands for reform or abolition of the Family Code have, at times, played into the hands of the Algerian government: the government has discovered in women's demands concerning the Family Code yet another political weapon to be deployed against its Islamist opponents. Although many women activists are independent, official and quasi-official organs have embraced aspects of the movement's platform, making it another element in the political battle against "fundamentalism."

The situation in Tunisia has been the most precarious. Despite its progressive Family Code the repressive Tunisian regime has impeded actions of human rights organizations and other associations, including women's groups. As many groups of women activists have been denied official status by the government, women have been forced to act as individuals and groups as autonomous, unofficial units. As a result, the Collectif's platform has reportedly been less accessible to the population than in either Morocco or Algeria.

## Prospects and Strategies for the Future

Prospects for the future, whether adoption of the Egalitarian Code or simply the implementation of reforms, cannot be separated from the political realities of the Maghreb. The repressive character and poor human rights records of all three governments make it unlikely that the struggle to protect women's rights will succeed; fundamental rights continue to be denied in most other spheres. Even if the government appears to join forces with women, as in Algeria, or to observe silently, as in Morocco, the ever-present menace of political Islam in the region makes women's rights the most suitable area in which governments can make concessions to Islamists without paying a political price. The elusiveness of a political solution to the conflict in Algeria has not gone unremarked by its neighbors, who have followed a dual policy of repression and concession in an effort to avoid igniting internal conflicts of their own.

On a more practical level the women's movement in the Maghreb has been hampered by the lack of a regional framework or formal network of women's groups. Although many issues are common to the women of the region, they have generally been raised in country-specific contexts. The challenge facing the Collectif and the broader women's movement in the region is how to maintain momentum and motivation even in the face of slow progress.

The Beijing conference provided a temporary structure for collective activity and the opportunity to raise critical issues in an international context as well. To improve the chances of progress women in the Maghreb must continue to address regional and international fora in order to raise awareness of women's demands in the region. Some of the international structures already in place, such as the United Nations Human Rights Commission based in Geneva, which reviews the human rights practices of member states, and the periodic review of compliance with international conventions such as CEDAW provide opportunities to place regional issues on the international agenda and ensure scrutiny of governmental compliance with international standards they have pledged to uphold.

In the post-Beijing era, scrutiny of the significant yet nonbinding commitments made by governments during the Beijing conference is also needed. A larger network consisting of the Collectif and other women's groups in the region in the pursuit of this objective would strengthen each group's contacts and visibility and would make possible the development of a common advocacy strategy. By targeting the most discriminatory aspects of family codes in the region as well as the failure by governments to enforce laws that protect women such a network would increase the pressure on governments and bring about greater scrutiny of abusive practices.

The fact that the Collectif is still going strong one year after Beijing is testimony to the effectiveness of collective action. It also demonstrates that women in the Maghreb will continue the struggle for equality until laws and practices that discriminate against women are eliminated.

# 8

# Leadership Development
# for Young Women
A Model
Sharifah Tahir

The international women's movement has brought indisputable changes for the better to women all over the world. The improvements and positive changes, however, have yet to affect the majority of women. At the same time as many women benefited from the women's movement, class and regional differences were created that resulted in widening gaps in lifestyles and access to resources among women. Furthermore, decision making in the women's movement is concentrated in a small group of core women. As a result of these differences, many women are marginalized and their diverse concerns are not addressed.

To represent all women the women's movement has to bridge these gaps and to develop effective mechanisms to ensure that the voices of all women are heard and respected. Expanding the base of the movement not only will broaden the issues and concerns to be addressed but also will encourage wider participation in decision making. Only by involving women from all walks of life in the political process and in program development will the varied needs of women be addressed effectively. It needs a conscious effort to identify new problems, to be flexible in formulating agenda, and to broaden leadership in the women's movement to make it more representational and more successful.

Thus, the nurturance of the next generation of women leaders is of crucial importance for the future of the women's movement. Young women traditionally have been excluded from the process of defining issues concerning women in general and concerning themselves in particular. They also have very little opportunity to voice their concerns and opinions anywhere. The lack of structures that would enable young women to capitalize on the experiences and expertise of older women and to formulate their own points of view has resulted, on the one hand, in a lack of in-depth understanding of various issues that concern them and, on the other, in a lack of leadership and administrative skills that would be crucially important for their own success in the future. Moreover, weak leadership resulting from lack of leadership skills and a superficial understanding of issues concerning women easily may jeopardize the continuation of the women's movement altogether.

The impact of structural adjustment programs, national debt to foreign lenders, transnational capitalism, and the growth of so-called religious fundamentalism threatens to undo the gains achieved by women in Muslim countries over the last few decades. In light of these threats the need for strong leadership over a wide spectrum of human affairs is higher than ever at all levels of society, within communities and in national and international organizations, in governmental and nongovernmental institutions. Women need to increase their efforts to develop future leaders and to put in place mechanisms for leadership development.

## Leadership Development for Young Women

The Platform for Action at the Fourth World Conference on Women dedicated a section to women in power and decision making and made recommendations to promote the development of young women leaders. But how are these recommendations to be translated into action? What are the specific strategies for leadership development of young women?

In this chapter I am concerned with such questions as they pertain to young women in Muslim countries. An analysis of the factors affecting the development of young women is followed by recommendations for specific interventions. Neither the analyses nor the recommendations, however, are equally applicable in all countries because women's experiences and the social and cultural realities in which they live are highly diverse. In developing the leadership training model, I have relied heavily on my experiences working in leadership development and in youth reproductive health programs in Asia and initiating a young women's caucus in Kuala Lumpur in which they strive to establish dialogues with older women activists.

The term *leadership* is used widely but carries different meanings for different individuals and in different contexts. Astin and Leland suggest that leadership is "integral to social change and is a creative process that empowers others to organize collectively for action."[1] This kind of leadership should be present on all levels of human affairs: at the grass roots, in national and international bodies, in NGOs, in local groups, in the professions, in religious communities, the private sector, political parties, and in the media.

Although some people are "natural" leaders, leadership is strongly influenced by environmental factors such as culture and training.[2] Leadership traits and skills can be cultivated, and anybody can become a leader if taught properly. For such training to be effective for women a strategic program of action is required.

## Leadership and Muslim Women

Although some very prominent, strong Muslim women leaders exist, leadership among Muslim women, especially young ones, generally lags behind that of women elsewhere. The reasons for this lag are multiple and complex. Culture and tradition are significant.

### Culture and Tradition

The Muslim girl child, like most other girl children, is discriminated against from the moment of birth. In Muslim societies it is customary to regard a son as a gift from God and a daughter as a burden or trial. Girls are unlikely to receive an education that will help them to become aware of their potentials. They are kept at home to help with household chores and to care for younger siblings. Their education is strongly oriented toward teaching them to fulfil their duties as wives and mothers. Early marriage for women is common. Girls move from obeying their parents, especially their fathers, to obeying their husbands and in-laws. Dependency and obedience are praised. From the beginning almost all decisions are made for them.

Under these conditions young Muslim women have extremely limited opportunities to develop decision-making and leadership skills. They are not exposed to alternative styles of living. Their ways of life are prescribed by the male-dominated community. They have few, if any, role models who could show them different ways of life, and thus, as mothers, they will enculturate their own daughters just as they themselves had been enculturated before and thereby continue the cycle through the next generation.

In Muslim societies that offer young women more choices and opportunities young women, nevertheless, often choose not to be leaders, especially not leaders for women's rights movements. This unwillingness is attributable to several factors. First, *women's rights* is viewed as a *feminist* concept, a term with negative connotations. This point came up clearly at a workshop for young women in Malaysia when discussing women's rights and in conversations I held with young women leaders from Muslim countries. Young women do not want to be labeled feminist lest they be seen as aggressive and un-Islamic. Equally important is the lack of support for young women's engagements with women's groups from families and friends, who would rather encourage young women to behave in traditional ways than to become leaders in social movements.

To increase leadership among young women, a critical analysis of how culture and tradition contribute to the devaluation of young girls and women in any given Muslim society, how limitations are imposed on their options, must precede plans for action.

### Resources and Opportunities

In societies or communities where culture and tradition provide few opportunities for women to develop themselves lack of resources likely becomes a further decisive hindrance. If families have to pay for education, for example, or for job training, sons are most likely to be supported and not daughters. Thus, many empowerment opportunities are barred for young women. At the national level, discriminatory priorities result in very few resources allocated for development opportunities for young women. Like parents, the government, too, fails young women. Although international agencies have started to emphasize the development of young women, resources available from these agencies are still very scarce.

Young women who, nevertheless, are willing to assume leadership roles and have some relevant skills often find themselves without much of a chance to exercise their skills in various women's and human rights organizations. They are regarded as "too young" to lead and are given insignificant tasks that do not strengthen their leadership qualities. For example, they are given few opportunities to participate in meetings or seminars or to attend, let alone speak at, conferences.

Some opportunities do exist for resource mobilization, but young women are mostly unaware of them or else lack the know-how to access them. This disadvantage clearly was evident at the Fourth World Conference on Women. Although girls and young women were represented fairly from Western countries, only a few from Muslim countries and developing nations were present. Furthermore, participation at many educational and leadership events organized regionally and internationally for girls and young women is dominated by delegates from developed nations.

These realities of life leave young women from Muslim societies with few opportunities for self-development, including the development of leadership skills. On a brighter side, however, the new global commitment to enhance the status of women and to honor women's human rights creates ample opportunities for change. International agencies such as UNICEF, UNFPA, and UNIFEM[3] are beginning to focus on young women in their planning.[4] Increasingly, young women are encouraged to help formulate development actions and priorities, using their own knowledge and life experiences. The regional youth consultations during the Beijing process are a case in point.

Despite existing efforts the road to developing leadership among young women is a long one. The pertinent recommendations in the Platform for Action are a good starting point, but what specific interventions ought to be taken?

## The Leadership Development Process

The development of leadership and participation of young women in decision making in Muslim countries requires men and women to challenge existing realities and practices, social and political structures, and policies that discriminate against women. It also calls for a comprehensive program of interventions, which, however, cannot simply be generalized across the great diversity of social, political, economic, and cultural contexts in Muslim societies. Nevertheless, a contour of interventions that aim to develop or to strengthen leadership skills among young women can be developed.

### The Educational System

Ideally, leadership development should begin in elementary school and continue through all educational levels. Astin and Leland report that the women leaders they sampled shared early leadership experiences and subsequent leadership skills, personal awareness, and self-confidence.[5]

The current educational system, not only in Muslim countries but also worldwide, to a large extent fails to include leadership training in its curricula. School systems, however, offer some opportunities, such as through Girl Scout groups, class speakers and class monitors, and prefectships. At higher educational levels, leadership positions in student unions, school newspapers, and student committees offer further opportunities of which girls especially should be encouraged to take advantage.

In addition to these programs schools should introduce special programs that involve teens either as part of the school curriculum or as extracurricular activities. For example, the government of Malaysia recently launched a nationwide program called Rakan Muda, which gives young people the opportunity to be involved in various activites, from sports to arts and from nature to community work. Although the purpose of the program is to keep young people meaningfully occupied, it also creates opportunities for young people, including young women, to develop leadership skills.

The education system is an excellent channel through which to expose girls and young women to positive role models. Unfortunately, even where school attendance of girls is high, curriculum and teaching materials to a large degree remain gender biased and still reinforce traditional female and male roles. Textbooks often show women in stereotyped roles as mothers and housewives rather than as leaders or in any other roles. These materials together with a widespread lack of gender awareness by educators reinforce existing discriminatory tendencies. They undermine girls' and young women's self-esteem and thwart their self-development. To promote girls' and young women's education and self-development effectively school systems and their curricula must be reevaluated critically. Educators and policymakers in the education system must be sensitized to gender issues, and curricula must be developed that are free of gender stereotyping. In Muslim countries examples from the Quran and life experiences of women around the Prophet Muhammad are relevant. Khadijah, the first wife of Muhammad, was a successful businesswoman. Aisha, the Prophet's last wife, was known for expressing her thoughts and for her leadership. The Prophet is reported to have sought the advice of these two women in political and social matters. Such examples are found in Islamic studies courses in Malaysian schools, but, unfortunately, they are not fully used to address gender stereotyping.

*Leadership Training Workshops*

Training workshops for women have become a popular intervention strategy for enhancing women's leadership and decision-making skills. These workshops, which are offered by governments, NGOs, and international agencies, have resulted in the emergence of formal and informal women leaders in social, political, and economic arenas. Unfortunately, however, such training has not been extended adequately to young women.

Young women will greatly benefit from workshops that address their particular concerns and teach them how to go about practical matters such as organizing, communicating, lobbying, advocating, networking, cooperating, strategic planning, and resource mobilizing. They can learn to speak in public, how to counter arguments from antiwomen's rights activists, and how to use religious scriptures to the advantage of women. Their positive awareness as women could be strengthened early in discussions of international instruments for social change such as the *Convention on the Elimination of All Forms of Discrimination Against Women (CEDAW)*, the Beijing Platform for Action, the International Conference on Population and Development in Cairo (ICPD), and the Vienna Program of Action, and by instruction in how to use these instruments effectively.

I was one of the thirty young women from twenty-eight countries who participated in the Young Women Leaders Program organized and sponsored by Caritas during the Beijing conference. We were guided through the whole Beijing experience and were given in-depth information about the conference and NGO forum process. Women experts taught us how to use the international instruments, particularly *CEDAW*. Although these introductory sessions were useful, we felt a need for intensive training which included in-depth discussions and examples of how these instruments have been mobilized.

In the Philippines, for example, the Women's Resource and Research Centre has taken initiatives to implement a program to strengthen emerging young leaders within the women's movement. The program will include workshops to identify and address the needs and concerns of young leaders and will bring in veteran feminists to teach leadership techniques and responsibilities to young women.

*Mentorship Programs*

Mentors and role models can inspire young women to set high goals for achievement. Through mentoring, young women can receive guidance from established leaders to learn successful techniques and to avoid making the same mistakes their mentors had made earlier.

Mentorship programs can be implemented easily within the educational system (e.g., student-teacher) and in informal interactions between leaders and young women. These programs do not require substantial resources but do demand time and commitment of the mentors. Established women leaders especially should be recruited to hand down to young women their wealth of knowledge and experience. Through mentoring, older women leaders who otherwise might feel threatened by young women "upstarts" can develop positive and nurturant relationships that benefit both themselves and the young women they tutor. Established leaders must realize the importance of succession of leadership and that through their guidance and commitment to mentoring they are coaching and empowering the next generation of leaders who will continue their struggle.

Although mentoring can happen by chance, programs must be developed for offering such opportunities systematically to as many young women as possible. Several women's groups and organizations in Malaysia are making progress in this area. Whereas some, such as Asian-Pacific Resource Centre for Women (ARROW), employ young women as their assistants, others, such as the Sisters in Islam, have invited their younger counterparts to become involved in their activities and meetings. In these arrangements young women are able to voice their opinions and at the same time learn from their more experienced sisters.

*Internship/Fellowship Programs*

Learning by doing allows young women to practice leadership skills while gaining other valuable experiences and insights. Especially for leadership development in the areas of human rights, women's rights, population, and environment, which are not readily available at institutions young women are customarily attached to such as schools, there is a special need for internship programs. The program can be implemented at organizations and offices that work on the regional, national, or international levels. Preferably, interns should be assigned to experienced persons who act as mentors. For example, the Population Institute in Washington, D.C., has a program called Young Leaders of America, which gives young women and men the chance to work in a population-related organization in developing countries for six to twelve months; the United Nations Volunteers are young people who are assigned to United Nations agencies for between several months and two years.

*Experience Sharing*

Young women need opportunities to share experiences and information with each other, to compare strategies, and to learn from the successes and failures of others. Regional, national, and international seminars and conferences provide such opportunities.

A good example of such sharing of experiences was the Caritas-supported Young Women Leaders Program described above. Throughout the event, young women leaders shared their success stories and failures, exchanged ideas, and discussed their experiences in their own countries. Furthermore, participants spent time with established women leaders who talked about their experiences fighting for women's rights.

Equally valuable is the documentation and dissemination of personal experiences of young women from different countries. For example, a collaborative project, Our Words, Our Voices: Young Women for Change, was initiated in preparation for the Beijing conference. It consists of a compilation of case studies by and about young women from every region of the world. The studies cover violence and rape, crimes of "honor," teen pregnancy, the plight of young women workers, sex trafficking, health issues, and education. Each case study is placed within a larger framework and concludes with proposals for action. Through such programs young women learn that their problems are not unique and can gain the self-confidence necessary to find solutions for them. For example, the Young Women's Caucus (YWC) in Kuala Lumpur published a booklet, *Young Women Speak Out*, which carries articles on a range of issues from Pakistan, Vietnam, Singapore, and Malaysia. The articles include a discussion between two generations of women activists, a discussion among young women on sexuality, reproductive health and gender, feminism and everyday life, and young women's responses to "feminism."

### Dialogue

Dialogues between young women and experienced leaders, particularly women leaders, policymakers, and professionals in various fields enable young women not only to learn various opinions and perspectives but also to get their own concerns heard. Indeed, the recognition of the importance of addressing the needs of young people has been an impetus to the organization of such dialogues. This momentum should continue. For example, the Young Women's Caucus organized a minidialogue with several women leaders before the Fourth World Conference on Women. The dialogue allowed members of the YWC to express their ideas and at the same time enabled the women leaders to listen to the younger women and to offer guidance. As mentioned earlier, several women's groups and organizations in Malaysia have included young people in their activities and meetings and, thus, offer them opportunities for meaningful dialogues.

### Networking

Networks consisting of young women, women's organizations, women leaders, and donor agencies that sponsor women's projects allow the exchange of information, experience sharing, and accessing of resources and provide much-needed support for young women. Such networks should be formed at regional, national, and international levels. Youth organizations ought to be brought into such networks because they already have access to young people, promote youth-related activities, and are likely to have leadership development programs that can be used to benefit young women concerned with women's rights.

### Issues

In implementing the suggested interventions, several issues must be addressed:

1. Continuing Advocacy. Although the need to empower young women and to address their needs is recognized widely, it is not a high-priority political concern in most nations. Thus, there is a strong need for effective advocacy to achieve long-lasting changes for girls and young women. Young women leaders and their supporters must raise awareness of young women's issues, and must change perceptions and attitudes in the family as well as in society at large. They must persuade decision makers in the social and political domain to place girls and young women at the heart of policy-making. They must insist that economic development projects and educational policies take the needs and contributions of young women into account. In other words, they must become politically active on all levels. Furthermore, religious leaders, who play an important role in shaping public awareness of social issues regarding women in many Muslim countries, must be persuaded to support the advancement of girls and young women. Women's advocates have to develop strategies for generating such support in as nonconfrontational and cooperative a way as possible so as not to alienate religious and traditional segments of the society and their leaders, and can look for suggestions to the Muslim nations of Malaysia and Indonesia where religious leaders indeed support women's issues.

2. Institutionalization of Interventions. Successful interventions must be institutionalized within public and private institutions to be sustained. If programs that support young women's leadership training are not incorporated into existing institutions and made part of standing budgets and policies, they run the great risk of being discontinued should immediate interest in them fade or patronage by individual politicians or groups be withdrawn or funds diminish.

3. Comprehensive Approach. Leadership development cannot be achieved in isolation from other interventions such as education, employment, health care, and family planning, which aim to ensure that young women are able to enjoy fully their rights and to become effective agents of change. Although special interventions for leadership development are necessary, other enabling conditions, such as a sup-

portive social and political environment, availability and access to opportunities, and allocation of resources, must be addressed at the same
time.

4. Active Participation. The development of programs must involve the active participation of young women at all levels, beginning
with the identification of needs. Young women must be involved in
the development and implementation of programs and in their evaluation if interventions are to be successful. Programs must be set up by
and for a target group. For this notion to be realized, efforts must be
made to include young women of all walks of life and from all parts
of a country to avoid the possibility that a minority of young women
leaders will speak for a large, marginalized, and silent majority.

# 9

## The Women Studies Program
## in Palestine

### Between Criticism and New Vision

### Eileen Kuttab

**Palestinian Women's Activism**

Since the beginning of the twentieth century the Palestinian women's movement has been an integral component of the Palestinian national movement, centering its activities around national issues. For example, different women's institutions were established to provide basic services to the devastated population after the 1948 and 1967 wars. Women's charitable societies, led by educated women of the upper classes, adopted a welfare strategy to meet the immediate needs of families in crises during political upheavals.

During the two decades following the occupation of the West Bank and Gaza Strip, the drastic changes that the Israeli occupation policies imposed on the Occupied Territories resulted in economic dependency on the Israeli market and the destruction of the local political, social, and economic infrastructure. In response new organizations were created to enlarge the social base of the Palestinian national movement and to expand the base of resistance. New mass-based Palestinian national institutions were created to address specific basic needs of the society in health, education, agriculture, and social services.[1] Along with students and workers, women were mobilized to participate actively in the national struggle.

This democratization movement of which the so-called women's committees were a part was led by educated youths of the middle class trained either in local institutions of higher education such as Birzeit University or in Western universities abroad.[2] The women's committees became the key component of the grass-roots movements. Although theoretically the differences and connections between na-

94

tional and social liberation (including women's liberation) were identified by these organizations, practically, the political and national issues remained their top priority. Occupation policies and practices complicated the social and national agendas. They made the implementation of a feasible, meaningful women's agenda impossible.

The unfortunate alliance between feminism and nationalism continued in the *intifada*, the popular national uprising in 1987. In its early stage women seized new opportunities with courage and persistence; in later stages women found themselves marginalized within the structure of the national movement, especially after the intifada moved away from mass mobilization.[3]

The decline of women's participation in the political process has been attributed by scholars and activists mainly to the inability of Palestinian women's committees to maintain effective mobilization because of a lack of agendas that expressed the dialectic relationship between social and national liberation struggles. This lack left the women's committees in a vacuum.

Furthermore, the decline in the activities of the democratic structures of the intifada as a result of repressive Israeli policies led to controversies over women's political participation, which resulted in women's gradual withdrawal from the political arena. In addition, the emergence of the so-called fundamentalist Islamic movement posed a challenge to the women's movement and at the same time exposed the weakness and the patriarchal nature of the national movement. The national movement had failed to understand the importance of promoting gender issues in a national struggle and had instead downplayed social issues involving gender relations.

In this situation class and gender issues became politicized. In the early 1990s a women's consciousness emerged from women's previous experiences, which promoted gender activism and led to the establishment of centers for women's research, development, and counseling, especially in the West Bank and the Gaza Strip. They addressed issues such as the patriarchal structures of the society, including the national movement; they promoted a national debate on women's rights and on women's place in the public sphere; they organized conferences, workshops, and publications that addressed gender issues. For example, a conference in Jerusalem, "The *Intifada* and Some Social Issues," for the first time addressed such women's concerns as early marriage, the imposition of modest dress, the representation of women in decision making, and female education, all within the national liberation struggle.[4] Task forces and advocacy groups were established to discuss and formulate strategies for empowering Palestinian women and for integrating them in the decision-making process.

## The Post-Oslo Period

The Oslo Agreement further marginalized Palestinian women and excluded their representatives from the decision-making process. In the various technical committees that were formed to serve the peace process women were minimally represented: of 410 members, only 5 were women. Concerned women launched a campaign that resulted in the establishment of a Women's Affairs Technical Committee that was responsible for addressing women's concerns. For example, under its umbrella different women's committees were mobilized to formulate gender-sensitive policies for the Palestinian authorities and strategies to redress gender imbalances and to ensure an increase in women's participation in decision making in the future.

Obviously, the women's movement in Palestine had come to realize that the Palestinian leadership must be pressured to adopt a women's agenda, to respond to women's needs and requirements, to appoint women to positions that reflect their contributions to the national struggle, and to become aware of the injustices created especially for the poor and for women in the economic processes of globalization and privatization. Now the women's movement's leadership addresses different issues, such as women's work, the relationships between feminism and nationalism, the impact of Palestinian political authorities on women's decision making, and the legislation of women's rights.[5]

## The Womens Studies Program:
## Philosophy and Practice

Members of women's organizations and research centers realized that the development of strategies to further women's agendas requires a new level of research, analysis, and activism. Thus, a group of women academicians from different departments at Birzeit University responded to the current political changes, community needs, and an academic interest in gender relations in the region by creating the Women Studies Program (WSP) at Birzeit University.[6] The Women Studies Committee, appointed by the University Council, prepared the plan for the program within the Faculty of Arts. It was approved in September 1994.

The new Women Studies Program concentrated on three major areas—teaching, research, and community outreach and gender intervention—to combine academic and activist activities that would be responsive to community needs and relevant to the political situation.

*Teaching*

From the beginning and keeping in mind women's experiences in the Palestinian women's movement, the educational goal of the program was to change attitudes about and of women and to find the reasons for women's devaluation and subordination. Thus, the program committed itself to the development of a critical approach to knowledge to be able to promote the process of increasing gender awareness. Furthermore, because the Women Studies Program had evolved in the contexts of national struggle and economic restructuring, issues such as the relationships between nationalism and feminism and the impact of global structural changes on women's political and economic participation became important. Most importantly, however, the program taught Palestinian students to understand social organization, relations within the family, and interpersonal dynamics in terms of gender relations and gender expectations in Palestinian as well as greater Arab society.

The WSP offers a minor consisting of eleven courses. Its introductory course is designed to be relevant to a wide range of students and has been received enthusiastically by male and female students alike. Other, more specific, courses increasingly are being cross-listed with different departments to ensure their availability to as many students as possible.[7]

One of the major problems in developing the curriculum is the paucity of texts, especially in Arabic. A Women's Studies Library and Resource Center is being established to further the acquisition of relevant books and journals, and the WSP has started a translation project of key works in feminist scholarship and plans to publish an interdisciplinary anthology that can be used as a text on feminist theory and gender relations in Palestinian society and in the Middle East generally. The translation involves the creation of new words for concepts that do not exist in the Arabic language and will necessitate the development of a dictionary.

After two years of teaching the Women Studies Program, the faculty noticed a high interest in the WSP by women outside the university and responded to it by creating a professional diploma program based on several core courses and a practical component in policy-making, planning, and training. This degree program, which will start in 1997–98, targets women, nongovernmental activists, development planners, civil servants, and teachers; it is designed as a postbachelor degree program and as the first stage of a planned master's program in Gender, Development, and Law in the WSP.

*Research*

The founding members of the WSP agreed that academic research should not be separated from community activism because a gap between theory and practice constitutes an obstacle to successful identification and solution of the problems of Palestinian women. Thus, the members rejected the standard scientific approach of the "dualistic compartmentalization of life" into thinking and doing, theory and practice,[8] and instead saw research as a tool of change for women and the community at large.

In this context in September 1994 the WSP started a fifteen-month collaborative research project on "Palestinian Women in Society" with four teams, including all members of the WSP, other faculty members from Birzeit University, and researchers from other Women's Research Centers. The project was to make a critical assessment of the state of research and writing on Palestine in the economy, education, social entitlements and support systems, and culture and society, with emphasis on gender relations.

The project included an international workshop at Birzeit University, "Palestinian Women in Society: State of Research and New Directions," in December 1994 to clarify the project's methodological and theoretical framework. Four working papers and a research report, "Status Report on Palestinian Women," issued in Arabic and English, have been well received. The WSP aims to make its research results available in a form easily accessible to activists, planners, and decision makers.

Among others, the project found a lack of policy research and public debate on women's issues. This prompted the WSP to initiate a second phase of the Palestinian Women in Society project, which will end in 1998. It has the goal of monitoring rapidly evolving Palestinian social policies and of assessing their impact on women and men at the level of the household and the family. Furthermore, it aims to promote social policies more equitable to women and the poor and to address the major social issues and inequities in Palestinian society today.

During the first research project two areas were identified for further research: social security and support, and educational curriculum reform.

In the social security and support area the research project identified formal and informal support structures and their inadequacies and suggested strategies for improvement and for further research on informal economic and social networks. To this effect the second research phase will concentrate on the investigation of the role of the family and of kin networks in providing social support, of household coping strategies in economic crises, of pressures and burdens on family members, particularly on women within the household, and will investigate to what extent support institutions and programs actually address women's concerns. In cooperation with other local researchers the project will identify priority issues for the women's movement agenda for the near future.

In the educational curriculum and reform area the first project found that, despite a rising educational level of Palestinian women in the West Bank and the Gaza Strip over the 1980s and 1990s, women's formal participation in the labor force remains low and professional opportunities for women remain few, even if one takes into account that temporary, seasonal, and informal work of women generally is underestimated. The second research project will address this gap between educational attainment and economic opportunities for women. A gender diagnosis of vocational education and training in the first research project found a marked gender bias in this type of education and a curriculum that does not meet women's or men's needs. In the second phase of the project educational policies and curricula, therefore, will be examined for gender biases and structural weaknesses, and suggestions for effective interventions will be made.

*Community Outreach and Gender Intervention*

In the ongoing debate about how to build a democratic society of equal citizens the WSP contributes to gender awareness and to the development of policies that address the social, cultural, economic, and political issues confronting Palestinian women. Various tools have been identified that are useful in accomplishing these goals. One is gender planning training of government officials, and of members of nongovernmental organizations and international agencies. A Gender Planning Manual will be tested in pilot training sessions in 1998. Another tool is the organization of workshops and seminars on policies affecting Palestinian women, such as, for example, on the Palestinian labor legislation and on reports, "Poverty in the West Bank and Gaza" and "The Future of Palestinian Women's Activism." Yet another tool is the use of local mass media to circulate information of strategic importance to women and other marginalized groups. Finally, the WSP established a scholarship fund to support needy female students in an attempt to draw women from poorer segments of the society to higher education.

## Conclusion

There is a big difference between women studies as practiced at Birzeit University and other traditional disciplines. The Women Studies Program there has emerged from political and social activism outside the university and has been able to combine academic pursuits, feminism, and community activism ever since. Generally, women's studies programs arose partly as a critique of the traditional disciplines that excluded the experiences of women and scholarship on and by women and partly to identify and to dismantle the patriarchal bases inherent in the traditional disciplines.[9] The WSP at Birzeit University is no exception. It is committed to taking an activist stance in promoting women's rights and gender equality in Palestinian society through dynamic, multidisciplinary cooperation with all sectors of the population.

# 10

## Imperiled Pioneer
### An Assessment of the Institute for Women's Studies in the Arab World
### Laurie E. King-Irani

Long before some leading women's studies programs had been established in Europe and North America, the Institute for Women's Studies in the Arab World (IWSAW) was founded in Beirut, Lebanon, in 1973. It was part of the Beirut College for Women, a respected American-affiliated institution that attracted young women students from the Arab world, Iran, and Turkey. Soon after the founding of the IWSAW, the college became the coeducational Beirut University College, which developed into the Lebanese American University in 1994. Despite the many changes in the College and the chaos and destruction visited upon Lebanon during seventeen years of war, the IWSAW successfully carried on its work as a center for research and documentation and continued to publish a quarterly journal and many studies on women's conditions in the Arab world.[1]

During the twenty-five years of IWSAW's existence, social, political, and economic realities at the local, national, and international levels have changed dramatically and with them have changed Arab women's lives, needs, and priorities. These changes necessitate a critical appraisal of IWSAW's mission today.

A pioneer in the field of women's studies in the 1970s and 1980s, the institute in the 1990s no longer is at the forefront of research, education, publication, or advocacy regarding Arab women. Scholars affiliated with the institute neither have undertaken nor published major research projects on Arab women since the end of the war nor have they offered courses in women's studies since 1994. In 1995 the extent of IWSAW's marginalization became apparent when not one representative of IWSAW was officially invited to join the Lebanese mission to the Fourth International Women's Conference in Beijing.

The reasons for IWSAW's current lethargy and marginalization range from the cessation of wartime relief funding to the cumulative negative effects of a long war on research and academic standards, from social and economic instability and increasing political repression in postwar Lebanon to a lack of fresh ideas and intellectual openness among the institute's and the university's current leadership. Behind these reasons, however, lies a more fundamental problem—a permanent crisis of identity that has hindered the work of IWSAW since its very inception. I delineate here this identity crisis, survey the institute's achievements, examine the challenges the institute is facing, and discuss the strategies the institute might pursue to regain leadership in women's studies in the Arab world. Despite its current problems IWSAW has not lost its resources: an inspiring history, a rich documentation center, a potentially vital institutional infrastructure, and talented, creative, and energetic members. It remains the only institution in Lebanon capable of drawing together scholars, activists, policymakers, students, and nongovernmental organizations concerned with improving the condition of Lebanese women.

Although housed in a university in the heart of an important Arab capital, IWSAW lacks deep roots in the local culture and has not sustained interactions with all sectors of the society. Despite its self-declared "pioneering" approach to Arab women's issues, the institute's leadership consistently distances itself from feminist philosophy and agendas and increasingly avoids speaking or doing research on potentially controversial topics. Trying not to offend anybody, IWSAW has failed to satisfy those who could benefit most from its resources.

Because of its ambivalent identity, IWSAW has not been able to engage fully in vital debates concerning women's human rights in the Arab-Islamic world, women's reshaping of religious and legal texts, and critical appraisals of traditional gender roles and cultural practices. Yet, considering Beirut's long-standing contacts with East and West, with Christianity and Islam, IWSAW would be well placed to link women academics and activists from the Arab world and the West into an international network of dialogue and cooperation.

## IWSAW's Identity Crisis

IWSAW did not develop organically out of an Arab-Islamic social and intellectual milieu, nor was it founded on feminist principles and goals. Its ancestry can be traced to the American Presbyterian missionary educators and reformers who founded the American University of Beirut and the forerunner of the Beirut College for Women in the waning days of the Ottoman empire, an institution then known as the

Beirut Girls' College or Junior College. In its first brochure IWSAW cited this impressive pioneering educational heritage to stress its identity as the first Arab women's studies institute in the first women's college in the Arab world. Fittingly, IWSAW named its journal *al-Raida* (The Woman Pioneer).

In 1972 the leaders of a consortium of nine Asian colleges decided to establish centers for women's studies at each institution.[2] These centers were to compile basic statistical data for comparative research, introduce courses on women's issues into the curricula of each college, provide career counseling for women students, and emphasize the important role of university education in changing local women's consciousness.

IWSAW, the first of the centers, and the other women's studies centers in the Asian Women's Institute, as the consortium was called, were funded by the North American Cooperating Agencies of Overseas Women's Christian Colleges. Julinda Abu Nasr, a U.S. trained specialist in early childhood education, has served as its director since it was founded in 1973. According to Julinda Abu Nasr, she was appointed director not because of any training in women's studies or a commitment to feminist goals (most of which, she says, she does not support), but because she was the only Arab woman teaching at the Beirut College for Women who held a doctorate at the time.

The very first issue of *al-Raida* featured an editorial by the then president of the college, Albert Badre, on the rationale for the institute and on its goals. These had less to do with the pursuit of social justice and gender equality than with the socioeconomic progress of the Arab nation. Badre decried the Arab world's "failure to exploit the full potential of the Arab women as we have exploited the potential of Arab oil," adding that whatever hindered Arab women's development also hindered the social and economic progress of the entire Arab world.[3] Thus, a primary goal of IWSAW was to "instill faith and self-confidence in the Arab woman . . . to enable her to bring forth the full flow of her capacities for the betterment of the Arab nation, its development and renewal" in the face of the key obstacles of ignorance and rigid cultural traditions within Arab society itself.[4] The implicit message was that Arab women's salvation (and with it the salvation of the entire Arab nation) depended on women's detachment from the native cultural milieu and the adoption of progressive, modern, Western ways of thinking and acting. He did not even consider the possibility that Arab women might find their own solutions to their problems. Solutions would come from proper education and "the use of relevant documents and statistics, creative scientific research, and analytical studies." IWSAW was to become a documentation center and to conduct objective research "in order to advance a better understanding of issues pertaining to Arab women and children." [5] In the same issue of *al-Raida* research priorities were listed: "The role of women in development; Working women; Social and legal status of Arab women; Women's achievements; Women's self-conceptions; Women and education; Social taboos which hinder women's development; Population and health issues."

Twenty years later, in early 1996, nearly all of these topics were listed again in *al-Raida* as subjects in need of examination. Little had changed in two decades. Yet, quite obviously, something more than college courses and quantitative research for and by educated, Westernized elite women was needed to address the problems of ordinary Arab women. Indeed, from the very beginning IWSAW lacked an open, egalitarian dialogue between researchers and educators, on the one hand, and women from all socioeconomic backgrounds, on the other. Instead, only two women, including the director herself, served on the first Board of Directors of IWSAW; all but one board member were Christians; two members were Westerners. Clearly, Muslims and women were grossly underrepresented in the leadership of an institute officially devoted to Lebanese women.

The early issues of *al-Raida* have a paternalistic tone. The educators and researchers are certain that they have the answers to all problems; a little social engineering and formal education as defined by Western-trained professionals would solve the problems of Arab women. The voices of Arab women talking about lived experiences, quandaries, beliefs, and practices did not even begin to appear in *al-Raida* or other IWSAW publications until well into the war years, after 1980.

The war in Lebanon, which began in early 1975 and lasted until late 1990, quickly changed and focused IWSAW's mission and identity, particularly between 1977 and 1987. Most women interviewed for this chapter referred to this decade as "IWSAW's golden years."

## Crucible of Change and Achievement: The War's Impact on IWSAW

The Lebanese war, which brought about untold suffering, destruction, and chaos to the Lebanese people, made many Lebanese women question traditional assumptions about their culture and the boundaries of their lives. With the collapse of the state and most systems of centralized authority, familial and communal roles and social relationships readjusted, often to women's disadvantage, but occasionally in ways that gave women more decision-making power and freedom of action than before.[6] This change gave IWSAW social relevance and new directions for research. IWSAW also benefited from generous wartime relief funding, mostly provided by charitable and educational foundations in Europe and North America.

The combined effects of increased funding, decreased control by centralized authorities, and the challenges of the war created an atmosphere conducive to creative, ground-breaking research on issues of importance to Arab women. Under the able leadership of Julinda Abu Nasr and Research Director Irini Lorfing the institute shifted from collecting basic statistical data to the analysis and interpretation of women's responses to the war, particularly in economy and employment. The results of these projects were published as monographs by UNESCO, the International Labor Organization, and the University of California Press,[7] but IWSAW produced so much research during that time that it became a publishing house itself.[8]

The war also prompted IWSAW's staff to become involved in the lives of many women from all social backgrounds. By 1980 staff members, particularly Anita Nassar, were providing crucial services, training, and counseling to the ever-increasing numbers of displaced women and their families who inhabited bombed-out buildings throughout Beirut. From this activism IWSAW developed its acclaimed Basic Living Skills Project (BLSP), an action-oriented program designed to educate and train women in survival skills and to provide them with useful knowledge. It covered topics such as family planning and health care, civic education, environmental awareness, employment skills, and legal rights. The individuals interviewed for this paper cited the BLSP, along with the institute's own survival, as the institute's greatest accomplishment to date.

The Basic Living Skills Project drew upon IWSAW's resources and also involved collaboration with nongovernmental organizations, educators, medical personnel, governmental agencies, researchers, and community leaders. But the project also directly involved displaced women, many of whom were poverty-stricken and initially uneducated, in decision-making processes affecting their lives. Thus, the BLSP broke with conventional charitable social service practice and instead aimed to put women in charge of their own lives by helping them to reclaim their dignity and self-sufficiency, giving them information, skills, and tools with which they could understand their position and could learn strategies necessary to survive in the market and to defend themselves legally. The BLSP was not dictated from above but arose from dialogue and collaboration of IWSAW staff with women from all walks of life who suddenly found themselves widowed, displaced, impoverished, and in charge of their families' welfare. The project's focus on these women's own cognitive and emotional realities produced a highly effective program. In addition to helping nearly one thousand women become economically self-sufficient, the BLSP also generated a rich body of knowledge about women's roles in economic decision making, the development and maintenance of community support networks, women's leadership capacities, factors hindering women's empowerment, and women's evolving roles in Lebanese and Arabic society. It is very likely that without the war and the BLSP experience IWSAW would have remained isolated from the realities, needs, and experiences of nonelite, noneducated, economically disadvantaged women, who, unfortunately, represent the majority of Lebanon's female population. The theoretical and practical insights gained from the project ought to be reviewed for possible use in postwar Lebanese and other Arab societies instead of being filed away in the archives.

## Losing Direction and Relevance:
## IWSAW in the Postwar Period

With the end of the war in 1990 IWSAW entered a period of "downsizing" of its research and outreach activities. This resulted in a sense of uncertainty about IWSAW's role in Lebanese society and the wider Arab world that has continued until today. The end of the war brought about a decrease in funding and, consequently, in independence. Independence was further curtailed by the resurrection of centralized systems of authority at the university and in the government. Now, both the government and the Lebanese American University favor money-making enterprises and "pragmatic" programs. Accordingly, IWSAW is neglected while new undergraduate and graduate programs are launched in computer science, pharmacy, and engineering. The social sciences and the humanities are marginalized in the universities just as social services and humanitarian projects are marginalized by the Lebanese government. Women are little, if at all, involved in the decision making of either the university or the state, which, since the end of the war, increasingly tends toward political repression and censorship of print and media.

In this atmosphere of limited resources, economic hardship, political restrictions, and postwar exhaustion, controversial issues such as those regarding Muslim women are avoided, and the institute is in danger of losing its direction and social relevance. This development is especially distressing because IWSAW, situated in a society that has experienced a protracted war, extreme poverty, population displacements, and economic restructuring, is well-positioned for research on the two key issues identified at the Beijing conference: the impact of all kinds of violence on women and the feminization of poverty. Furthermore, Lebanon's cultural pluralism presents a natural sociological "laboratory" in which one can study Arab women in a variety of social, cultural, and religious circumstances.

In spite of these problems and hardships the institute had some positive developments recently. Since 1992 *al-Raida* has focused on topics at the juncture of academia, activism, and policy-making, such as women's human rights and women in sustainable human development programs. Encouraging, too, has been the increasing interest in feminist theory and feminist issues of women students at the three universities in Beirut.[9] The students have formed a consciousness-raising group, the Friends of IWSAW, which organizes occasional public education programs on women's rights and concerns. Last but not least, the automation of the holdings of the institute's documentation center will enable the institute to make its collections available on the Internet.

Although the sociopolitical atmosphere in postwar Lebanon is not conducive to intellectual debate and activism on any social issues, especially not on those concerning women, two promising developments should be explored by the institute. First is the return of many well-educated, articulate young professional Lebanese women who spent most of the war years in the West. Their views on gender roles and women's rights, which they learned while abroad, are at odds with those they find at home. Their experiences and knowledge ought to be tapped by the institute. The other development is the establishment of a new women's research association, al-Baahithat (Women Researchers), which includes all women researchers, not just those who specialize in women's issues and feminism. It has published two issues of an informative academic journal and has organized a regional conference for Arab women scholars. A representative of al-Baahithat expressed dismay about the current marginalization of IWSAW. Unlike al-Baahithat, the institute specializes in women's issues and has a solid institutional infrastructure through which it can reach out to nongovernmental organizations and policymakers much more effectively than can the new women's association.

## New Frontiers for an Old Pioneer

To ensure that this pioneering women's studies center will continue to explore new frontiers for Arab women in the coming millenium Lebanese researchers, activists, and feminists interviewed for this chapter suggest that the leadership of the institute and the university consider the following strategies and ideas:

1. Establish an endowment fund to gain some independence from the short-term cycles and restrictive philosophies of conventional funding sources.

2. Decentralize authority within the institute with leaders serving as coordinators of programs. Information and power ought to be shared among the staff members. IWSAW should be a model for open dialogue, cooperation, and exchange among academics, NGO activists, journalists, educators, and policymakers.

3. Design long-term, interdisciplinary research projects on issues of concern to all Arab women, such as on women's human rights, women's roles in agriculture and environmental stewardship, and the impact of poverty on women, and then develop educational programs and strategies for activism and lobbying based on these research data.

4. Avoid the "ghettoization" of women's studies in Lebanon and the wider Arab world by focusing research not so much narrowly on women as an isolated category but, for example, on gender aspects in institutions, social change, and community interactions. For such research ethnographic methodologies that contextualize social research, such as participant observation, the collection of oral histories, and case studies, are more relevant to current realities than is the collection of purely quantitative, baseline statistical data focused exclusively on women.

5. Assert IWSAW's political independence as an academic institution and take the risks to design and publish research that breaks social taboos and encourages creative thinking.

6. Become a pioneer in the search for common ground between Islamic, feminist, and Christian points of view on women and, thereby, facilitate dialogue and collaboration among Arab women from all ideological and confessional backgrounds.

7. Publish the institute's findings in Arabic, English, and French and distribute publications extensively throughout the Arab world.

8. Establish "sister" relationships with women's studies institutes in Europe and North America to facilitate joint research projects and faculty and student exchanges.

9. Strengthen communication and collaboration with women's studies centers in other Arab countries and organize regular joint planning meetings.

There is no lack of ideas, hopes, and enthusiasm for the future of the institute. What is not certain is if the administration of the Lebanese American University has the vision and the will to make it possible for the institute to be a pioneer again working for Arab women.

# I I

## Claiming Our Rights

A Manual for Women's Human Rights

Education in Muslim Societies

Mahnaz Afkhami

The Platform for Action identified twelve focus areas for the improvement of women's human rights: poverty, education, health, violence against women, effects of armed conflict, economic structures and politics, inequality of men and women in decision making, gender equality, women's human rights, media, environment, and the girl child. A reasonably efficient national human rights policy must include the identification, articulation, and transmission of women's human rights in these areas. Women must be able to learn about these rights and how they fit local traditions, including religious ones; they must be able to compare their own situations to the postulates of "rights" and to form and formulate their own opinions and arguments if they are to benefit from human rights policies.

The purpose of this manual, therefore, is to facilitate transmission of the universal human rights concepts as inscribed in the major international human rights documents to grass-roots populations in Muslim societies.[1] Because the transmission process is affected by the prevailing economic, social, cultural, and political conditions, the education model that forms the basis for the manual aspires to be multidimensional and to develop a framework that can easily be used to convey universal concepts in association with indigenous ideas, traditions, myths, and texts rendered in local idiom. It was developed in close cooperation with Muslim women scholars and activists and with workshops in Bangladesh and Iran. In various ways it uses Islamic and universal human rights-related sources[2] and classic and modern literary texts such as the Iranian *Book of Kings* and *A Thousand and One Nights*. Presently, the manual is being tested and refined in workshops in six Muslim countries to ensure its adaptability to various local conditions and will continuously be evaluated and adjusted as it is implemented.[3]

## Major Premise

The manual and the education model informing it are based on the premise that there are no contradictions between universal human rights and the spirit of Islam. Because most Muslims believe that Islam includes the essentials of human rights and that its content, as God's revelation, is superior to ordinary law, human rights documents must be presented as consonant with Islamic tenets if they are to succeed in Muslim societies. They must be able to address and contravene the argument that women's human rights contradict Islamic tenets. The following propositions are relevant to this task:

1. As the written word of God, the Quran is eternal, infinite, and mystical and is understood in its eternal and infinite scope by the Prophet only. All other mortals understand it according to their human gifts. The religious experience, i.e., the experience of the Word of God, therefore, is by definition a personal experience, whereas obeying the religious law, the Shari'a, is obedience to manmade law.

2. The Shari'a, the rules by which Muslims have been governed throughout the centuries, is historically determined and situated in time and place because it has had to be understandable to each age and community's specific situation.

3. The original Word of God is infinite in depth and scope and, hence, applicable to innumerable circumstances and evolving conditions. Because most human societies have been organized hierarchically and patriarchally, the Shari'a, just like other religiously inspired laws, reflects this social reality. Consequently, the Quran and the other scriptures as well have been interpreted by the *ulama* to reflect the historical reality of their respective societies.

4. Specific verses in the Quran attest that God enjoins the Prophet not to force human beings in religious matters. Where the Quran clearly states that some social policy must be followed, the statement is, by implication, always bound to the requirements of time and space.

5. The moral impulse of the Word, its eternal thrust, is toward equality for all. Because the Quran values the human person as God's creation, it also values the individual person's right to live in equality with other persons under God. Thus, all instances of inequality are time and space dependent.

6. These points produce a moral imperative for gender equality within Islam's ethical compass. It is, therefore, morally incumbent on the political systems to promote gender equality.

7. These positions can be substantiated by reference to the Quran and the *sunna* (actions and sayings of the prophet Muhammad), provided that one moves outside the traditional epistemology of Shari'a. They also are directly supported by the Islamic Gnostic tradition.

## The Model

As a communications model, the educational model on which the manual is based requires a communicator, a medium, a message, and an audience. Interactively, these components mesh, that is, the communicator and the audience become participants in the production and interpretation of the message and in the construction and validation of the medium as well. When successful, the process leads to constructive discourse. A successful communications model, therefore, is open-ended and produces dialogues that facilitate the transport of ideas that may be entrenched in tradition or presented as dogma to a level of interactions where the participants can start to define their relevance and validity themselves. In other words, the appropriate goal of a human rights education model is to promote "rights" by facilitating individuals' participation in the definition of law or truth, in problematizing and politicizing familiar concepts, and in designing and defining freedom for themselves. This the present model hopes to achieve.

*The Communicator*

Although the transmission of women's human rights messages may take place anywhere, the most likely places will be women's organizations, human rights organizations, and appropriate government agencies. The originator and facilitator in this model are assumed to be women's organizations and to be aided by local and international women's rights advocates and human rights organizations. In many cases governmental agencies can be expected to assist as well.

Women's organizations in Muslim societies are mostly composed of women in public and private institutions, particularly of women teachers in intermediate and higher education. Because women teachers can reach a large audience of young people, they are in an excellent position to promote human rights concepts widely. Many of them are well educated and versed in values that transcend parochial boundaries. More importantly, their position as teachers gives them the moral authority and social acceptability to serve as role models. Under constraints of political and cultural local conditions their role as government-approved professional communicators gives them an important advantage.

Human rights groups everywhere exist to defend the rights of individuals under existing constitutions and to promote rights yet to be achieved. Although they may not possess the direct means of person-to-person communication available to women's organizations, their members are usually better-equipped theoretically and better-connected to the media.

Most Muslim states historically have accepted women's rights as a component of their modernization policies. This support has been diminished or reversed in recent years because of a resurgence of militant fundamentalism. It is more important to mobilize governments in support of women's human rights if the goals of the Platform for Action are to be met. A function of a human rights education model, thus, is to help facilitate state mobilization. When governments are not directly controlled by fundamentalists, the model ought to help women's organizations and human rights groups to empower the state to confront fundamentalism by opening the political space to women, by affirmative action, and by legal reform. To achieve these goals women's advocacy groups need to network and to build constituencies.

### The Audience

The model is based on interaction, reciprocity of roles, and exchange of positions between communicators and their audiences. Its aim is to establish dialogue, not to teach a particular truth. It foresees communication among equals. The audience varies depending on the purpose of communication: it may be the members of a government agency or a religious group, a village gathering, women in a workshop, or family members. The most important audience, however, must be the youth. The young are not only more receptive intellectually and ethically but, as students, they are also more accessible. They constitute a significant majority of the population in the model's target societies. They are the future leaders. Given the criteria of rights education delineated above, their participation in the discussion of rights, in itself, is a strong impetus to the development and democratization of civil society.

The model assumes that any sustained dialogue promotes rights, regardless of the content of the dialogue. For example, the social and ethical constraints in a traditional community will make it possible for a young woman to maintain an ongoing discussion about her rights as an individual with her father, brother, or teacher only after a significant degree of consciousness of rights has been achieved on all sides.

### The Medium

The medium is multivariate, including the mass media, formal and informal organizations, and groups and individuals. The more extensive and numerous the communications channels, the more successful will be the human rights project. A good medium allows for dialogue. But even one-way channels such as radio or television are better than none at all, even though radio and television usually are controlled by governments that may advocate views that are contrary to universal human rights.

The model assumes that most governments officially promote rights even though those rights may be defined in terms of values that are not in line with those of universal human rights and that government officials can be put into positions where they have to defend or explain the difference. Human rights advocates can use the mass media, even if they are controlled by the government, as direct and indirect vehicles of dissemination either by persuading them to broadcast the human rights version of rights or by forcing adversaries into defensive positions in public as often as possible.

This model primarily employs face-to-face communication. It is assumed that all participants will bring a wealth of personal knowledge and experiences to the dialogue and that the discussions will produce not only an awareness of rights but also concrete plans to disseminate insights through the mass media whenever practicable. A political dimension is inherent in any dialogical process.

*The Message*

An efficient model designs messages that can be made operational in the existing cultural, political, and technological environments. An efficient model facilitates the problematization of patriarchal values by encouraging individuals to think about them and to discuss them in relation to the existing sociocultural conditions, on the one hand, and to the universal precepts of rights, on the other. The message must be designed with attention to the cultural and technological environment of the target population so that it can be received and understood widely. The operative concepts are identity and authenticity in a context of freedom and equality.

As does any collective social good, achieving women's human rights also requires an understanding of the political process and the importance of organizing for political action. Human rights messages, therefore, should include suggestions for the following kinds of activities: building constituencies, networking, affirmative action, legal reforms, and resisting extremists.

*The General Structure of the Model*

The model has three parts: an introductory statement about goals, premises, and method; the learning exercises with specific topics and materials used to discuss various aspects of women's rights; appendices with notes to facilitators, texts of four international documents of rights, biographies of several of Islam's early heroines, a list of human rights and women's organization in selected Muslim societies, and a selection of relevant Quranic verses, *hadith*, and proverbs.

The learning exercises comprise nine major topics of rights:

1. Women's rights within the family
2. Women's rights to autonomy in family planning decisions
3. Women's rights to bodily integrity
4. Women's rights to subsistence
5. Women's rights to education and learning
6. Women's rights to employment and fair compensation
7. Women's rights to privacy, religious beliefs, and free expression
8. Women's rights in times of war
9. Women's rights to political participation

These rights optimally are discussed in twelve weekly sessions, each lasting approximately two and one-half hours. The model is flexible enough, however, to allow other arrangements to meet the needs and circumstances of the participants. The sessions begin with the more personal and familiar experiences of home and family life and gradually move to the more distant subjects of community-oriented activities, including economic and political participation. Each session is composed of several exercises designed to problematize routine social practices that impinge on women's basic rights and to stimulate audience participation. In fact, the success of the exercises may be gauged by the extent of interaction of members in each session.

One of the facilitator's main goals is to encourage members to speak up so that the sessions will be lively and interactive. In most cases the facilitator will be reasonably familiar with the basic ideas and principles of the international documents of rights. The most relevant of these documents are provided in the appendix to the manual in the respective national or local language. The model, however, has been designed to work even in the absence of such familiarity by stressing every participant's right to take positions on each issue and by promoting her discussion rather than on imparting or receiving "correct" answers and solutions. Thus, this model is a first approximation of a truly dialogical and fully participatory model for promoting women's rights in Muslim societies.

The following session-program is an example of the methodologies used in the manual.

**Session VIII: Women's Rights to Employment and Fair Compensation** (2 hours 30 minutes)

*Exercise 1: Working Out of the Home*

Supplies needed: none

Time Frame: 1 hour—1 hour 15 minutes

Objectives: To promote women's rights to employment out of the home, to fair compensation, and to their choice of employment.

Instructions:

(1) Arrange yourselves in a semicircle.

(2) One by one, starting with the workshop participants and ending with the facilitator, answer the following questions:

- (Have) you work(ed) outside of the home? If so, what is the nature of your employment?
- Why have (did) you decide to/not to work outside the home?
- When did you start/stop working out of the home?
- Did (Has) your employer treat(ed) you differently from the men in your workplace?
- How do (have) the male members of your family (brother, father, husband, etc.) feel (felt) about your working out of the home?

(Each person should take no more than five minutes so that every participant will have the opportunity to speak.)

(3) As a group, ask yourselves and discuss the following questions:

- Why is women's employment outside of the home important to you? To the family? To the community?
- Does your family, community, and/or government favor men over women in certain types of work? In what types of work?
- Are women and men paid the same wages for the same work?
- If your family, community, and/or government limits the availability of, choice of, and compensation for women's employment, how does that make you feel?
- If a woman works outside of the home, should the male members of the family share in the household chores?
- How does (may) employment outside of the home affect your life?

(This portion of the discussion should take 30–40 minutes.)

*Exercise 2: Earning Equal Pay for Equal Work*

Supplies needed: none

Time frame: 1 hour 15 minutes—1 hour 30 minutes

Objectives: To raise consciousness about gender discrimination in compensation for work; to evaluate women's strategies for negotiating with employers about this issue.

Instructions:

(1) Read aloud the following scenario between "Fatima" and "Dr. Rahbari." (The facilitator may read or select a volunteer from among the workshop participants; the reading should take no more than 10 minutes.)

Fatima's New Job: "I Deserve to Be Paid Fairly!"

While studying medicine in the capital, Fatima decides that she should find a job to earn some money and experience. One of her professors at the university, Dr. Rahbari, a pediatrician, hires Fatima to administer vaccinations to the children who come to his office. Fatima loves her job because she is learning about the medical profession and enjoys working with children.

Soon after starting her position, however, she discovers that Dr. Rahbari's other medical assistant, Samir, is receiving five dinaris an hour for vaccinating adults, whereas she makes only two dinaris an hour. When Fatima asks Dr. Rahbari why her salary is lower than Samir's, the doctor explains that his clinic operates with a limited budget and that Samir must support his wife and children. Fatima insists that she also must support her daughter by herself because she is a widow and that working with children is more difficult than with adults. The doctor resents Fatima's question, explaining that women are naturally inclined to work with children and should be grateful when they are allowed to work out of the home.

Fatima has continued to work at Dr. Rahbari's office because she needs the money, but she is upset about the difference between her pay and Samir's. She has even considered discussing this issue with Rahbari's supervisor and primary benefactor, Dr. Habibi, who runs numerous clinics throughout the country, including one in her hometown.

(2) As a group listening to this scenario, consider Fatima's dilemma. Ask yourselves and discuss the following questions:

- What are Fatima's rights in this situation?
- What conversation should Fatima have with Dr. Rahbari? Should she enlist Samir's help in resolving the problem? Why or why not?

- Should Fatima talk to Dr. Habibi about her disagreement with Dr. Rahbari? What are the advantages and disadvantages of approaching Dr. Habibi? Will the conversation with Dr. Rahbari's supervisor be easier or more difficult if Dr. Habibi is a woman?
- Should Fatima explore the possibility of organizing other women workers, particularly in the field of health care? Should she appeal to organizations such as the local women's group(s), labor union(s), and health care trade association(s)? Should she discover what the law says about the issue of fair compensation for women employed outside of the home?
- Some argue that women are more naturally inclined to do certain types of work such as child care, cleaning, sewing and clothing repair, and so on, whereas men are suited to work that is intellectually or physically challenging such as accounting, engineering, and medicine, or carpentry, electrical repair, and plumbing. What do you think about this claim? Are women capable of working in the same professions as men? Why or why not?
- What aspects of your religious and cultural experience support a woman's right to employment and fair compensation?

(This portion of the discussion may take the session's duration.)

## Session IX: Women's Rights to Privacy, Religious Beliefs, Free Expression—The Relationship Between Rights (3 hours)

*Exercise 1: Considering Your Right to Privacy*

Supplies needed: none
Time frame: 45 minutes
Objective: To introduce the concept of a woman's right to privacy.
Instructions:
  (1) Arrange yourselves in a semicircle.
  (2) As a group, ask yourselves and discuss the following questions:
    - How would you define the term *privacy*? Does privacy refer to a separate physical space? Does privacy refer to mental space? Can you exercise the right to privacy without having a separate physical space?

- What aspects of your life do you consider private? Your relationship with your husband? The income you or someone else in your family earns? Your family's disagreements? Your religious beliefs? Your political opinions?
- How do you feel when somebody violates your right to privacy? Has this ever happened to you?

*Exercise 2: Defining Your Right to Freedom of Religion*

Supplies needed: none
Time frame: 45 minutes
Objectives: To promote a woman's right to practice her religion freely; to encourage tolerance of religious diversity.
Instructions:
  (1) As a group, ask yourselves and discuss the following questions:
    - What does being a Muslim mean to you? Do you consider yourself a religious individual?
    - What role does your family, community, or government play in determining how you practice your faith? Should any of these play a role? Why or why not?
    - Do you interact regularly with individuals who practice other faiths or who practice Islam differently from you? Do these religious differences affect your interaction? How?
    - What do you have in common with these individuals?
    (This portion of the discussion should take 20–30 minutes.)
  (2) Consider the meaning of the following verses from the Quran:
    (a) Sura 2, al-Baqara [the heifer]; verse 256
        Let there be no compulsion in religion: Truth stands out clear from error: whoever rejects evil and believes in God hath grasped the most trustworthy handhold that never breaks. And God heareth and knoweth all things.
    (b) Sura 5, al-Ma'ida [the table spread]; verse 69. Those who believe [in the Quran], those who follow the Jewish [scriptures], and the Sabians and the Christians,—Any who believe in God and the Last Day, and work righteousness,—on them shall be no fear, nor shall they grieve.
    (c) Ask yourselves and discuss the following questions:
        - What do these injunctions say about the nature of Islam in particular? Of faith in general?
        - How should faith be practiced?
        - How should Muslims treat people of other faiths?
    (This portion of the discussion should take no more than 15–20 minutes.)

*Exercise 3: Exercising Your Right to Freedom of Expression*

Supplies needed: none

Time frame: 1 hour

Objectives: To recognize the political validity and consequences of women's expressions (i.e., art, dance, music, writings, etc.); to promote a woman's right to express herself freely—without self- or other kinds of censorship.

Instructions:

(1) Read aloud the following scenario between Leila, Huda, the Association for Women's Advancement, and the university's board of directors. (The facilitator may read or select a volunteer from among the workshop participants; the reading should take no more than 10 minutes.)

Huda's Writings: "I Have the Right to be Heard!"

Months after Adil divorces Huda, she decides to return to her passion—writing poetry and short stories. She writes a series of articles and poems, reflecting on her personal experience as a victim of domestic violence who is seeking to find a new direction for her life after a bitter divorce from the man who beat her. Huda calls the series of articles and poems "Piece by Piece: Rebuilding a Shattered Life." When the local newspapers refuse to publish the series, Huda asks Leila, who has recently joined the Association for Women's Advancement, to review the articles and poems.

Leila is so impressed by Huda's work that she recommends to her colleagues in the association that they arrange a public forum for Huda to read the articles and poems. Upon reading Huda's work the association members agree with Leila's recommendation.

The association asks the university's board of directors for permission to hold the public reading of Huda's work at the auditorium. After reviewing the articles and poems, however, the board of directors refuses the association's request, claiming that Huda's work will "create tensions between husbands and wives." Consequently, the board becomes embroiled in a battle with the Association for Women's Advancement over what is "suitable for women to see and hear."

Leila and the other association members quickly come to Huda's defense, seeking to rally other women and their male relatives behind her. Feeling pressured by the association's persistent and vigorous defense of Huda, the university's board of directors acquiesces to a meeting with Leila and a few other women to discuss Huda's work.

(2) As a group listening to this scenario, consider the dilemmas faced by Huda, Leila, and the other members of the Association for Women's Advancement. Ask yourselves and discuss the following questions:

- What are Huda's rights in this situation? What are the rights of the members of the Association for Women's Advancement?
- What conversation should Leila and her colleagues from the association have with the university's board of directors? Should they ask Huda to join them for the meeting with the board? Why or why not?
- Should Huda and the association members explore what the law says about her right to read her works in a public forum? Should they take legal action against the university's board of directors in the court system? Should the association organize a petition drive in support of Huda? Should the association distribute Huda's work to all members of the community?
- Do you think that artistic works such as Huda's series of articles and poems have political consequences? If so, how and why?

(This portion of the discussion may take 45–50 minutes.)

*Exercise 4: Exploring the Relationship Between Rights*

Supplies needed: pen(cil) and paper optional
Time frame: 30 minutes
Objectives: To analyze the relationship between women's rights to privacy, religious beliefs, and free expression.
Instructions:

(1) As a group, ask yourselves and discuss the following questions:

- How do you exercise your rights to privacy, to religious beliefs, and to free expression in your daily life?
- What aspects of your religious and cultural experience support a woman's rights to privacy, to her faith, and to free expression?

(2) Homework: Collect your thoughts clearly and/or write an essay of one to two pages to consider the following questions about your rights: Can you exercise any one of these rights without the other? If so, how? If not, why not?

Your essays will be discussed at the beginning of the session on political participation.

# PART THREE

International Organizations
and the Implementation
of the Platform for Action

# 12

## International Human Rights Organizations and Advocacy for Change

### Maryam Elahi

This chapter is an exploratory exercise in assessing the overall value of the Fourth United Nations World Conference on Women in Beijing for providing tools, mechanisms, and opportunities for protecting the rights of women. I examine three basic areas:

1. The impact of the Beijing conference and the Platform for Action adopted there as an advocacy tool for nongovernmental organizations (NGOs) and women activists;

2. The roles and actions that the United Nations needs to assume and undertake to promote the rights of women;

3. The measures that governments must put into place to implement the Platform for Action.

The United Nations-sponsored world conferences in Mexico, Nairobi, Vienna, Cairo, and Beijing have created a momentum leading to a profound change in the advocacy approach of both international and domestic NGOs to women's rights issues. Some international NGOs are struggling to find adequate operating procedures and to define a framework within which the slogan, "Women's Rights Are Human Rights" will mean more than ink on paper. Other international NGOs have invested in specific projects on women's rights and have contributed significantly there by documenting human rights violations against women and by advocating substantive government action. Yet other international human rights groups have been established with the sole purpose of advocating for the promotion and protection of women's human rights around the world. All of these international advocacy groups work toward the theoretical and practical integration of women's rights into broader human rights discussions.

The dynamic fusion that has taken place between women's rights groups and international human rights organizations has established powerful allies. The women's rights coalition proved to be the most effective advocacy movement in Vienna. Women have emerged as a force to contend with, and human rights have emerged as a powerful framework for the promotion of equality. In a matter of years the women's movement has changed from lobbying for the recognition of women's rights to an advocacy and monitoring position with the power to mobilize a large international grass-roots base for mass action.

## Impact of the Beijing Conference as an Advocacy Tool

Hard work by the nongovernmental community assured that the concluding message of the Beijing conference was to reaffirm the universality and indivisibility of rights. A number of countries, particulary some in Asia, sought to nullify the universality principle by demanding that cultural and religious norms need to be considered in the application of human rights principles. This position posed a serious threat to the very basic framework of the *Universal Declaration of Human Rights* and to the principles that are enshrined in that document and in the other human rights conventions. Women's groups managed to turn around the debate on cultural relativism in Cairo, Vienna, and Beijing so that in Beijing the resulting Platform for Action unequivocally supported the principles of universality and indivisibility of all rights.

The conference provided an opportunity for education and mobilization of women by women advocates by insisting on international human rights standards and on mechanisms to advance their cause and claims. It also was used appropriately to get the international media to publicize women's rights issues around the world and to challenge governments that had ignored and violated women's rights.

As had previous world conferences on women's issues, this conference, too, provided an excellent opportunity for networking and coalition-building between groups and advocates from different parts of the world. Such contacts and networking have made it possible for this movement to mobilize successful actions. For example, Amnesty International members wrote to the Moroccan authorities about the case of Kelthoum Ahmed Labid el-Quanat, a twenty-four-year-old Sahrawi woman who had been sentenced to twenty years in prison in 1993 by a Moroccan military court. She had been arrested with four others at a time when hundreds of youths were demonstrating and calling for independence in the Western Sahara and for the release of political prisoners. She had not advocated or used violence but had been arrested, nevertheless, merely for her peaceful political activities. During the ten months in secret detention she was completely cut off from the world and was allegedly beaten, tortured, and severely abused. A massive call to action by Amnesty International on her behalf was launched on Women's Day 1995. Women's groups around the world were asked to appeal to the Moroccan authorities. She and several of the other detainees were released a few days before the Beijing conference, partly, without a doubt, as a result of the pressure put on the Moroccan authorities by activists around the world.

A broad range of U.S.-based NGOs monitoring the Dayton Accords have noted the invisibility of the high number of severe violations of women in the armed conflicts in the Balkans in these accords. The NGOs put the issue on the agenda of high-level U.S. authorities and made a series of recommendations to the U.S. government and the United Nations to ensure that the victimized women would receive necessary assistance and that preventive action would be taken in the context of other conflicts.

The lobbying efforts of a number of organizations, using networks developed during the conference, put pressure on the United Arab Emirates (UAE) government not to execute Sarah Balabagan, a sixteen-year-old domestic worker from the Philippines who had been raped by her employer and had killed him. A UAE court initially had found her guilty of manslaughter and a victim of rape and had sentenced her to seven years imprisonment and a large fine. The president of the UAE demanded a retrial by a different court, which found her guilty of murder and sentenced her to death. At this time an international campaign was launched on her behalf. An appeal court heard her case, suspended the death sentence, and sentenced her to one-year imprisonment and one hundred lashes.

As these examples show, networking for the purpose of disseminating information and organizing protests and appeals can create very effective tools of intervention on behalf of women's rights.

The conference charged international human rights organizations to ensure that women's rights and investigations of gender-specific violations are fully incorporated into their work. Amnesty International, for example, recently has focused much more on gender-sensitive issues in areas of armed conflict and in countries where rape in custody is prevalent. In all such missions Amnesty International attempts to ensure that women researchers are available to carry out interviews with women refugees or former detainees on gender-specific violations.

## The Future Role of the United Nations
## and the Platform for Action

The Platform for Action supported the drafting of an optional protocol to the *Convention for the Elimination of All Forms of Discrimination Against Women* (the Women's Convention [*CEDAW*]), one of the most significant and concrete outcomes of the Beijing conference. This optional protocol will operationalize the committee that monitors the Women's Convention by enabling it to hear complaints and receive petitions from women's groups around the world and by enabling it to initiate its own inquiries into situations that merit its attention and expert advice. This structure will be a very important tool to women advocates around the world once it is operational. The drafting and adoption of the optional protocol will take a few years and will require close monitoring, expert assistance, and constant nudging by the nongovernmental organizations, the United Nations Center for Human Rights, and the United Nations High Commissioner on Human Rights to become effective.

A high-level post in the U.N. Secretariat now advises the secretary-general on gender-related issues. Although it is too early to assess the new office's success, nonetheless, it is an important achievement in highlighting the importance of gender-specific concerns.

The U.N. Center for Human Rights has drafted gender-specific guidelines, which were submitted to the Beijing conference and to the U.N. Human Rights Commission. It is critical that all United Nations expert bodies use these guidelines in their monitoring and reporting.

The United Nations has expressed its commitment to the integration of women's issues into the agenda of all its special rapporteurs and theme rapporteurs. It is too soon to determine how well the integration of gender-specific issues is proceeding at the United Nations. The expectation in the NGO community is that the U.N. High Commissioner on Human Rights will ensure that this integration takes place effectively.

### Implementation of the Platform for Action

To implement the Platform for Action governments around the world must:

1. Publicly condemn violence against women and refrain from engaging in violence against women.

2. Address the issue of impunity by investigating and bringing to justice those who are responsible for violations of women's human rights.

3. Create national institutions and promulgate legislation that protect and promote women's rights in all areas of life.

4. Ratify the *Convention for the Elimination of All Forms of Discrimination Against Women* and other international human rights instruments and support the draft optional protocol to the Women's Convention.

5. Develop national plans of action to implement the commitments made in the Beijing Declaration and in the Platform for Action. These plans of action should have reasonable time-bound targets and include strong national educational programs. The U.N. High Commissioner on Human Rights should follow through with governments to ensure that the national plans of action are comprehensive.

There is a great need for advocacy, education, monitoring, and mass public mobilization by nongovernmental organizations to ensure that the issues that have been placed on the agenda in Beijing become a priority for governments and remain a priority in coming years and that a true commitment to promoting women's rights in all arenas of life is sustained.

# 13

## International Organizations, National Machinery, Islam, and Foreign Policy

Mervat Tallawy

In this chapter I highlight the importance of the interrelationships between national and international bodies for the advancement of women in Muslim countries. I focus on three topics: the historical perspective of the accomplishments and shortcomings of the national machinery, with a brief reference to the case of Egypt; the effect of *CEDAW* on women's rights in Muslim societies; and the influence of foreign policies of donor countries and these policies' compatibility with the Beijing commitments toward gender equality.

The Beijing conference was one of the rare occasions during which the potential power of women received due attention, as demonstrated by the massive participation of delegates from governments, NGOs, and the press. The dissemination of a wealth of knowledge on women's roles in modern societies led to radical changes in the perception of gender issues and despite prevailing conservative trends worldwide resulted in commitments by a great many governments to advance women's causes. Despite many unsolved problems the Beijing conference was a success.

For this success the NGOs largely must be credited. Their preparatory work proved to be vital in the struggle for gender equality, and their engagement will urgently be needed for the implementation of the Beijing Platform for Action in the future. Another factor in the success was that women were in charge of negotiations and were presiding over the committees and workshops in contrast to earlier women's conferences in which women were mainly represented by men.

This shift in participation reflects the gradual development of the status of women in international diplomacy from Mexico to Beijing.

In Mexico and Copenhagen, for example, several male delegates controlled the negotiation process and insisted on introducing controversial subjects totally irrelevant to women's issues to score points in the ideological power plays of the two superpowers. Counting on the women participants' lack of political expertise, these men delegates used the U.N. women's forum for their own national political interests. This usurpation of the negotiation process resulted in divisiveness, hampered the implementation of the final documents, and diffused the momentum that was generated in favor of gender equality.

In contrast, in Beijing the women who headed committees and working groups worked together in harmony and supported each other. For example, they met every evening to decide on a strategy for the following day, and members of the NGO Forum informed the women negotiators of problems or adversarial political moves in advance. The negotiations succeeded despite the many controversial issues under discussion and despite the hard-line positions of certain delegations because women and men worked together and reached agreements without sacrificing women's causes. For example, the working group on health, discussing controversial issues such as abortion, reproductive health, and family planning, managed to reach agreement on more than ninety problematic pending paragraphs that were potentially a great threat to the success of the conference. It is worth noting that this working group was presided over by a woman from a Muslim country, namely myself, who had to work, on the one hand, with tough, religiously traditional Muslim and Catholic men and, on the other hand, with the most liberal delegates from northern European countries.

This empowerment of women through women leaders in negotiating processes was inspiring. Women will need to build on this experience in the implementation of the Platform for Action.

## The National Machinery

During the preparatory work for the first U.N. Conference on Women in Mexico City in 1975 the idea for setting up so-called national machineries as a vehicle for the advancement of women was formulated.[1] Since then many countries indeed have established different national machineries within different legal frames.

*National machinery* as defined by the United Nations is any organizational structure established with particular responsibility for the advancement of women and the elimination of discrimination against women at the central national level. It may include governmental,

Table 1.   National Machinery, by Region

| Countries with National Machinery | Region | | | | Total |
|---|---|---|---|---|---|
| | Africa | Asia and Pacific | Europe and Others | Latin America and Caribbean | |
| Percentage | 55.8 | 41.9 | 88.9 | 66.7 | 61.6 |
| Number | 52 | 43 | 36 | 33 | 164[a] |

*Source:* U.N. document E/CN.6/1991/3, 12 Dec. 1990.
[a] All member states plus four observers.

nongovernmental, or joint governmental-NGO bodies and may consist of one or several agencies all of which are recognized by the government as the national machinery for the advancement of women.

The recommendations of most U.N. conferences on women, particularly those adopted in Nairobi in 1985, emphasized the importance of the national machinery to monitor and to improve the status of women, to promote and to integrate women's needs and concerns into government policies and programs, to mobilize grass-roots support, and to provide information at the national and international levels.

The United Nations has undertaken several reviews and appraisals of national machineries. A seminar on national machineries organized by the United Nations in 1987 in Vienna provided qualitative information. In 1989 the first directory on national machineries was prepared; in 1990 the review of the results of the Nairobi conference included a chapter on national machineries; in 1991 a questionnaire collected more detailed information from member states; and in 1993 a second directory was published.

According to the first U.N. directory of national machineries in 1989, 101 countries reported the existence of a national machinery; 54 percent of developing countries and 89 percent of developed countries had a national machinery in place. National machineries in different regions are shown in table 1.

Almost three-quarters of the countries that have signed or ratified the *Convention on the Elimination of All Forms of Discrimination Against Women* have a national machinery in place. By contrast, only one-third of the countries that have not signed or ratified the convention have a national machinery as indicated in table 2.

The first directory on national machinery states that although most countries have a national machinery in some form, most of these do not function as effectively as they could and will need more support on all levels to perform their assigned role. Indeed, most national machineries lack a strong technical capacity or are precariously located

Table 2. Countries with a National Machinery

| Countries with National Machinery | Signed or Ratified the Convention | Neither Signed nor Ratified the Convention | Total |
|---|---|---|---|
| Percentage | 71.5 | 37.5 | 61.6 |
| Number | 116 | 48 | 164[a] |

*Source:* U.N. Document E/CN.6/1991/3, 12 Dec. 1990.
*Note:* By signatory status of the *Convention on the Elimination of All Forms of Discrimination Against Women.*
[a] All member states plus four observers.

in the government structure. Frequently, they lack resources for staff and equipment. For example, whereas 90 percent of national machineries in developed countries reported that they had headquarters, only 44 percent in developing countries did so. Of these, only 20 percent had more than one computer compared to 65 percent in developed countries, and no national machinery in developing countries belonged to a computer network.

The latest directory, published in 1993, provides the following information about 128 states with national machineries.

1. Although many countries have a national machinery located in the government, others still use nongovernmental organizations as national machinery.

2. Although some countries[2] have ministers of women's affairs, others[3] include women's affairs in the title of ministers reporting to the cabinet, such as in the ministries of Youth, Social Affairs, and Education.

3. In some countries lower-level-organizations such as the council for equality, the office of ombudsman for women, or parliamentary commissions are responsible for national machinery tasks.

4. The weakest national machineries are located only as focal points in ministries with other responsibilities.

Just as the structural location of national machineries varies greatly from country to country, so do mandates. Some are clearly delineated, backed by laws, and funded adequately, whereas others are less well integrated and, therefore, are less effective. In Asia many national machineries are nongovernmental because of active women's NGOs. The support for ministries for women's affairs in Europe to a large extent depends on the political party in power and, therefore, can change rather fast.

Although national machineries can be useful tools for the advancement of women, in twenty years many have not been very effective.

For a national machinery to be effective and successful it must have a clear identity and a well-defined mandate, an appropriate, firm location within the government structure independent of the interests of political parties, adequate financial and human resources, and it must maintain close working relationships with local women's NGOs.

The Beijing platform recognizes the importance of national machinery by including it in its three objectives, namely: the strengthening of the national machinery; the integration of gender perspectives in legislation, public policies, and programs; and the generation and dissemination of gender-disaggregated data for planning and evaluation. National machineries further were charged with monitoring the prevailing political trends to prevent any potential setback to women's rights as a result of political and economic changes in the country, particularly the rise of extremist ideologies and any radical and ultra-conservative trends.

Moreover, the national machinery must institutionalize women's gains to prevent setbacks such as the weakening of affirmative action in the United States or the abolishment of quotas for seats in the parliament and the municipal councils of Egypt. National machineries must take a proactive rather than a defensive stance by setting new goals for decision making for women in high political levels to prevent setbacks.

One of the weaknesses in the operation of national machineries is the concentration of activities in the capital and in urban areas, which excludes many women. Only if women from all areas and all social backgrounds are reached can a national movement for gender equality be generated.

The U.N. Committee on the Elimination of All Forms of Discrimination Against Women is entitled to monitor governments' compliance with the articles of the convention on women. Its evaluations and criticisms should be acted upon promptly by the national machinery to ensure that the suggestions for the advancement of women at the international level are reflected on the national level. National organizations can promote change by comparing local conditions with international norms and experiences; close partnerships between national and international organizations facilitate the exchange of ideas and experiences and foster women's global solidarity.

## Interrelationships Between the National and International Levels: The Case of Egypt

In the 1970s I participated in the drafting of the convention that had affirmative action for the advancement of women as the subject of

ARTICLE 4. Egypt was aware of this subject and of the growing trend toward allocating special quotas for women and passed a law in 1979 allowing women a quota of thirty seats, close to 9 percent, in the parliament, and 15 percent to 20 percent of the seats in local and municipal councils. In 1986, however, the quota system was abolished after a court ruling proclaimed it to be unconstitutional and to represent reverse discrimination. The advocate of this ruling was a conservative antifeminist lawyer on the Supreme Court. Since the quota system was abolished, women's representation in the parliament has fallen to 2.2 percent.

The national machinery in Egypt was established in 1975 with the preparation for the Mexico conference and has had many ups and downs since then. For example, after the first chairperson was replaced, not much was achieved for women by the national machinery. In 1993 its mandate was renewed and strengthened with a new leadership and the preparation for the Beijing conference. It organized its first general conference in 1994 and its second one in 1996 to discuss the implementation of the Beijing Platform for Action. Egypt's First Lady, Mrs. Mubarak, the president of this committee, announced the main guidelines for action. The most important result of this meeting was the integration of the policies for the advancement of women with the Five-Year National Development Plan.

The recommendations emphasized among others the importance of women's education and, particularly, the eradication of illiteracy by increasing the number of single-class-schools in rural and remote areas to three thousand and by establishing community schools funded jointly by the government, individual donors, and communities. Furthermore, the general school curriculum is to include information on women's rights to ensure that the new generation of men and women become more aware of gender equality.

A publicity campaign was planned to change traditional attitudes that are detrimental for women, and a review of laws was recommended to remove contradictions in the legal code and laws that could be used to limit the progression toward gender equality.

The current status of women in Egypt must be seen in the light of Egypt's long and complex history, which spans civilizations in which women such as Hatchepsut, Cleopatra, and Shagaret-El-Dorr participated in the governance of the society, and times when women had little input in the political domain. Egypt's many different roots in African, Arab, and Mediterranean traditions, and its geographical position at the crossroads of East and West have enabled it to borrow widely and to be open to new and universal trends. In 1956 Egypt's Constitution gave all women political rights. A series of legislations was passed to promote women's legal and social equality with men. This progressive development was a result of a long reformist evolution in Egypt whose origins go as far back as the mid-nineteenth century when Mohamed Ali Pasha established the first school for girls. At the turn of the twentieth century, several reformists called for the emancipation of women, including Mohamed Abdou, Kassem Amin, and Mostafa Abdel Razik. Their writings advocated the importance of women's education as investment for the future of Egypt's society and propagated the slogan "Educating a Woman is Educating a Whole Generation."

Mohamed Abdou and other reformers were well-respected theologians and graduates of the prestigious Islamic University, al-Azhar al-Sharif, the first university in the world and a global center for Islamic teaching. Graduates of al-Azhar are leading Muslim theologians in many countries in Africa and Asia today. In Egypt their reformist ideology created a climate that favored women's equality and led to the creation of Egypt's first women's movement, chaired by Hoda Sharawy, the first woman to represent Egypt in international conferences even before Egypt's independence. She led the struggle against veiling in the early 1920s, organized the participation of women in the struggle against the British occupation, and joined the Egyptian revolution of 1919.

Thus, the reformist ideology behind the movement for the emancipation of women in Egypt ultimately came from the highest authority in Islamic theology and jurisprudence, al-Azhar. It was guided by Islamic teaching, which recognizes women's importance for progress, and shows how misconceived and unfounded are today's fundamentalist ideas about women's rights in Islam. If Muslim theologians thought progressively about Muslim women's positions in a Muslim society almost one hundred years ago, one must seriously ask whether modern fundamentalists' contrary claims are not so much related to theology and religion as they are to political goals.

Current Egyptian laws follow the spirit of the constitution in treating men and women much the same. Moreover, several important measures have been taken toward gender equality. These include the ratification of a number of U.N. treaties, including the international *Convention to Eliminate All Forms of Discrimination Against Women* in 1981; the creation of the National Council for Childhood and Motherhood in 1988; the establishment of a Ministry for Population and Family Planning in 1993; the consolidation of departments concerned with women's issues in the Ministries of Social Affairs, Health, and Agriculture; the passing of the law on Childhood and Motherhood in 1996, which goes a very long way toward asserting women's and children's rights; the recent adoption of a law concerning legal procedures in family law, which ensures that decisions in legal disputes are reached promptly; the amendment of family law with the aim of curtailing polygyny. A national law to grant citizenship to children of Egyptian women married to foreigners is currently under review.

Today, Egyptian women hold 12 percent of all high positions in the diplomatic corps; twelve women ambassadors are in charge of different embassies, missions, or general consulates. Women represent 23 percent of the total work force, 38 percent of the informal sector, and 17 percent of the business community. In the parliament are seventeen women representatives in the Lower House, that is, 2.2 percent of all representatives, and 4.7 percent in the Upper House. (As mentioned earlier, these figures constitute a decline from the 1970s when women constituted 9 percent of the members of parliament. The decline was the result of a court order that abolished the quota system for women.)

Despite considerable achievements toward gender equality, many problems and obstacles remain, particularly those posed by the resurgence of outdated and backward models of how a society should work and by ideologies about women's roles in it that are propagated under the influence of or in the name of religious extremism. There is strong hope, however, that the fight against this wave of extremism will be won by the Egyptian people, men and women together, who constitute an overwhelming moderate majority, supported by the international community of all those who believe in tolerance, coexistence, and equality. This support and solidarity between international bodies and local women's movements is essential for sustaining the momentum toward gender equality not just in Egypt but everywhere.

## The Implementation of the Platform for Action in Muslim Societies

The following experience is an example of the linkage between national and international levels of activity and of the need for international support of women's rights in a particular country or region.

In 1987 three Muslim governments' reports submitted to CEDAW included assertions of practices they called Islamic but which constituted grave breaches of women's rights and were challenged by other Muslim authorities. The first report came from an Asian Muslim country and stated that throwing acid in a woman's face for punishment is supported by the Shari'a, Islamic law. The second report was submitted by an African Islamic country and stated that when a husband dies, his wife is considered part of his movable property to be inherited by his brother. This, too, was attributed to Shariʿa law. The third report allegedly attributed a great many degrading treatments of women in the delegate's country to Shariʿa law.

The only Muslim expert in *CEDAW* at the time challenged the content of these reports and protested against such wrong interpretations of Islam being submitted to the United Nations in official governments' reports from Muslim countries. When questioned about the source of such obvious misrepresentations of Islam, the representatives from these three countries could not provide answers and instead were taken aback because they had not been aware of the problematic content of these passages. *CEDAW*'s experts then decided to request the Economic and Social Council of the United Nations (ECOSOC) to call for the preparation of a compilation of women's rights as stipulated in Islamic scriptures. This compilation was to be done in cooperation with a renowned religious Islamic authority such as al-Azhar and to be made available to *CEDAW*'s members, most of whom had no prior understanding of Islam, to use as a reference in future considerations of various governments' reports regarding basic Muslim women's rights.

This decision never passed ECOSOC because of the strong opposition from representatives of Muslim countries who considered the decision biased against Islam because there were no similar requests for other religions.

The opposition against the decision was instigated by one of the countries whose report had included a controversial claim and had supported it by a—for many Muslims blasphemous—reference to Islam. Obviously, the country now wanted to shift the blame for the mistake on the committee and its female experts.

The rejection, however, was based also on the fear that this study, once translated into six official U.N. languages and disseminated widely, would, in fact, embarrass many Islamic countries that are known for their hard-line policies against women, policies that now would be declared to be against Islamic teaching. Moreover, it would make it obvious that no unanimity exists among Islamic countries on the interpretation of Islamic scriptures, especially in regard to the Shariʿa. Ironically, the *CEDAW* decision, which was aimed at defending Islam and showing it to contain women's rights, was turned around and used as an example of the alleged bias the United Nations, and especially *CEDAW*, has against Islam.

This is a clear case of the old and complicated issue of the interpretation of Islamic scriptures in different cultural settings and of how Muslims and non-Muslims understand Islamic teaching. The issue is not easily settled, especially because centuries ago the religious leaders closed the door to the kind of flexible interpretation of the Shari'a that would reflect the actual situation of a society and cultural changes over time.

The difficult problem of the interpretation of Islam and the Shari'a raises the following questions: Can the Platform for Action be implemented in Muslim societies at all? How can one help Muslim women who struggle against the rise of extremism? How dangerous are the misconceptions of Islam for women? What is the impact of the media on the next generation? Answers to these questions lie in the wider context of the ongoing debate on Women and Islam with its numerous contradictory and confusing claims.

It is wrong to assume that the status of women is the same in all Muslim societies. Local cultural backgrounds and histories affect the status of women so much, despite a common religion, that there are profound differences even among Arab countries that share the same language and a common identity. One must take respective cultural backgrounds into consideration.

Islam, just like all other religions and faiths, can enrich and enhance the lives of people, including women. It is wrong to assume that Islam itself is against women. Women must correct the widespread misinformation in the world mass media on this point. A clear distinction must be made between the rights and principles as stipulated in the religion and the practices in the name of religion by some Muslim people who interpret Islam to justify misogynist cultural customs.

A complex and serious problem is the imposition by new radical so-called Muslim groups of detrimental ideas about women's and men's allegedly different rights and duties in Islam. Rather than sound theology, this is a political tool to suppress women and to take away their rights as stipulated in religious texts. These rights were preached by Muslim theologians fourteen centuries ago and are similar to those formulated by modern advocates of equal rights movements. People all over the world need to be educated about the basic tenets of Islam to counter the dangerous and self-serving new ideologies of so-called fundamentalist groups. Women need to demonstrate that Islam was, and still is, a force for emancipation that gave women unprecedented rights, such as the right to independent legal and economic identity; to payment for work; to own and inherit property; to learn and to have the liberty of thought and movement; to perform the pilgrimage and to take part in Holy War; to control important aspects of their lives through marriage contracts in which they can stipulate the right to initiate divorce proceedings, to financial compensation, to monogamy, or to the custody of children, for example. The rights are there, but sadly, women do not know them, or they choose, for many reasons, not to use them. Efforts must be made to teach women their rights and to give them the legal means to use them to their advantage.

The veil and polygyny are the two most obvious and most exploited issues for negative propaganda about Islam. Yet they are trumped-up issues; total veiling is not required by Islam. Indeed, during the pilgrimage to Mecca, the most sacred religious event, women must not cover their faces and their hands in the mosque if their pilgrimage is to be valid. The Quranic injunction on polygyny was used to limit the practice to certain social necessities such as wartime widowhood. Before Islam, the number of wives a man could have was unlimited. Furthermore, there is an explicit Quranic order for a man to have only one wife if he cannot treat his wives absolutely equally.[4]

When talking about Islam, the international media almost exclusively reports on the views of extremists and thereby supports them. Giving the title "Women in Islam" to a large picture of a totally veiled woman in a newspaper is catchy but is stereotyping and misleading. This is a serious problem because it means that the media is taking sides in the ongoing debate between moderates and radicals in the Islamic world at the expense of women's rights. It also means that it tacitly supports the fundamentalist view that the Shari'a is a static body of laws against the many Muslim scholars who call for more flexible interpretations.

These practices by the international media jeopardize Muslim women's battles for exercising their rights as stipulated by their religion and will propagate the fundamentalist view of Islam in Muslim countries and abroad. The current media campaign also strengthens the extremists' position by introducing extremist ideas in every aspect of life. Thus, the cultural and religious gap between Muslims and non-Muslims and between mainstream-Muslims and extremists will widen as a result of polarizations of opinions and an increasing lack of tolerance and dialogue between adherents to different religious ideas.

To implement the Beijing recommendations the attitude of the mass media toward Islam in regard to women must be countered and corrected, and the current use of religion as a means to suppress women and other segments of society must be discussed to overcome the dangers that these new movements pose to women. Instead of being told that their religion veils and marginalizes them, women must be educated by the mass media about their rights in Islam.

## Implications of the Beijing Process
## on the Foreign Policy of Donor Countries

The relevant issues for the foreign policies of donor countries are: human rights, democracy, population issues, and official development assistance.

*Human Rights.* Although I have great reservations about using human rights arguments, democracy issues, and offical development assistance as political tools in imposing policies of donor countries on recipient countries, such noninvolvement can go too far. Some donor countries' own concerns with women's rights and gender equality not only are not expressed in their foreign policies, but these donors' support of repressive regimes and governments as far as women's rights are concerned is contrary to their commitment to the Beijing recommendations.

Unfortunately, many Western countries and international organizations as well defend the rights of opposition groups, extremists or fundamentalists on the grounds of human rights, whereas the fate of millions of women who suffer under blatant discrimination and physical and mental abuse and violence does not raise similar concerns and does not motivate much international action.

*Democracy.* The quest of most donor countries to promote democratic political systems in recipient countries does not extend to women. There are few official inquiries into the participation of women in so-called democratic processes or into the extent to which women benefit from the kind of democracy that is sponsored. Because women are badly underrepresented in many political and legal democratic processes, there should be discussions about the workings of democracy and about possible constitutional measures to reach more equitable participation in the democratic process. Donor countries could do a lot more by initiating such debates and by linking their assistance to women's political inclusions.

*Population.* The population issue is closely related to women's status, their rights, and their prospects for the future. National and international bodies that handle population problems and make decisions about the allocation of resources for population issues, therefore, should give priority to the affected women's perspectives and needs. To be more effective, donor countries' policies regarding population issues should be long term and stable rather than change widely according to the policies of different political parties who win and lose elections.

*Official Development Assistance (ODA).* Although recently there has been some improvement in how funds are allocated, the ODA still does not give enough attention to women's programs, especially in areas of basic needs such as health, education, human resource development, economic development, and lending facilities, especially in light of the fact that most women are self-employed and have little access to existing insurance possibilities or governmental programs for workers.

Radical change is needed in the concept and methods of using aid for gender issues. ODA resources should be used according to a comprehensive plan that would assist rather than duplicate or undermine national efforts at the governmental and nongovernmental levels. Helping the NGOs' activities alone is not enough. Particular responsibilities require governmental intervention. Such activities need bilateral regional and international support.

At present, women of the Middle East and other Muslim countries are paying the price for some Western foreign policies in the region. Such policies are seen by many as humiliating for Muslims and as biased against the people's customs and religion even in times of peace. They create deep animosity, even hatred, against the West and its cultures and ideologies and against those who support or defend it inside the Muslim countries. The more the West is seen as the force behind campaigns that are locally perceived as being against Islam or humiliating for Muslims, the more difficult it is for women in Muslim countries to exercise rights that are seen as ultimately coming from the West.

# 14

## Muslim Law and Women Living under Muslim Laws

### Seema Kazi

*It is that act of speech, of "talking back," that is no mere gesture of empty words, that is the expression of our movement from object to subject — the liberated voice.*

—bell hooks

### Universalizing Women's Rights

The acknowledgment of the universality of women's rights implies the inclusion of women's rights within the family.[1] This is important because it renders visible the discrimination of women in what was hitherto considered the "private" realm. "Extensive discrimination against women continues to exist"[2] together with "the lack of respect for and inadequate promotion and protection of the human rights of women."[3] This is particularly relevant for countries ranging from theocracies to secular states where laws or legal systems governing marriage and family relations derive from interpretations of religion or are legitimized by them.

Family laws, that is, laws that govern relations between men and women in marriage, divorce, inheritance, guardianship and custody of children, provoked considerable debate at the Fourth World Conference on Women in Beijing. Women from Muslim societies discussed the contradiction between the affirmation of the universality of women's rights and the principle of legal equality in the Platform for Action and the existence of contrary family laws.[4] The failure of numerous Muslim states to adopt and implement nondiscriminatory family laws is as disturbing as are the arguments justifying their nonimplementation. This state of affairs camouflages what one feminist asserts to be a "visceral rejection of the principle of equality."[5]

Recent feminist research reveals a tradition of male monopoly over religious (mis)interpretation in Muslim societies. Indeed, the question

141

no longer is what Islam says or does not say but who has said what on behalf of Islam and for what purpose.[6] Arguments justifying discrimination in family codes and laws mirror the political projects of regimes and are a reminder that law is not a neutral agent but reflects dominant power relations in society.[7]

Given the complexity of Muslim societies and their different schools of jurisprudence and legal practice, it is necessary for women's rights activists to develop channels of communication for facilitating a cross-cultural discussion of the diverse laws and legal systems existing within the Muslim world.[8] Such exchanges will aid in the development of practical strategies for increasing women's critical understanding of laws that influence the nature and scope of their autonomy.

The network Women Living under Muslim Laws (WLUML) seeks to achieve this goal through its ongoing Women and Law project.[9]

## WLUML and Muslim Laws

The WLUML *dossier* 3, July 1988, states:

> Women living under Muslim laws invariably lack information regarding their official, legal rights, both in terms of Muslim personal laws and/or civil codes. They remain ignorant about the differences that may exist between customary laws applied to them and Muslim laws. They also have no access to information that might enable them to challenge the validity of either type of law. Furthermore this situation is reinforced by a deliberate policy of misinformation. Given the existing monopoly and control over the matters relating to Islam, we feel the need to evolve a network for information, solidarity and support amongst women living under Muslim laws.

WLUML was initiated in 1984 when ten women attending the Reproductive Rights Tribunal in Amsterdam formed the Action Committee of Women Living under Muslim Laws. This committee was established in response to situations arising out of the application of Muslim laws in India, Algeria, and Abu Dhabi that resulted in the violation of women's human rights.

In India Shehnaz Sheikh filed a petition in the Supreme Court, arguing that the application of minority religious law violated her constitutional right to equality. In Abu Dhabi a pregnant woman was sentenced to be stoned to death, and in Algeria women fought to gain custody of their children from their ex-husbands.[10] WLUML believed that each of these situations, although geographically scattered, were "symptomatic of a much wider problem confronting women in the Muslim world."[11]

Two years later, in 1986, WLUML drafted a Plan of Action which identified the centrality of the public-private dichotomy in arguments justifying the denial of freedom and equality to women and acknowledged the existence of laws, both written and unwritten, drawn from interpretations of the Quran that merge with local tradition to influence the lives of Muslim women. Sharing experiences of the manner in which this dichotomy is used to deny women's rights in different cultural settings was considered an urgent priority of the network.[12]

In 1988 WLUML initiated an Exchange Programme, involving twenty-four women from fifteen different countries,[13] twelve of whom went to different host countries.[14] The Exchange Programme facilitated a deeper understanding of the varied cultural settings, the diverse political systems, and the multiple legal systems/customary laws existing in the Muslim world. The notion of a homogenous Muslim world was demystified as was the idea that laws operative in different countries are similar. The difference between what is often categorized as "Islamic" and Muslim practice was highlighted when women from India learned about the "Islamic"[15] practice of genital mutilation in Egypt and the Sudan or when the "Islamic" practice of veiling in parts of Asia was compared with its nonexistence in parts of Muslim Africa.

The Exchange Programme generated empirical information on the legal rights of Muslim women in different cultural contexts and also highlighted the role of law as a major factor in influencing and defining the scope of women's autonomy in Muslim societies. Given the importance of law as an agent of social change and given the fact that in several countries marriage and family relations operate with reference to Islam, the documentation of such laws, legal systems, and their social practice was considered a first step toward women's empowerment. "Intended for practical use rather than academic discussion," research conducted in the ongoing WLUML Women and Law Programme analyzes "the determinants of changes impeding or promoting women's autonomy and legal rights."[16]

## WLUML and the Platform for Action

At the U.N. Conference on Human Rights in Vienna women human rights activists exposed the gendered hierarchy of the mainstream human rights movement by pointing to the exclusion of the family from the definition of human rights. The existence of discriminatory family laws symbolizes this exclusion. Subordination through family codes and personal laws operates at two levels: at the local level of social practice and on the political level of the state.[17] At the societal level discriminatory personal laws violate women's rights to equality within the family while at the political level governments retain patriarchal family laws to maintain the gendered boundaries of their own political priorities. It is in these two contexts that the WLUML Women and Law country projects contribute locally and internationally toward advancing the aims of the Platform for Action.[18]

The documentation of information in the Women and Law country projects highlights the gap between formal law (or civil code) and its social practice in a particular country, captures the variance in legal interpretation and schools of jurisprudence operative within a specific national context, and reveals the intermeshing of legal and cultural patriarchy in determining women's location in Muslim societies.

A flexible research methodology allows women from different cultural settings to arrive at their own definitions of self-empowerment. For example, during the implementation of the India project its national coordinator was part of a small group of women activists who worked together to formalize a preliminary version of a Muslim marriage contract that would safeguard the interests of women, thus demonstrating the practical implementation of women's legal empowerment using religious law.

The information generated in the respective country projects in collaboration with NGOs and community-based organizations ensures local participation in developing a critical understanding of Muslim laws and their implications for women's autonomy. The Women and Law India project has been successful in establishing a network of Muslim women within the country. These women met several times during the project to discuss issues of common concern. Two women from this network subsequently attended a WLUML international meeting in Lahore in 1994. The Women and Law country projects thus facilitate the formation of information and solidarity networks within a particular country that might not have existed before and link these local networks with those of another country project within the region. These networks establish and strengthen regional links among women mobilizing for change.

Furthermore, country projects highlight the existence and application of Muslim law in countries where Islam is not the state religion. A case in point is India where the issue of Muslim family law is interlinked with constructions of so-called communal identity.[19] The term *communal* in South Asia has negative connotations. It is based on the notion that people belonging to a particular religious community also share common social, political, and economic interests. The merging of cultural identity with the issue of Muslim family law in India and its negative fallout for women's rights was shared by WLUML with South African women. In 1993 at an international seminar in

Capetown women from WLUML cautioned South African women against the potential drawbacks of demands for religion-based family laws that might erode their constitutional right to equality.[20]

Women and Law country projects also draw attention to states that are publicly committed to *CEDAW* yet fail to modify or to legislate against discriminatory personal laws. By highlighting the inherent contradictions between a public policy that affirms women's rights and the retention of family laws that undermine these very rights WLUML constantly alerts women within and outside the network to the implications of what Mayer appropriately terms the *new world hypocrisy* on women.[21] In a statement prepared for the 1994 World Conference on Human Rights in Vienna WLUML pointed to the "retention of personal laws based on religion, tradition and custom" in violation of the fundamental rights of women and, in some cases, of their constitutional right to equality with men.[22]

On national and international levels the WLUML projects operate on a reciprocal basis and feed into each other. The information generated by country projects strengthens local and regional networks of women working in human rights advocacy while the international dimension of the WLUML Women and Law project facilitates a cross-cultural and international network of information, support, and solidarity among women from Muslim societies.

An international comparison of regressive laws in certain countries to relatively liberal laws in others dislodges the myth of a homogeneous Muslim world. This awareness allows women to resist imposed identities and to develop their own definitions of self-empowerment.

By 1994 twenty-five countries were associated with WLUML either as Women and Law country projects or as inputs.[23] Shaheed writes that "with the development of the WLUML Women and Law Programme, the network appears to have entered a new phase in which a common project has merged with solidarity action and networking."[24]

As the Women and Law project unveils the violation of women's rights in the Muslim world, it also reclaims the centrality of women within the discourse on Islam and women's rights. As Mernissi observes, "Muslim history, from the first century to the present, has had to struggle with women's refusal to conform to such models" (of sexual segregation).[25] WLUML acknowledges this history of resistance—through documentation, affiliation, and joint action—and by doing so, ensures that it will continue.

The presence and participation of women from WLUML at the Beijing conference reflected the specificity of Muslim women's struggles within the larger women's movement. The Beijing conference reaffirmed the universality of humanhood as being independent of racial, cultural, or religious identity. It also underscored the importance of cross-cultural networks of solidarity among women from Muslim societies for working toward the realization of women's human rights in the face of the rising challenge from forces opposed to women's self-determination.

# 15

## Gender Equality and the World Bank
Roslyn G. Hees

In his speech to the Fourth United Nations World Conference on Women in Beijing in 1995 the president of the World Bank, James Wolfensohn, declared: "I need no persuading that women are absolutely central to sustainable development, economic advance and social justice." He promised the conference participants: "We [the World Bank] will commit our finance and our energy as an advocate and as a partner in the fight for equity."[1]

One year later, one may ask: Has the World Bank lived up to this promise? How is it helping to advance gender equality in Muslim societies? I answer these questions with examples of the kinds of activities the bank supports as part of its commitment to gender equality.

The bank can promote greater gender equality in three main ways:

1. The bank can ensure that its analyses of the factors constraining economic development include consideration of gender inequalities and that gender concerns are highlighted in its economic policy dialogue with governments.

2. The bank can provide targeted support for national agencies that promote gender equality in bank member countries.

3. Most importantly, the bank can address gender issues directly in the development projects financed by its loans in a wide variety of fields.

Although Muslim countries share a common religion and many cultural traditions, they differ substantially in levels of economic development, social indicators, income distribution, patterns of production, and cultural practices that affect women's status. Thus, although gender goals such as equal access to education or to income-earning opportunities may be shared, strategies to reach those goals will differ. For example, in some Muslim countries, girls and boys are educated in separate schools; in others, children of both sexes attend school together from primary school through university. In some Muslim countries women are active in business and industry as professionals, wage earners, and microentrepreneurs; in others, women do not work outside the home. Because of these differences in the status and role of women among countries, no universal solution to gender inequality can be appropriate. For each country it is essential to understand the specific situation of women and to work with men and women in that particular society to determine the best approach to enhancing gender equality.

Therefore, the first step for the bank is to work with agencies in the country to identify what specific constraints are hampering women from contributing to social and economic development. In many cases such analysis is carried out as part of a so-called poverty assessment or in studies on the labor force or on rural development. In the past, to carry out such studies, a team of World Bank staff and consultants would descend on the country, spend a few weeks gathering all available data, and return to Washington to analyze what the data meant and what the country should do. Now, however, the bank has learned to rely on local organizations and universities to help gather the data, interpret it in light of country circumstances, and advise what strategies will or will not work to address the problems identified. These partnerships can help both the bank and the local groups: the bank gains valuable insights from grass-roots reality checks, and the bank's reports and policy dialogue can bring messages from the grass roots to the attention of economic and financial decision makers.

For example, the bank's chief economist, a hard-headed macroeconomist, Larry Summers, was able to generate interest in girls' education among the finance ministers and central bankers attending the World Bank/International Monetary Fund annual meetings in 1992 when he said: "Concrete calculations demonstrate the enormous economic benefits of investing in women. I would dare to suggest that over time, the importance of female education will dwarf many of the financial issues on which we will focus during the next few days." The fact that it was a noted macroeconomist from the World Bank speaking undoubtedly had greater impact on that particular audience.

Recently in Morocco, one of the countries I work with, a national Living Standards Measurement Survey supported by the bank indicated a strong linkage between poverty and access to basic public services, such as education, health care and family planning, drinking water, and household fuel. This link was underlined in the bank's *Poverty Assessment Report* and discussed at all levels of the Moroccan government. A complementary study worked through local nongovernmental organizations (NGOs) to reach out directly to women in a sample of poor communities to learn what the women themselves saw as their priorities and how they thought their needs could best be met.

This participatory exercise showed that unless women and girls have access to clean water and household fuel, they will not be able to take advantage of educational or income-earning opportunities because gathering water and fuelwood will take up too much of their time. This was an important finding for the design of programs that could be supported by bank loans to enhance the condition of disadvantaged women and their families. The study was an innovation for both the bank and the Moroccans.

The bank also pays increasing attention to ensuring that the impact on women is taken into account in macroeconomic policy reforms. After the first round of so-called Structural Adjustment Programs in the 1980s, bank staff realized that budget cuts were often affecting social services disproportionately because of their predominance in recurrent budgets and, thus, negatively affecting the poor and especially women. More recently, bank macroeconomic dialogue has emphasized the importance of protecting basic services under public expenditure reforms. This has been the case in Algeria, for example, where the structural adjustment program has actually increased public expenditures on basic health, education, and social assistance. Moreover, the increase in export-oriented manufacturing that results from trade liberalization often benefits women, who account for most of the workers in the textile, garment, and electronics industries. This has been the case in Indonesia and Tunisia.

The second way in which the bank enhances gender equality is by supporting national institutions in its member countries that address gender constraints. For example, a small grant from the bank's Institutional Development Fund is helping the Office of Women's Affairs in the Islamic Republic of Iran to gather and analyze gender-disaggregated statistics to better understand the status of women in Iran. It allows the Office to link into the network of similar women's organizations in other countries and to access worldwide sources of documentation on women's issues. A similar grant has trained staff of the Tunisian Ministry of Women and the Family in techniques for evaluating the impact of development projects on women. The Tunisian team presented their methodology and results to an international conference on evaluation in Vancouver in 1995. Another such grant supports the newly established National Committee for Women in Yemen.

A new small grant program, the Consultative Group to Assist the Poorest (C-GAP), has been recently established under the bank with funds from several donors. Its purpose is to strengthen institutions that provide small loans or microcredit, which, as learned from the Grameen Bank example in Bangladesh, are often the only source of financing for women. Traditional financial institutions are generally not willing to make microloans, and community-based organizations that have the outreach capability may not have the financial skills. This program aims to strengthen community-based organizations so that they can provide sustainable financing to women and men whose small businesses provide the livelihood for their families.

The third and most important instrument by which the World Bank can promote gender equality, however, is the projects it finances. Such projects can help women in two ways: through supporting projects that target women directly, such as girls' education, maternal health, and family planning, or by encouraging the participation of women in development programs in a wide variety of sectors, such as agriculture and livestock, water supply, and microenterprise development.

Girls' education has been shown to be one of the highest-return investments in development. During the Beijing conference President Wolfensohn committed the World Bank to increase its lending for education by 20 percent over the next five years with nearly two-thirds of this increase to benefit girls. These examples show how an increase in girls' education in countries where the education of women has traditionally lagged can be accomplished.

The bank, along with other donors, has financed a project in the Baluchistan Province of Pakistan specifically aimed at increasing the enrollment of girls in primary school. Before the project began, only 15 percent of girls in Baluchistan were receiving primary education; 90 percent of the primary schools were for boys only. The Pakistani government has undertaken a number of highly innovative measures under the project to increase girls' schooling, including intensified hiring of female teachers, provision of mobile teacher training for village women, and the introduction of coeducational community schools. One of the most important innovations has been the establishment of Village Education Committees made up of fathers of students to encourage parental interest in the education of girls and to help counter the high dropout rates that have prevented girls in the past from completing the primary cycle. These committees are launched by community education promoters from a local NGO, the Baluchistan Society for Community Support for Primary Education, founded by a Pakistani educator named Quaratul-Ain Bakhteari and staffed mainly by young women leaders. The project has expanded girls' enrollments to 87 percent in target villages and radically changed community attitudes toward the importance of girls' education. This kind of cooperation between the World Bank, government, and NGOs illustrates the bank's new approach to addressing gender issues.

Other projects include women as both change agents and beneficiaries. For example, in Tunisia the Northwest Mountainous Area Development Project targets rural development in three hundred poor
villages *(douar)* through improved agricultural production, establishment of basic infrastructures, and community-based savings and credit
programs. Women account for a high proportion of farm and off-farm
labor in the project area, particularly when men migrate to the cities to
search for wage work. The project organized teams of male and female
extension agents to work with the village development committees to
help identify their needs and priorities and to design the douar (village) Development and Action Plans. Because of this participatory
approach, women now represent about one-third of the members of
the development committees and have influenced village decisions on
how to select and implement project-financed programs. Women have
particularly benefited from the components of the project, which improved access to drinking water and microcredit.

In Egypt, women are benefiting from the Egypt Social Fund,
another World Bank-financed multisectoral project. Launched during
the Gulf War crisis, this project was intended to mitigate the social
impact of that crisis and of a parallel Economic Reform and Structural
Adjustment Program, particularly through supporting employment
promotion and community development efforts. These included labor-
intensive public works programs, community social services, and support for small and microenterprise development. Special efforts were
made to target women. It has been estimated that 60 percent of the
community development activities under the first phase benefited
women and that between one-quarter to one-third of the small and
microentrepreneurs who were sponsored were women, much higher
than the average for other enterprise development programs. One of
the reasons for this success was that the project worked extensively
with Egyptian NGOs, which managed about one-half of the Social
Fund enterprise and community development subprojects.

If gender concerns are so important to the World Bank's agenda
for development, why do these problems persist in bank member
countries? Some of the reasons can be explained by the following
incident, which took place recently in one of the Middle East–North
African countries that particularly prides itself on promoting the status
of women. A bank mission was discussing with a senior government
official a proposal to carry out an in-depth study on the factors influencing the high dropout rates in basic education. The senior official
actually said, "I don't understand why you are so worried about these
dropout rates; you know they mainly affect girls." "It is for precisely
for that reason we are so gravely concerned," replied the mission. In

the face of such attitudes, which luckily are rapidly changing, an external agency cannot have much impact. Nonetheless, the World Bank can and intends to do much more to promote gender equality. The three strategies described above—integrating gender concerns in the macroeconomic dialogue, supporting national agencies working on gender issues, and targeting women in development projects—can help Muslim countries achieve greater gender equality. But the World Bank cannot promote social change alone. It must rely on women and women's groups in member countries to articulate women's special needs, to bring gender issues to the attention of their governments, to insist on the consideration of gender concerns in policy reforms, and to implement the policies adopted to realize the enormous potential of one-half of their population.

# 16

## UNIFEM and Women's Climb to Equality

### No Turning Back

### Noeleen Heyzer and Ilana Landsberg-Lewis

More than one hundred countries and most United Nations organizations made formal commitments to further women's human rights at the Fourth World Conference on Women in Beijing. Women from Muslim countries voiced their concerns with passion and with conviction and placed their vision for equality, development, and peace squarely on the regional and international agendas. After the success of the Beijing conference, women now face the challenge of transforming words into action. The implementation of the Platform for Action (PFA) needs commitment and resources on all local, national, and international organizational levels. The United Nations Development Fund for Women (UNIFEM), which was established to give the world's women a space within the United Nations system, has a strong mandate to concretize the commitments made in the PFA.

Women's impact at the recent U.N. conferences shows that women are a global force in international development debates and in providing directions for sustainable human development. The 1992 U.N. Conference on the Environment and Development, the 1993 U.N. Conference on Human Rights, the 1994 International Conference on Population and Development, and the 1995 World Summit on Social Development, although not directly concerned with women's issues, were turning points for the international women's movement. Women introduced gender perspectives into all development issues. The advocacy of the women's movement at these international conferences was spearheaded by a strategic coalition that spanned international, national, and nongovernmental organizations. UNIFEM played a prominent role in this strategic coalition. From these coalitions emerged the consensus that global development issues cannot be addressed adequately without the inclusion of women's realities and perspectives. At the World Conference on Human Rights, for example, a coalition of women's human rights advocates insisted that women's rights be treated as human rights and that states are accountable for them.

UNIFEM sees itself as critical to ensuring that the U.N. system is responsive to the realities of women's everyday lives. UNIFEM evolved out of women's aspirations in Mexico City in 1975, and now is a bridge between the U.N. system and women living in the most remote communities. During the Beijing preparation process, UNIFEM worked closely with networks of women's organizations, policy makers, and grass-roots women. UNIFEM draws on these diverse partnerships to implement the Platform for Action at the national level in the following ways—UNIFEM

1. works with governments to translate the PFA into national strategic plans and programs for the economic and political advancement of women;

2. involves women in the development of national strategies and measurable outcomes and in the monitoring and implementation of the PFA;

3. builds women's leadership skills and capacities to interact with governments and markets to advocate for gender-sensitive development;

4. creates gender-sensitive policies during development planning, in national budgets, and within national development priorities frameworks;

5. encourages exchange of experiences on gender-sensitive policy options, strategies, and best practices among developing countries and across different regions;

6. ensures that there are operational directives and administrative guidelines in policy documents on women's empowerment;

7. translates the PFA into local languages where necessary.

As the operational and advocacy organization for the empowerment of women, UNIFEM, then, serves as a much-needed base for women within the U.N. system. It works to ensure that the realities of women's lives are not lost from sight and that women's gains achieved at the international level also reach the periphery of societies. This is accomplished by making sure that key recommendations of U.N. world conferences are translated into innovative and catalytic programs that will empower women in the developing world; by ensuring that UNIFEM's operations and advocacy activities strengthen gender perspectives in development interventions by the U.N. system as a whole; and by creating incentives for change in program-design and -implementation processes to increase the involvement of women.

UNIFEM also looks for strategies to leverage funds from larger development agencies, national governments, donors, and lending institutions. It is learning how to mobilize resources that otherwise will not be directed toward women and how to design strategies that will ensure that resources within particular countries and within the U.N. system are used well and for women's benefit.

UNIFEM's vitality and uniqueness lie in its deep connections to a worldwide network of women's organizations, experts, activists, and grass-roots women. UNIFEM relies on the expertise in this network and, in turn, helps women's groups to place their issues on national and international agendas to find new choices and new solutions to problems. From its vantage point UNIFEM can provide substantial input to gender-in-development efforts of other entities in the U.N. system, which, in turn, enables those entities to carry out their work more effectively. Thus, UNIFEM is placed optimally within the United Nations to help realize the commitments made in Beijing to benefit the lives of women at the grass-roots level.

During the six months after the Beijing conference UNIFEM worked with governments and NGO partners in more than sixteen countries to implement the PFA. In several countries UNIFEM supported the translation of the PFA into local languages. In Asia, Latin America, and Africa UNIFEM helped to organize special post-Beijing meetings to address the issues of poverty, violence against women, power, and decision making as they relate to women. In the process UNIFEM has gained expertise in coordinating efforts among organizations and interest groups concerned with women on all levels.

## UNIFEM's Mandate: Political and Economic Empowerment for Women

Paragraph 336 of the Platform for Action mandates UNIFEM to "increase options and opportunities for women's economic and political empowerment." In the post-Beijing era, UNIFEM's work thus is focused on two key areas: women's economic and political empowerment.

Women's economic empowerment is based on women's entitlement to and control over all economic resources, including income, assets, opportunities, and benefits.

To reach this goal UNIFEM's Programme on Economic Empowerment focuses on globalization with attention to trade and new technologies, on women and enterprise development, and on natural resource management. The program supports and funds catalytic and innovative programs that make macroeconomic policies gender sensitive and assists women in participating in the policy-making process. The program enhances women's access to and control over economic resources on a long-term, sustainable basis. It supports women's livelihoods and builds their leadership skills and their capacity to make decisions in economic matters and to take advantage of economic opportunities.

Women's political empowerment is based on women's abilities to control their own lives within and outside the home and on their power to influence the direction of social change.

To empower women politically, UNIFEM's Programme on Political Empowerment is designed to strengthen the role of women in governance and decision making at all levels. It promotes women's leadership and management, strengthens women's organizations to advocate for women's human rights at the national and international levels, strives to bring a gender perspective to the international human rights machinery, and assists in the prevention of violence against women and girls. The program promotes a gender-sensitive and development-oriented response to emergency situations and strengthens the role of women as agents in peace building and the setting of a peace agenda.

UNIFEM believes that women's economic and political empowerment is essential for the eradication of poverty, the elimination of violence against women, and the establishment of sustainable livelihoods. This agenda is based on rights with equal weight given to economic and political rights. The fund places great importance on the use of a rights-based framework with the pursuit of sustainable human development as a fundamental human rights issue.

## U.N. Systems Initiatives

UNIFEM participates with other U.N. agencies in the follow-up on the PFA recommendations. The U.N. secretary-general has established three interagency task forces to provide coordinated assistance to countries for transforming the outcomes of recent major U.N. conferences into concrete national policies and programs via the Resident Coordinating System. These task forces will address the issues of basic social services, employment and sustainable livelihoods, and the enabling environment for social and economic development.

At the request of the U.N. Population Fund, UNIFEM was the lead agency for a working group to make recommendations on the empowerment of women to an interagency task force in the implementation of the International Conference on Population and Development. Guidelines for this work identify five key components of women's empowerment:

1. Women's sense of self-worth
2. Their right to have and to determine choices over their lives
3. Their right to have access to opportunities and resources
4. Their right to have the power to control their own lives both within and outside the home
5. Their ability to influence the direction of social change to create a more just social and economic order nationally and internationally.

The former U.N. secretary-general appointed a high-level adviser on gender issues to oversee U.N. system-wide implementation of the Beijing PFA. Rosario Green, in this capacity, has established the Inter-Agency Committee on Women and Gender Equality. This committee will monitor the implementation by the U.N. system of the PFA and gender-related recommendations emanating from recent U.N. conferences and summits; it will advise the U.N. Administrative Committee on Coordination on how to ensure cooperation within the U.N. system; it will support the mainstreaming of a gender perspective within the U.N. system. UNIFEM will serve as a liaison to ensure that a gender perspective is integrated into the other task forces.

The U.N. Commission on the Status of Women has been turned into an intergovernmental forum for the exchange of policies, best practices, and lessons learned regarding the implementation of the PFA. The commission will take up three critical areas of the PFA at each of its sessions up to the year 2000. In 1997 it will focus on women and the environment, women and power and decision making, women and the economy, and women and education. In 1998 it will focus on women and armed conflict, violence against women, women's human rights, and the girl child.

**Regional Imperatives**

The 1995 *Human Development Report (HDR)*, focusing on gender and development, makes the powerful statement that

> the four critical elements of the human development concept—productivity, equity, sustainability, and empowerment—demand that gender issues be addressed as development issues and as human rights concerns. The compelling reason: development, if not engendered, is endangered. Only when the potential of all human beings is fully realized can we talk of true human development.[1]

UNIFEM concurs. Although it understands that the implementation of the PFA in Muslim countries and elsewhere will not happen overnight, it insists that it has to be an essential process in the development of a society. To this effect UNIFEM is determined to make women's voices heard wherever decisions about the direction of the development of their societies are being made. Although some progress has been made in this regard in Muslim countries, the challenges are still great. For example, the 1996 *HDR* reports that in the Arab states the number of girls per one hundred boys enrolled at the secondary school level rose from forty-seven to seventy-seven between 1970 and 1990 and at the tertiary educational level rose from thirty-four to sixty-five. According to the same *HDR* documents, however, only 25 percent of Arab women participate in the formal labor force, compared with 39 percent in the developing countries as a group; further, women hold only 4 percent of parliamentary seats, well below the 10 percent average in the developing world. Many Arab states have yet to sign and/or ratify the *Convention on the Elimination of All Forms of Discrimination Against Women (CEDAW)*; others have ratified only with significant reservations.[2] The *HDR* states that in Arab states in general, "women have been more successful in overcoming cultural barriers to *building* their capacities than in overcoming the barriers to *using* these capabilities."[3] In striving to bring about the empowerment of women UNIFEM seeks to enable women to both build and exercise their capacity.

## UNIFEM's Follow-up Operations in Western Asia after Beijing

Development programs assisting women in the Middle East region must address both the commonalities and the considerable cultural, political, and economic differences of local women. The diversity of political systems and social structures, political environments, and income disparities in Arab countries, for example, necessitates implementation plans for the PFA that are carefully considered and negotiated between individual governments and NGOs to ensure their feasibility and success. Wars, structural adjustment programs, and the alarming rise of religious extremism present challenges to women's participation in the region's decision-making fora. Although indicators on education, economic and political participation, and health generally show positive trends, women in the region still lack full access to both political and economic spheres and have yet to attain the full enjoyment of their human rights.

In the post-Beijing era the United Nations is increasingly sensitive to the necessity of examining the effects of such situations on women and to the monitoring of compliance with obligations of states under international agreements such as the PFA and U.N. human rights instruments. For example, the former secretary-general of the United Nations recently spoke out strongly against the oppression of women in Afghanistan, citing both the *CEDAW* and the Beijing Platform for Action as strong authorities that would disapprove of the restrictions placed on women in that country.[4] UNIFEM views these uses of the PFA and the Women's Convention as great advancements for women within the United Nations and in their countries.

In UNIFEM's experience the role played by NGOs and civil society in general in ensuring women's involvement in development has depended greatly on the tolerance and support provided by governments, but government allocations for the establishment and operation of institutions concerned with gender-sensitive issues vary considerably. UNIFEM, therefore, attempts to initiate programs that involve governmental agencies and NGOs as well and to be a broker between them, insisting that women's perspectives are not just given a cursory hearing but that women themselves are brought to the negotiating table.

In Arab countries the process of establishing national machineries for addressing women's issues is under way: in Jordan a national Strategy for the Advancement of Women has been formulated along with an institutional framework for promoting the status of women. In Palestine a National Commission for Women is being established. Yemen has set up a Women's National Committee after the interest generated by the Arab region preparatory conference for the Beijing conference, held in Amman, Jordan. Lebanon, Kuwait, and Qatar have drawn on their Ministries of Social Affairs to carry out a welfare model of support for women. In some countries women's unions take on the role of a national machinery although these unions do not carry the same weight in all countries. In Syria, Palestine, Iraq, and, to some extent, Yemen women's unions are a political body aligned with the ruling party and receive support from the government.

During the preparations for the Beijing conference national multidisciplinary committees were established with representatives from government agencies, NGOs, women activists, and the private sector. In many countries this arrangement worked effectively and led to the establishment of firm networks. To ensure a strong and effective participation of Arab delegates and Arab women at the Beijing conference UNIFEM trained NGO representatives and others to work effectively within the context of a U.N. conference. Accomplishments of the preparatory phase included the establishment of national committees, the preparation of national reports on the status of women, the raising of awareness of gender issues and of the global Platform for Action, and the establishment of networks among NGOs, government agencies, donors, experts at think tanks, and delegates concerned with gender issues.

As a result of its participation in this process and with the support

of the European Commission, UNIFEM has started a project to implement the recommendations of the PFA in Western Asia. The strategy
for the project is to build upon networks and institutions that were put
in place during the preparations for the Beijing conference, with the
goal to translate the PFA into national priorities for policies and strategies that will benefit local women.

The project will involve NGOs and the governments of Jordan,
Lebanon, the Occupied Palestinian Territories, Syria, and Yemen. It
will

1. use the activities started in preparation for the Beijing conference, including the mobilization of local women's groups to lobby for
national policies that benefit women, and for the implementation of
the PFA;

2. provide financial and technical support to existing networks of
women NGOs at the regional and national levels to strengthen their
capabilities as disseminators of information;

3. encourage youths to get involved in issues of gender and development because today's youths are tomorrow's women and men who
will bear the responsibilities for carrying out today's policies and will
bear the consequences of today's policies.[5]

During the first phase of the project, the preparatory assistance
stage, UNIFEM works with the respective governments to develop a
national plan for the implementation of the PFA. A series of strategic
planning sessions includes national and NGO committees, key policymakers, and government officials. The national plan has to assess
the status of women in the country, to identify priority areas for intervention, and to recommend specific activities, which then are to be
carried out by NGO and governmental institutions with clear and
specific time frames and resources needed.

Training sessions will strengthen the capacity of governmental and
nongovernmental organizations and leaders to mobilize resources and
to implement national platforms for action. UNIFEM can offer expertise in the building and maintenance of interagency working relationships, in facilitating dialogues, and in implementing training programs
in the skills of negotiation, leadership, coalition building, lobbying,
and brokering between governments and NGOs.

Finally, believing that continuous NGO involvement in the process
will be absolutely critical to the success of the process, UNIFEM will
facilitate the consolidation of NGO coordination and networking at the
national, regional, and international levels, developing and supporting
NGO information systems (an electronic newsletter), and holding
workshops to facilitate the exchange of information and experiences.

This pilot project has captured the interest of other governments in the region. When the Arab League recommendation to organize an Arab Regional Conference one year after Beijing was followed, UNIFEM provided technical support and leveraged resources for this major event. At this conference, which included a ministerial-level meeting with the participation of experts and NGOs, consensus was reached on mechanisms for regional cooperation. UNIFEM, leading a joint technical committee of U.N. agencies and organizations, provided technical expertise and coordinated several workshops. Delegations from the Arab Gulf countries expressed interest in following a similar process as the one promoted by the United Nations through the regional project and requested UNIFEM's assistance to replicate this initiative in their countries.

UNIFEM will continue to play an active and forceful role as a supporter of women in the region by acting as a broker among United Nations bodies, governmental initiatives, NGOs' activities, and local women's interests. The fund also will continue to advocate within the U.N. system to realize womens' visions for a transformed world of equality, peace, and development within the context of their universal, indivisible, interdependent, and interrelated human rights.

Notes
Bibliography
Index

# Notes

## Introduction

1. See also, for example, *Universal Declaration of Human Rights* (1948); *International Covenant on Economic, Social and Cultural Rights* (1966); *International Covenant on Civil and Political Rights* (1966); *Convention on the Elimination of All Forms of Discrimination Against Women (CEDAW,* 1981); U.N. *Declaration of the Elimination of Violence Against Women* (1993); *Vienna Declaration and Programme of Action* adopted by the *World Conference on Human Rights* (1994); and *Report of the U.N. Fourth World Conference on Women in Beijing* (1995). Most of these documents may be found in United Nations, *Compendium on International Conventions Concerning the Status of Women* (New York: United Nations, 1988). For a comprehensive collection of the UN instruments of human rights see the two volumes of United Nations bluebooks, *Human Rights: A Compilation of International Instruments* (New York: United Nations, 1996), sales no. E. 94, XIV.1.

2. A/RES/50/203: 23 Feb. 1966.

3. See Netin Desai, *Keeping the Promises* (WEDO Workshop Report, New York, 10-12 Sept. 1996), 8–10.

4. This is Deniz Kandiyoti's very useful concept, implying the specific dynamic in relationships of women (or other subordinates) in authoritarian, paternalistic structures. By agreeing to their position and its demands women can elicit the good will of their superiors, be they men or older women, and, eventually, can gain some authority over specific resources and relationships themselves.

5. "Beijing and Beyond: Implementing the Platform for Action in Muslim Societies" (international conference presented by Sisterhood Is Global Institute, 11, 12 May 1996, George Washington Univ., Washington, D.C.).

## 1. Beyond Beijing: Obstacles and Prospects for the Middle East

1. This was already apparent during the International Conference on Population and Development held in Cairo in 1994 but became more visible at the Beijing conference.

2. Bina Agarwal, "From Mexico '75 to Beijing '95," *Indian Journal of Gender Studies* 3, no. 1 (1996).

3. There is nothing inherently antiauthoritarian about secularism as opposed to governments that claim legitimacy from religion. Contemporary totalitarianisms of the Left and Right have been vigorously secular.

4. For an interesting, if somewhat inconclusive, set of exchanges on this question among Michael C. Hudson, Farhad Kazemi, Augustus Norton, Suad Joseph, Clifford Chanin, and Ellis Goldberg, see Hudson, Michael C., "Obstacles to Democratization in the Middle East," *Contention* 14 (1996): 81–106.

5. Saad Eddin Ibrahim, "Thinking of Assassination and the Assassination of Thought," *Civil Society* (Cairo) 3, no. 35 (1994): 3.

6. Hudson, "Obstacles to Democratization," 81–106.

7. Yahya Sadowski, "The New Orientalism and the Democracy Debate," *Middle East Report* 183 (July–Aug. 1993): 14–26.

8. See, for instance, Deniz Kandiyoti, *Women, Islam and the State* (London: Macmillan, 1991). I have also argued elsewhere that the notion of secularism itself is a debatable one in contexts where Islam and Arabism are made coterminous as items of cultural nationalism. See Deniz Kandiyoti, "Identity and Its Discontents: Women and the Nation," in *Colonial Discourse and Post-Colonial Theory*, ed. Patrick Williams and Laura Chrisman (Harvester: Wheatsheaf, 1993).

9. Suad Joseph, "Gender and Citizenship in Middle Eastern States," *Middle East Report* 198 (Jan.–Mar. 1996): 4–10.

10. Ibid., 10.

11. Andrea B. Rugh, "Reshaping Personal Relations in Egypt," in *Fundamentalism and Society*, ed. Martin E. Marty and R. Scott Appleby (Chicago: Univ. of Chicago Press, 1993), 151.

12. Leila Ahmed, *Women and Gender in Islam: Historical Roots of a Modern Debate* (New Haven, Conn.: Yale Univ. Press, 1992); Deniz Kandiyoti, "Gendering the Modern: On Missing Dimensions in the Study of Turkish Modernity," in *Rethinking the Project of Modernity in Turkey*, ed. Sibel Bozdogan and R. Kasaba (St. Louis, Mo.: Washington Univ. Press, in press).

13. Hudson, "Obstacles to Democratization."

14. This point was fully articulated in Nira Yuval-Davis and Floya Anthias, eds., *Woman, Nation, State* (London: Macmillan, 1989). See also Kandiyoti, *Women*; idem, "Identity," cited in n. 8.

15. Parvin Paidar, "Feminism and Islam in Iran," in *Gendering the Middle East: Emerging Perspectives*, ed. Deniz Kandiyoti (London: I. B. Tauris, 1996).

16. Massoud Karshenas, "Economic Liberalization, Competitiveness and Women's Employment in the Middle East and North Africa" (paper presented at the Seminar on Economic Liberalization and Women's Employment in the Middle East and North Africa, Nicosia, Cyprus, 10 Nov. 1995).

17. Günseli Berik and Nilufer Cagatay, "Industrialization Strategies and Gender Composition of Manufacturing Employment in Turkey," in *Women's Work in the World Economy*, ed. Nancy Folbre et al. (Hong Kong: Macmillan, 1992).

### 2. Fundamentalism and Women's Rights: Lessons from the City of Women

1. These riots were hastily and wrongly labeled "bread riots" by the international press.

2. ARTICLE 2 of the constitution declares Islam the religion of the Algerian state.

3. In Iran, for example, such young women are already challenging the patriarchal views of the mullahs and other "guardians" over their lives. See "Femmes Iraniennes contre le clergé," *Le Monde Diplomatique*, Nov. 1996.

### 3. Women, Islamisms, and State: Dynamics of Power and Contemporary Feminisms in Egypt

1. This paper is based on fieldwork carried out between 1991 and 1996 (Azza M. Karam, *Women, Islamisms and the State: Contemporary Feminisms in Egypt* [London:

Macmillan, in press]) on women activists in Egypt and in various international fora such as the International Cairo Population and Development Conference (1994) and the Beijing women's conference (1995).

2. John L. Esposito, *Islam and Politics* (Syracuse, N.Y.: Syracuse Univ. Press, 1984); Nazih Ayubi, *Political Islam: Religion and Politics in the Arab World* (London: Routledge, 1991); François Burgat, *L'Islamisme en face* (Paris: La Découverte, 1955); Martin F. Marty and R. Scott Appleby, eds., *Fundamentalisms Observed* (Chicago: Univ. of Chicago Press, 1994).

3. Such as, Fatima Mernissi, *Beyond the Veil: Male-Female Dynamics in Muslim Society* (London: al-Saqi, 1985); Valentine M. Moghadam, *Modernizing Women: Gender and Social Change in the Middle East* (Boulder, Colo.: Lynne Rienner, 1993); Kandiyoti, *Women*; John S. Hawley, ed., *Fundamentalism and Gender* (New York: Oxford Univ. Press, 1994).

4. See also Margot Badran, "Competing Agenda: Feminism, Islam and the State in Nineteenth and Twentieth Century Egypt," in *Women, Islam, and the State*, ed. Deniz Kandiyoti (London: Macmillan, 1991).

5. Amany Farag, personal communication, Sept. 1995. When pressed to give an example, she mentioned punctuality and the respect for commitments in the West.

6. Chandra T. Mohanty, "Cartographies of Struggle: Third World Women and the Politics of Feminism," in *Third World Women and the Politics of Feminism*, ed. Chandra T. Mohanty, Alice Russo, and Lourdes Torres (Bloomington: Indiana Univ. Press, 1991), 7.

7. Chandra T. Mohanty, "Under Western Eyes: Feminist Scholarship and Colonial Discourse," in *Third World Women and the Politics of Feminism*, ed. Chandra T. Mohanty, Alice Russo, and Lourdes Torres (Bloomington: Indiana Univ. Press, 1991), 52–53.

8. Mohanty, "Under Western Eyes," 54.

9. Amrita Basu, ed., *The Challenge of Local Feminism: Women's Movements in Global Perspective* (Boulder, Colo.: Westview Press, 1995), 20.

10. Kumari Jayawardena, *Feminism and Nationalism in the Third World* (London: ZED Books, 1986), 2.

11. Linda J. Nicholson and Nancy Fraser, "Social Criticism Without Philosophy: An Encounter Between Feminism and Postmodernism," in *Feminism/Postmodernism*, ed. Linda J. Nicholson (London: Routledge, 1990), 34.

12. This typology can be used to distinguish among different feminisms within many Muslim communities.

13. *Jihad* means effort. It is usually linked with *fi sabil illa* (for the sake of God), that is, for a religiously commendable aim, and has various meanings. Islamists often use it synonymously with revolutionary struggle for Islamist ideals.

14. Heba Ra'uf, interview with author, May 1993, Cairo.

15. Prominent, internationally known writers and scholars who advocate this stance include Fatima Mernissi (Moroccan), Azizah al-Hibri (Arab-American), and Riffat Hassan (Pakistani).

16. *Ijtihad* means independent inquiry into the religious sources, that is, the Quran, the texts about the exemplary behavior of the Prophet Muhammad—peace be upon him—and the Hadith. The main goal of this inquiry is to formulate interpretations of the religious texts that are suitable for the conditions and exigencies of modern life.

17. For an interesting and informative comparative situation in Algeria see Susan Slyomovics, "Hasiba Ben Bouali, If You Could See Our Algeria: Women and Public Space in Algeria," *Middle East Report* 192 (Jan.–Feb. 1995): 8–13.

18. Moustapha K. el-Sayed, "The Islamic Movement in Egypt: Social and Political Implications," in *The Political Economy of Contemporary Egypt*, ed. Ibrahim M. Oweiss (Washington, D.C.: Georgetown Univ. Press, 1990), 234.

19. Hassan al-Banna was the founder of the Muslim Brotherhood (MB) Association in Egypt in 1928. The MB became a prototype for similar movements in other parts of the Arab and Muslim world. The brotherhood's main aim has been and is the gradual Islamization, through Islamic education and implementation of Islamic values and laws, of the society and the state. For a study on the brotherhood see Richard Mitchell, *The Society of the Muslim Brothers* (Oxford: Oxford Univ. Press, 1993).

20. The fact that certain colonial authorities often used the woman question to belittle and critique the Islamic culture has tainted the whole feminist enterprise in the former colonies and protectorates. See Ahmed, *Women and Gender;* and Margot Badran, "Gender Activism: Feminists and Islamists in Egypt," in *Identity Politics and Women: Cultural Reassertions and Feminisms in International Perspective,* ed. Valentine M. Moghadam (Boulder, Colo.: Westview Press, 1994), 202–27.

21. Al-Azhar, in Cairo, is the oldest center of religious learning in the Arab world. In Nasser's time during the 1950s certain reforms rendered al-Azhar subject to state control. Many Islamists tend to accuse al-Azhar of being a state-organ to legitimize state actions rather than an impartial institution. An example which is often cited regarding al-Azhar's role as the state's official Islamic sponsor is the *fatwa* (edict) issued by al-Azhar during Sadat's visit to Jerusalem in 1978, declaring Sadat's action Islamically justified.

22. Azza M. Karam et al., *Islam in een ontzuilde Samenleving* (Islam in a nonpolarized society) (Amsterdam: Royal Tropical Institute Press, 1996).

23. Ann Elizabeth Mayer, "Rhetorical Strategies and Official Policies on Women's Rights: The Merits and Drawbacks of the New World Hypocrisy," in *Faith and Freedom: Women's Human Rights in the Muslim World,* ed. Mahnaz Afkhami (London: I. B. Tauris, 1995), 104–32.

### 4. Aberrant "Islams" and Errant Daughters: The Turbulent Legacy of Beijing in Muslim Societies

1. *Report of the Fourth World Conference on Women* (Beijing, 4–15 Sept. 1995), U.N. doc. ACONF.177/20 para. 230.

2. The original Libyan reservation is in a useful report, "Meeting of States Parties to the Convention on the Elimination of All Forms of Discrimination Against Women," Committee on the Elimination of All Forms of Discrimination Against Women, 7th Meeting, Provisional Agenda Item 6, at 18, U.N. doc. CEDAW/SP/1994/2 (1993).

3. Supplement to ST/LEGSER.E13. IV.8 *Convention on the Elimination of All Forms of Discrimination Against Women,* IV.8, p. 2.

4. Special rights are secured for wives under the Shari'a by virtue of the subordinate, dependent status that is assigned to them pursuant to which they could have "rights" such as claiming maintenance from their husbands.

5. Http://www.un.org/Depts/Treaty/reg.htm. The Pakistani reservation is recorded at Treaty/bible/Part_1_E/ IV_/IV_8.html.

6. See Ann Elizabeth Mayer, "Reflections on the Proposed United States Reservations to CEDAW: Should the Constitution Be an Obstacle to Human Rights?" *Hastings Constitutional Law Quarterly* 23 (1996): 756–65.

7. Ibid., 789–92, 811.

8. Ibid., 793–96.

9. See Rubya Mehdi, *The Islamization of the Law in Pakistan* (Chippenham: Nordic Institute of Asian Studies, 1994), 95–108. The Islamic features in the constitution were expanded under the rule of President Zia. If enshrining an enlightened version of Islam in the constitution had been the objective, this could have amounted to a positive

change. In context, however, Islamic provisions in Pakistan's laws have resulted in setbacks to women's rights. See Khawar Mumtaz and Farida Shaheed, *Women of Pakistan: Two Steps Forward, One Step Back* (London: ZED Books, 1987). When Pakistan made its "constitutional" reservations to *CEDAW*, this was tantamount to opening the door for using vague Islamic qualifications that could override women's human rights.

10. "Pakistan—Human Rights: Can a Muslim Woman Choose Her Partner?" Inter-Press Service, 16 Oct. 1996, available in LEXIS, NEXIS Library.

11. "Love Marriage Sparks Legal Battle over Islam, Human Rights," Agence France Presse, 23 May 1996, available in LEXIS, NEXIS Library.

12. "Pakistani Women Fight to Choose Husbands," United Press International, BC cycle, 7 May 1996, available in LEXIS, NEXIS Library.

13. "Pakistani Woman Fights to Keep Husband," Reuters World Service, 20 May 1996, available in LEXIS, NEXIS Library.

14. "Pakistan—Human Rights."

15. Ibid.

16. A chronology of events in the Abu Zaid case, editorials, and a translation of parts of the Court of Cassation ruling are presented in *People's Rights, Women's Rights*, no. 2 (Cairo: Legal Research and Resource Center for Human Rights in Cairo, 1996), 2–4. For further information on this case see "Shari'a or Civil Code? Egypt's Parallel Legal Systems. An Interview with Ahmad Sayf al-Islam," *Middle East Report* 197 (Nov.–Dec. 1995): 25–27; Nasr Abu Zaid, "The Case of Abu Zaid. Academic Freedom in Egypt," *Index on Censorship* 4 (1996): 30–39.

17. The court order was suspended in September. See " 'Heretic' Professor Wins Legal Right to Stay Married," Agence France Presse, 25 Sept. 1996, available in LEXIS, NEXIS Library. The couple, however, remained in exile in the Netherlands, a prudent move as long as Abu Zaid bore the label of apostate, which extremists would say provided sufficient justification for killing him.

18. "Arab Writers Liken Cairo Court Rule to Inquisition," Reuters, Ltd., 23 June 1995, available in LEXIS, NEXIS Library.

19. Mayer, "Rhetorical Strategies," 106–10.

20. For background on the jurisprudential debates see Jonathan P. Berkey, "Circumcision Circumscribed: Female Excision and Cultural Accommodation in the Medieval Near East," *International Journal of Middle East Studies* 28 (1996): 19–38.

21. "Lawsuits Filed Against Health Minister over Ban on Female Circumcisions," Agence France Presse, 2 Oct. 1996, available in LEXIS, NEXIS Library.

22. In one of the cases that aggravated the Egyptian controversy a fourteen-year-old girl bled to death in August 1996 as a result of a botched female genital mutilation (FGM) operation. The girl died not at the hands of a traditional practitioner of FGM in some primitive setting but as a result of an incompetently managed surgical procedure by a medical doctor.

23. "Sudan's Capital Bans Mixing of Sexes in Public," *New York Times*, 27 Oct. 1996, 6.

24. "Sudan Defends Sexual Segregation Laws," United Press International, 24 Oct. 1996, available in LEXIS, NEXIS Library. The very marginal role accorded to women judges in the fundamentalist Sudan is covered in Lawyers Committee for Human Rights, *Beset by Contradictions: Islamization, Legal Reform and Human Rights in Sudan*, New York: Lawyers Committee for Human Rights (July 1996), 42, 79.

25. "Iranian Cleric Blasts Taliban for Defaming Islam," Reuters North American Wire, 4 Oct. 1996, available in LEXIS, NEXIS Library.

26. "Afghan Taliban Says Iran Provocation Continues," Reuters North American Wire, 11 Oct. 1996, available in LEXIS, NEXIS Library.

27. "Kabul Citizens Call for End to Foreign Intervention in Afghanistan's Affairs," BBC SWB, FE/D2747/A, 19 Oct. 1996, available in LEXIS, NEXIS Library.

28. "Deputy Foreign Minister Meets German Diplomat," BBC SWB, FE/D2767/A, 12 Nov. 1996, available in LEXIS, NEXIS Library.

29. "How to Be an Iranian Islamic Feminist," *Financial Times*, 21 Nov. 1996, 6.

30. "Iran Considering Women to Be Judges," Agence France Presse, 27 Oct. 1996, available in LEXIS, NEXIS Library.

31. "Iran Conference Urges Halt to Afghan War," Reuters World Service, 30 Oct. 1996, available in LEXIS, NEXIS Library.

32. "Iran Starts Enforces [*sic*] Tough New Islamic Law," Reuters North American Wire, 10 July 1996, available in LEXIS, NEXIS Library; "Iranian Women Disrespecting Dress Code to Face Imprisonment," Deutsche Presse Agentur, 30 July 1996, available in LEXIS, NEXIS Library.

33. "Iran Considers Establishing Anti-vice Ministry, says MP," Deutsche Presse Agentur, 4 Sept. 1996, available in LEXIS, NEXIS Library.

34. "President Rafsanjani's Daughter Interviewed on Women's Issues, Society," BBC SWB, ME/D2753/MED, 26 Oct. 1996, available in LEXIS, NEXIS Library.

### 5. Muslim Women's Islamic Higher Learning as a Human Right: The Action Plan

1. This chapter and the research that led to its conception would not have happened without the special efforts and ecouragement of my husband, Muawia Barazangi. His comments and suggestions and those of Rahel Lidda Hahn and Gisela Webb were invaluable.

2. Nimat Hafez Barazangi, *Muslim Women's Islamic Higher Learning as a Human Right: Theory and Practice* (forthcoming).

3. Nimat Hafez Barazangi, "Viceregency and Gender Justice," in *Islamic Identity and the Struggle for Justice*, ed. Nimat Hafez Barazangi, M. Raquibuz Zaman, and Omar Afzal (Gainesville: Univ. Press of Florida, 1966), 77–94.

4. P. J. Stewart, *Unfolding Islam* (Reading, United Kingdom: Ithaca Press, 1994), ix.

5. United Nations, *Covenant for the New Millenium: The Beijing Declaration and Platform for Action*, Fourth World Conference on Women (Santa Rosa: Free Hands Books, 1996), 7.

6. Marnia Lazreg, *The Eloquence of Silence: Algerian Women in Question* (New York: Routledge, 1994), 2.

7. Stewart, *Unfolding Islam*, xiii.

8. United Nations, *Covenant*, 7.

9. Hafez Barazangi, "Viceregency," 78.

10. Ibn Sa'ad, M. bin M. al-Basri, *Al-Tabaqat al-kubra* (Leiden: Brill, 1904) v. 8, 4–5:205–9.

11. Annemarie Schimmel, *Deciphering the Signs of God: A Phenomenological Approach to Islam* (New York: State Univ. of New York Press, 1994), 114. Fazlur Rahman, *Major Themes of the Quran* (Chicago: Bibliotheca Islamica, 1980), 1.

12. Rahman, *Major Themes*, 29.

13. Ibid., 1.

14. Hafez Barazangi, "Viceregency," 91–92.

15. Schimmel, *Deciphering the Signs*, 114.

16. Mervyn Hiskett, "West Africa," in *The Oxford Encyclopedia of the Modern Islamic World*, 4 vols. (New York: Oxford Univ. Press, 1995), 37–40.

17. Rahman, *Major Themes*, 1.

18. Ibid., 2,3.

19. Nikki Keddie, "Afghani, Jamal al-Din" in *The Oxford Encyclopedia of the Modern Islamic World*, 4 vols. (New York: Oxford Univ. Press, 1995), 23–27.

20. Nimat Hafez Barazangi, "Educational Reform" and "Religious Education," in *The Oxford Encyclopedia of the Modern Islamic World*, 4 vols. (New York: Oxford Univ. Press, 1995), 406–11, 420–24.

21. Holly Sims, "Western Models, Indian Women: The Legacy of Foreign Aid," in *Bridging Worlds: Studies on Women in South Asia*, ed. Sally J. M. Sutherland (Berkeley and Los Angeles: Univ. of California at Berkeley, 1991), 225–39.

22. Fazlur Rahman, *Islam and Modernity* (Chicago: Univ. of Chicago Press, 1982), 15.

23. Elizabeth Fiorenza Schussler, *In Memory of Her* (New York: Crossroad, 1983, 1990).

24. *World's Women, 1995: Trends and Statistics* (New York: United Nations, 1995); *National Report* (Damascus, 1995), 15.

25. Amal Abd al-Rahim, "The Female Image in the Media" (paper presented at the American Cultural Center in Damascus, Syria, March 1996). Amal al-Hussaini, "The Come-back of the Hijab in Syria." Al Nahj, Center for Socialist Research and Studies in the Arab World, no. 5 (1995), 162–66. Hanan Lahham, *Min hadi al-Quran*, (Riyadh: Dar al-Huda, 1989). Bouthaina Sha'ban, "The Muslim Woman in Syria." Al Nahj, Center for Socialist Research and Studies in the Arab World, no. 5 (1995), 87–99.

26. Madeline Arnot, "A Crisis in Patriarchy? British Feminist Educational Politics and State Regulation of Gender," in *Feminism and Social Justice in Education*, ed. M. Arnot and K. Weiler (London: Falmer Press, 1993), 187.

27. In Islam there is no separation of mental and physical being. "Soul" implies the totality of the person and her disposition or the close relation between human heart and mind (Rahman, *Major Themes*, 17).

28. 'A'isha Abd al-Rahman, *Al-I'jaz al-Bayani Lil al-Quran* (Cairo: Dar al-Ma'arif 1987), 34.

29. Rahman, *Major Themes*, 17.

30. 'A'isha, Abd al-Rahman, *Al-Tafseer al-Bayani Lil al-Quran* (Cairo: Dar al-Ma'arif, 1968) 1:18.

31. Yousuf A. Ali, *The Holy Quran: Text, Translation and Commentary* (n.p.: McGregor and Werner, 1946).

32. Jane I. Smith and Yvonne Y. Haddad, "Eve: Islamic Image of Women," in *Women and Islam*, ed. al-Hibri, Women's Studies International Forum, vol. 5, no. 2 (1982), 135–44.

33. Roger Garaudy, *Islam habite nôtre avenir*, (Paris: Desclée de Brouwer, 1981), trans. Abd al-Majid Baroudy, *Al-Islam diin al-mustaqbal* (Damascus: Dar al-Iman, 1983), 179.

34. United Nations, *From Nairobi to Beijing: Second Review and Appraisal of the Implementation of the Nairobi Forward-Looking Strategies for the Advancement of Women*, report of the secretary-general (New York: United Nations, 1995), 211. United Nations, *Women: Looking Beyond 2000* (New York: United Nations, 1995).

35. Hafez Barazangi, "Viceregency," 87.

36. Seyyed Hossein Nasr, "Comments on a Few Theological Issues in the Islamic-Christian Dialogue," in *Christian-Muslim Encounters*, ed. Yvonne Yazbeck Haddad and Wadi Zaidan Haddad (Gainesville: Univ. Press of Florida, 1995), 463.

37. John Renard, "Islam, the One and the Many: Unity and Diversity in a Global Tradition," in *Islam: A Challenge for Christianity*, ed. Hans Küng and Jürgen Moltmann, *Concilium*, special issue (London: SCM Press, 1994), 32.

38. Sims's interpretation of Western models and the legacy of foreign aid in the

form of home economics and women's domesticity since World War II is a good example of the views that predated the U.N. *Universal Declaration of Human Rights* (Sims, "Western Models").

39. V. J. Cornell, "Tawhid: The Recognition of the One in Islam," in *Islam: A Challenge for Christianity*, ed. Küng and Moltmann (London: SCM Press, 1994), 61–66, 66.

40. Margot Badran, *Feminists, Islam, and Nation: Gender and the Making of Modern Egypt* (Princeton, N.J.: Princeton Univ. Press, 1995), 107.

41. Hafez Barazangi, "Viceregency."

42. Schimmel, *Deciphering the Signs*, 133.

43. Diane Singerman, *Avenues of Participation: Family, Politics, and Networks in Urban Quarters of Cairo* (Princeton, N.J.: Princeton Univ. Press, 1955).

44. Ibid., xi.

45. Muhammad Zubayr Siddiqi, *Hadith Literature: Its Origin, Development, and Special Features* (Cambridge: Islamic Text Society, 1993), 105, 116–23.

46. Rahman, *Islam and Modernity*, 137.

47. Abdullah Adhami, "Understanding Shari'ah Through Its Language," *Message* June 1996: 39–40.

48. Hafez Barazangi, "Religious Education," 407 f.

### 6. Imagination as Subversion: Narrative as a Tool of Civic Awareness

1. Jane Austen, *Pride and Prejudice* (New York: Avenel, 1985). Muriel Spark, *Loitering with Intent* (New York: Coward, McCann and Geoghegan, 1981).

2. Jack D. Zipes, *Arabian Nights* (New York: Signet Classic, 1991).

3. Arthur Conan Doyle, "The Greek Interpreter." In *The Annotated Sherlock Holmes*, vol. 1, ed. William S. Baring-Gould (New York: Clarkson N. Potter, 1967), 591–605.

### 7. Personal Status Codes and Women's Rights in the Maghreb

1. Collectif '95 Maghreb Egalité, *Maghreb Women "With all Reserve,"* (Stuttgart: Friedrich Ebert Stiftung, 1995).

2. Ibid.

3. Constitution of the Kingdom of Morocco, 1992, ART. 5.

4. Morocco, Code du statut personnel et des successions, 10 Sept. 1993, ART. 16(b).

5. Ibid., ART. 11–13.

6. Ibid., ART. 16(c).

7. Fatna Sarehane, Legislation comparée: Maroc, le statut personnel: Droit commun, capacité, mariage, filiation, 104, pt. 2–1, Aug. 1993, Editions Techniques-Juris-Classeurs, 1993.

8. Code du statut personnel, ART. 48.

9. Ibid., ART. 48(2).

10. Ibid., ART. 30. The official figure for polygyny in Morocco is 3 percent, but the actual rate is higher, according to the Democratic Association of Women in Morocco. One reason for the inaccuracy of the official figure is that many men hide new marriages from existing wives.

11. Code du statut personnel, ART. 30(2).

12. Ibid., ART. 148(2).

13. Ibid., ARTS. 35, 36.

14. *CEDAW*, ART. 16.

15. Code du statut personnel, ARTS. 53–58.

16. Author's interviews with human rights activists conducted in Morocco in May and June 1995.

17. Ibid.

18. Ibid.

19. Department of Statistics, Morocco, 1995, as quoted in Agence France Press, 27 Apr. 1995.

20. Constitution of the Kingdom of Morocco, ART. 6, 19.

21. Emad Eldin Shahin, "Under the Shadow of Islam: Morocco's Diverse Islamic Movements," *Middle East Insight* 11, no. 2 (1995): 40.

22. Republic of Tunisia, Aug. 1956 Family Code, ART. 18.

23. Ibid., ART. 3.

24. Ibid., ART. 23.

25. Republic of Algeria, June 1984 Family Code, ARTS. 9, 11.

26. Ibid., ARTS. 12, 13.

27. Ibid., ART. 12.

28. Ibid., ARTS. 37, 39.

29. Ibid., ARTS. 48, 53, 54.

30. Ibid., ART. 37.

31. Ibid., ART. 19.

32. "One Hundred Measures and Provisions," Collectif '95 Maghreb Egalité, ART. 6.

33. Ibid., ART. 7.

34. Ibid., ART. 13.

35. Ibid., ART. 27.

36. Ibid., ART. 26.

37. Ibid., ART. 63.

38. Ibid., ART. 64.

## 8. Leadership Development for Young Women: A Model

1. Helen S. Astin and Carol Leland, *Women of Influence, Women of Vision: A Cross-Generational Study of Leaders and Social Change* (San Francisco: Jossey-Bass Publishers, 1991), 156.

2. Ibid.

3. UNICEF: United Nations International Children's Education Fund; UNFPA: United Nations Population Fund; UNIFEM: United Nations Development Fund for Women.

4. Nafis Sadik, "The UNFPA Contribution: Theory to Action Programmes," *Development* 1 (1990): 7–12.

5. Astin and Leland, *Women of Influence.*

## 9. The Women Studies Program in Palestine: Between Criticism and New Vision

1. Liza Taraki, "The Development of Political Consciousness among Palestinians in the Occupied Territories, 1967–1987," in *Intifada, Palestine at the Crossroads,* ed. Jamal R. Nassar and Roger Heacock (New York: Praeger, 1990), 60.

2. Around 1977 Birzeit University changed from a two-year junior college to a four-year college that offered bachelor's degrees in different fields.

3. Eileen Kuttab, "Palestinian Women in the Intifada: Fighting on Two Fronts," *Journal of Arab Studies Quarterly* 14, no. 2 (1993), 69–85.

4. The conference was organized by the Women's Studies Committee of the Bisan

Research and Development Center in Rammallah. The proceedings of the conference were published by the Bisan Center.

5. These issues were prioritized by the women's movement in a round table discussion at Birzeit University hosted by the Women's Studies Program in March 1995.

6. Members of the Women Studies Program at Birzeit University are Ilham Abu Ghazaleh, Lamis Abu Nahleh, Rita Giacaman, Reema Hammami, Islah Jad, Penny Johnson, Eileen Kuttab, and Liza Taraki.

7. The courses offered by the WSP are Introduction to Women Studies; Women in Arab Society; Women in the Family; Women and Psychology; Women in Discourse; the History of International Women's Movements; Women and Development; Women and the Law; Theories in Women's Studies; Special Topics; Research Seminar.

8. Maria Mies, *Fighting on Two Fronts: Women's Struggles and Research* (The Netherlands: Institute of Social Studies, 1982).

9. Taly Rutenberg, "Learning Women Studies," in *Theories of Women Studies*, ed. Gloria Bowles and Renate Klein (London: Routledge, 1983), 72–78.

## 10. Imperiled Pioneer:
## An Assessment of the Institute for Women's Studies
## in the Arab World

1. This assessment is based on answers to a questionnaire distributed to twenty-five individuals who are or were closely associated with the Institute for Women's Studies in the Arab World (IWSAW); on open-ended interviews with four women—a researcher, a program officer, a board member, and an activist—who have worked with IWSAW for several years; on archival research; and on my own experiences as editor-in-chief of IWSAW's quarterly journal, *al-Raida*, during 1995 and 1996.

2. These colleges had been founded by various American church organizations in Lebanon, Iran, India, Pakistan, Japan, South Korea, and the Philippines before the Second World War. All but one were women-only institutions.

3. Albert Badre, "Editorial," *al-Raida* 1, no. 1 (1976): 2.

4. Ibid.

5. Ibid.

6. For further insights into the impact of the war on women see Jean Said Makdisi, *Beirut Fragments* (Oxford: Pergamon Press, 1991); Miriam Cooke, *Women Write War: The Centering of the Beirut Decentrists* (Oxford: Centre for Lebanese Studies, 1987); and the double issue of *al-Raida* devoted to "Women in Post-War Lebanon," 12, nos. 70, 71 (1995).

7. See, for example, J. Abu Nasr, I. Lorfing, and J. Mikati, *Identification and Elimination of Sex Stereotypes in and from School Textbooks: Suggestions for Action in the Arab World* (Paris: UNESCO, 1983); I. Lorfing, "Women Workers in the Lebanese Industry," in *Women and Work in the Third World*, ed. Najat M. Sanbary (Berkeley and Los Angeles: Univ. of California Press, 1983); J. Abu Nasr, N. Khoury, and H. Azzam, eds., *Women, Employment and Development in the Arab World* (Berlin: Mouton, 1985); and I. Lorfing and M. Khalaf, *Economic Contribution of Women and Its Effect on the Dynamics of the Family in Two Lebanese Villages* (Geneva: International Labor Organization, 1985).

8. For example, IWSAW published the monographs *Tasks of Women in Industry* (Beirut, 1985) and *Contemporary Arab Writers and Poets* (Beirut, 1985).

9. The Lebanese American University, the Lebanese University, and the American University of Beirut.

## 11. Claiming Our Rights:
## A Manual for Women's Human Rights Education
## in Muslim Societies

1. This article is a slightly modified version of the introduction to Mahnaz Afkhami and Haleh Vaziri, *Claiming Our Rights: A Manual for Women's Human Rights Education in Muslim Societies* (Bethesda: Sisterhood Is Global Institute, 1996). The sample sessions are ibid., 35–45.

2. These documents include, among others, United Nations, *Universal Declaration of Human Rights*, 1948.

3. The components of the model are to be tested in workshops in Bangladesh, Uzbekistan, Jordan, Malaysia, and Lebanon. These countries were chosen because of the diversity in their sociopolitical systems, cultures, and approaches to Islam. The facilitators in each country are human rights activists and educators; they will be in regular contact with the Sisterhood Is Global Institute. By summer 1997 the Project Advisory Group together with invited nongovernmental organization (NGO) representatives, scholars, human rights educators, and women activists will finalize the manual and identify sites for its use.

## 13. International Organizations, National Machinery, Islam,
## and Foreign Policy

1. U.N. documents used were "Insufficient Mechanisms at All Levels to Promote the Advancement of Women," EKNG/1995/3/Add.6.
"National Machinery for Monitoring and Improving the Status of Women," E/CN.6/1988/3.
"The Development of National Machinery for the Advancement of Women and Their Characteristics in 1985," SNMAW/1987/BP.1.
"The Context in Which National Machineries Operate and Their Role in Promoting Equality of Women and Men—Government Perspective," SNMAW/1987/BP.2.

2. For example, Australia, Austria, Bangladesh, Canada, Chile, Ivory Coast, Indonesia, St. Kitts—Nevis, and Uganda have ministers of women's affairs.

3. For example, Belgium, Cameroon, Chad, Germany, and the Netherlands include women's affairs in various ministerial portfolios.

4. The relevant verse says, "Marry women of your choice, two or three or four, but if you fear that you shall not be able to deal justly with them, then only one, and you will never be able to be just and fair between them," Quran, Sura 4.

## 14. Muslim Law and Women Living under Muslim Laws

1. "The World Conference on Human Rights recognized that the human rights of women and the girl child are an inalienable, integral and indivisible part of universal human rights. The universal nature of these rights and freedoms is beyond question" (*Beijing Declaration and the Platform for Action* adopted by the Fourth World Conference on Women: Action for Equality, Development and Peace, Advance Unedited Draft [Geneva: United Nations, 1995]).

2. The term *discrimination against women* is understood as "any distinction, exclusion or restriction made on the basis of sex in the political, economic, social, cultural or any other field" (*Convention on the Elimination of All Forms of Discrimination Against Women* [United Nations Department of Public Information, Feb. 1993]).

3. Critical Area of Concern (9). *Beijing Platform for Action* (1995).

4. "Ensure equality and non-discrimination under the law and in practice" (Strategic Objective 1.2, *Beijing Platform for Action*, Fourth World Conference on Women) (Beijing, Sept. 1995).

5. Fatima Mernissi, *Islam and Democracy: Fear of the Modern World* (London: Virago, 1993).

6. Mahnaz Afkhami, "Introduction," in *Faith And Freedom: Women's Human Rights in the Muslim World*, ed. Mahnaz Afkhami (London: I. B. Tauris, 1995).

7. Farida Shaheed, "Controlled or Autonomous: Identity and the Experience of the Network Women Living under Muslim Laws," *Signs* 19, no. 4 (1994): 997–1019.

8. The four major schools of jurisprudence are Hanafi, Hanbali, Maliki and Shafi'i. "All four schools agree on the fundamental dogmas, but differ in the application of the Koran and its interpretation" (Mernissi, *Beyond The Veil*).

9. Women Living under Muslim Laws (WLUML) has several activities. In this chapter, however, I focus on the ongoing WLUML Women and Law Programme—a major undertaking of the network, which seeks to advance the aims of strategic objective 1.2 in the *Beijing Platform for Action*.

10. WLUML *Dossier* 1, Feb. 1986, and WLUML *Dossier* 2, Apr. 1986. See also Farida Shaheed, "Linking Dreams: Network of Women Living under Muslim Laws," in *From Basic Needs to Basic Rights*, ed. Margaret A. Schuler (Washington, D.C.: Women, Law and Development International, 1995).

11. Shaheed, "Linking Dreams."

12. "In the case of women living under Muslim laws, this emphasis on the private and personal becomes critical since, unlike the differences which may separate us, similarities often relate to the private and personal domain. Thus for us, sharing experiences at this stage is not a question of just creating links and solidarity but is an integral part of our struggle" (WLUML Plan of Action, Aramon, 1986).

13. The twenty-four participants came from Algeria, Bangladesh, Egypt, India, Indonesia, Iran, Malaysia, Nigeria, Pakistan, the Philippines, Somalia, Sudan, Sri Lanka, Tanzania, and Tunisia.

14. The twelve women who participated in the exchange program went to receiving organizations in Egypt, Malaysia, Pakistan, Somalia, and the Sudan. See ISIS–Women's International Cross Cultural Exchange (WICCE), Women's World: Women Living under Muslim Laws (Geneva, 1989).

15. M. A. Helie-Lucas proposes to use *Islam* and *Islamic* for references to religion/ideal/utopia and *Muslims* and *Muslim* for believers and their actual practices. This terminology is essential in a conceptual understanding of Islamic law and its social practice. See M. A. Helie-Lucas, *Poverty and Development: Women and Islam in Muslim Societies* (The Hague: Ministry of Foreign Affairs, 1994).

16. WLUML, *Women and Law Country Project* (Shirkatgah, Lahore, 1992).

17. Shahnaz J. Rouse, "Gender(ed) Struggles: The State, Religion and Civil Society" in *Against All Odds: Essays on Women, Religion and Development from India and Pakistan*, ed. Kamla Bhasin (New Delhi: Kali for Women, 1994).

18. Strategic Objective 1.2, *Beijing Platform for Action*.

19. Bipan Chandra, *Communalism in Modern India* (New Delhi: Vikas, 1984).

20. Amy Biehl, "Custom and Religion in a Non-Racial, Non-Sexist South Africa," in *Women Against Fundamentalism*, 1, no. 5 (1994).

21. Ann Elizabeth Mayer, "Rhetorical Strategies."

22. Women Living under Muslim Laws' Statement on Women's Human Rights (prepared for the World Conference on Human Rights, Vienna, 1993).

23. Women and Law Programme country projects or inputs (in the form of information from countries where it has not been possible to implement a Women and Law

Programme) exist in Fiji, Indonesia, Malaysia, Singapore, the Philippines, Bangladesh, India, Sri Lanka, Pakistan, Iran, Turkey, Uzbekistan, Afghanistan, Yemen, Sudan, South Africa, Nigeria, Mali, Zambia, Senegal, Algeria, Morocco, and Tunisia. See "Women Laws Initiatives in the Muslim World": Discussions from the International Meeting, "Towards Beijing: Women, Law and Status in the Muslim World" (Lahore: Shirkatgah, Dec. 1994).

24. Shaheed, "Linking Dreams."

25. Fatima Mernissi, "Femininity as Subversion: Reflections on the Muslim Concept of Nushuz," in *Speaking Of Faith: Cross-Cultural Perspectives on Women, Religion and Social Change,* ed. Diana Eck and Devaki Jain (New Delhi: Kali for Women, 1986).

## 15. Gender Equality and the World Bank

1. From "Women and the Transformation of the 21st Century" (speech delivered by James D. Wolfensohn, president of the World Bank, to the Fourth United Nations World Conference on Women, Beijing, 1995, internal World Bank draft, World Bank, Public Information Office, Washington, D.C.).

## 16. UNIFEM and Women's Climb to Equality: No Turning Back

1. United Nations, *Human Development Report* (1995), 23.

2. United Nations, *Human Development Report* (1996), 38.

3. United Nations, *Human Development Report* (1995), 32.

4. U.N. Secretary-General, Press Release, 7 Oct. 1996.

5. The authors thank UNIFEM's Western Asia Regional Programme adviser for the information regarding this project.

# Bibliography

**Books, Articles, and Theses**

Abd al-Rahim, Amal. "The Female Image in the Media." Paper presented at the American Cultural Center in Damascus, Syria, March 1996.

Abd al-Rahman, 'A'ishah. *Al-I'jaz al-Bayani Lil al-Quran.* Cairo: Dar al-Ma'arif, 1987.

———. *Al-Tafseer al-Bayani Lil al-Quran.* Cairo: Dar al-Ma'arif, 1968.

Abu Nasr, J., N. Khoury, and H. Azzam, eds. *Women, Employment and Development in the Arab World.* Berlin: Mouton, 1985.

Abu Nasr, J., I. Lorfing, and J. Mikati. *Identification and Elimination of Sex Stereotypes in and from School Textbooks: Suggestions for Action in the Arab World.* Paris: UNESCO, 1983.

Abu Zaid, Nasr. "The Case of Abu Zaid. Academic Freedom in Egypt." *Index on Censorship* 4 (1996): 30–39.

Adhami, Abdullah. "Understanding Shari'ah Through Its Language." *Message* (June 1996): 39–40.

"Afghan Taliban Says Iran Provocation Continues," Reuters North American Wire, 11 Oct. 1996.

Afkhami, Mahnaz. "Introduction." In *Faith and Freedom: Women's Human Rights in the Muslim World,* edited by Mahnaz Afkhami, 1–15. London: I. B. Tauris, 1995.

Afkhami, Mahnaz, and Haleh Vaziri. *Claiming Our Rights: A Manual for Women's Human Rights Education in Muslim Societies.* Bethesda, Md.: Sisterhood Is Global Institute, 1996.

Agarwal, Bina. "From Mexico '75 to Beijing '95." *Indian Journal of Gender Studies* 3, no. 1 (1966).

Ahmed, Leila. *Women and Gender in Islam: Historical Roots of a Modern Debate.* New Haven, Conn.: Yale Univ. Press, 1992.

Ali, Yousuf A. *The Holy Quran: Text, Translation and Commentary.* N.p.: McGregor and Werner, 1946.

"Arab Writers Liken Cairo Court Rule to Inquisition," *Reuters Ltd.,* 23 June 1995.

Arnot, Madeline. "A Crisis in Patriarchy? British Feminist Educational Politics and State Regulation of Gender." In *Feminism and Social Justice in Education,* edited by Madeline Arnot and K. Weiler. London: Falmer Press, 1993.

Astin, Helen S., and Carol Leland. *Women of Influence, Women of Vision: A Cross-Generational Study of Leaders and Social Change.* San Francisco, Calif.: Jossey-Bass Publishers, 1991.

Austen, Jane. *Pride and Prejudice.* New York: Avenel, 1985.

Ayubi, Nazih. *Political Islam: Religion and Politics in the Arab World.* London: Routledge, 1991.

Badran, Margot. "Competing Agenda: Feminism, Islam and the State in Nineteenth and Twentieth Century Egypt." In *Women, Islam and the State,* edited by Deniz Kandiyoti, 201–36. London: Macmillan, 1991.

———. *Feminists, Islam, and Nation: Gender and the Making of Modern Egypt.* Princeton, N.J.: Princeton Univ. Press, 1995.

———. "Gender Activism: Feminists and Islamists in Egypt." In *Identity Politics and Women: Cultural Reassertions and Feminisms in International Perspective,* edited by Valentine M. Moghadam. Boulder, Colo.: Westview Press, 1994.

Badre, Albert. "Editorial," *al-Raida* 1, no. 1 (1976): 2.

Basu, Amrita, ed. *The Challenge of Local Feminisms: Women's Movements in Global Perspective.* Boulder, Colo.: Westview Press, 1995.

Berik, Günseli, and Nilufer Cagatay. "Industrialization Strategies and Gender Composition of Manufacturing Employment in Turkey." In *Women's Work in the World Economy,* edited by Nancy Folbre et al. Hong Kong: Macmillan, 1992.

Berkey, Jonathan P. "Circumcision Circumscribed: Female Excision and Cultural Accommodation in the Medieval Near East." *International Journal of Middle East Studies* 28 (1996): 19–38.

Biehl, Amy. "Custom and Religion in a Non-Racial, Non-Sexist South Africa." In *Women Against Fundamentalism* 1, no. 5 (1994).

Burgat, François. *L'Islamisme en face.* Paris: La Découverte, 1955.

Chandra, Bipan. *Communalism in Modern India.* New Delhi: Vikas, 1984.

Collectif '95 Maghreb Egalité. *Maghreb Women "With all Reserve."* Stuttgart: Friedrich Ebert Stiftung, 1995.

Cooke, Miriam. *Women Write War: The Centering of the Beirut Decentrists.* Oxford: Centre for Lebanese Studies, 1987.

*Contemporary Arab Writers and Poets.* Beirut: Institute for Women's Studies in the Arab World, 1985.

Cornell, V. J. "Tawhid: The Recognition of the One in Islam." In *Islam: A Challenge to Christianity,* edited by Hans Küng and Jürgen Moltmann, 61–66. London: SCM Press, 1994.

"Deputy Foreign Minister Meets German Diplomat," BBC SWB, FE/D2767/A, 12 Nov. 1996.

Desai, Netin. *Keeping the Promises.* Women's Environment and Development Organization (WEDO) Workshop Report, 8–10. New York, 1996.

Doyle, Arthur Conan. "The Greek Interpreter." In *The Annotated Sherlock Holmes,* vol. 1, edited by William S. Baring-Gould, 591–605. New York: Clarkson N. Potter, 1967.

Esposito, John L. *Islam and Politics.* Syracuse, N.Y.: Syracuse Univ. Press, 1984.

"Femmes Iraniennes contre le clergé," *Le Monde Diplomatique,* Nov. 1966.

Fiorenza Schüssler, Elizabeth. *In Memory of Her.* New York: Crossroad, 1983.

Garaudy, Roger. *Islam habite notre avenir.* Paris: Desclée de Brouwer, 1981. Trans. Abd al-Majid Baroudy, *Al-Islam diin al-mustaqbal.* Damascus: Dar al-Iman, 1983.

Hafez Barazangi, Nimat. "Educational Reform." In *The Oxford Encyclopedia of the Modern Islamic World,* vol. 1, edited by John S. Esposito, 406–11. New York: Oxford Univ. Press, 1995.

———. *Muslim Women's Islamic Higher Learning as a Human Right: Theory and Practice.* Forthcoming.

———. "Religious Education." In *The Oxford Encyclopedia of the Modern Islamic World,* vol. 1, edited by John S. Esposito, 420–24. New York: Oxford Univ. Press, 1995.

———. "Viceregency and Gender Justice." In *Islamic Identity and the Struggle for Justice,* edited by Nimat Hafez Barazangi, M. Raquibuz Zaman, and Omar Afzal, 77–94. Gainesville: Univ. Press of Florida, 1996.

Hawley, John S., ed. *Fundamentalism and Gender.* New York: Oxford Univ. Press, 1994.

Helie-Lucas, M. A. *Poverty and Development: Women and Islam in Muslim Societies.* The Hague: Ministry of Foreign Affairs, 1994.

" 'Heretic' Professor Wins Legal Right to Stay Married," Agence France Presse, 25 Sept. 1996.

Hiskett, Mervyn. "West Africa." In *The Oxford Encyclopedia of the Modern Islamic World,* edited by John S. Esposito, 37–40. New York: Oxford Univ. Press, 1995.

hooks, bell. *Talking Back: Thinking Feminist Thinking Black.* Boston: South End Press, 1989.

"How to be an Iranian Islamic Feminist," *Financial Times,* 21 Nov. 1996, 6.

Hudson, Michael C. "Obstacles to Democratization in the Middle East." *Contention* 14 (1996): 81–106.

al-Hussaini, Amal. "The Come-Back of the Hijab in Syria." Al Nahj, Center for Socialist Research and Studies in the Arab World, no. 5. 1995, 162–66.

Ibn Sa'ad, M. bin M. al-Basri. *Al-Tabaqat al-kubra.* Leiden: Brill, 1904.

Ibrahim, Sa'ad Eddin. "Thinking of Assassination and the Assassination of Thought." *Civil Society* (Cairo) 3, no. 35 (1994): 3.

Institute for Women's Studies in the Arab World. *Contemporary Arab Writers and Poets.* Beirut: Institute for Women's Studies in the Arab World, 1985.

Institute for Women's Studies in the Arab World. *Tasks of Women in Industry.* Beirut: Institute for Women's Studies in the Arab World, 1985.

"Iran Conference Urges Halt to Afghan War," Reuters World Service, 30 Oct. 1996.

"Iran Considering Women to Be Judges," Agence France Presse, 27 Oct. 1996.

"Iran Considers Establishing Anti-vice Ministry, Says MP." Deutsche Presse Agentur, 4 Sept. 1996.

"Iran Starts Enforces [*sic*] Tough New Islamic Law," Reuters North American Wire, 10 July 1996.

"Iranian Cleric Blasts Taleban for Defaming Islam," Reuters North American Wire, 4 Oct. 1996.

"Iranian Women Disrespecting Dress Code to Face Imprisonment," *Deutsche Presse Agentur*, 30 July 1996.

Jayawardena, Kumari. *Feminism and Nationalism in the Third World*. London: ZED Books, 1986.

Joseph, Suad. "Gender and Citizenship in Middle Eastern States." *Middle East Report* 198 (1996): 4–10.

"Kabul Citizens Call for End to Foreign Intervention in Afghanistan's Affairs," BBC SWB, FE/D2747/A, 19 Oct. 1996.

Kandiyoti, Deniz. "Gendering the Modern: On Missing Dimensions in the Study of Turkish Modernity." In *Rethinking the Project of Modernity in Turkey*, edited by Sibel Bozdogan and R. Kasaba. St. Louis, Mo.: Washington Univ. Press, in press.

———. "Identity and Its Discontents: Women and the Nation." In *Colonial Discourse and Post-Colonial Theory*, edited by Patrick Williams and Laura Chrisman. Harvester: Wheatsheaf, 1993.

———. *Women, Islam and the State*. London: Macmillan, 1991.

Karam, Azza M. *Women, Islamism and the State: Contemporary Feminisms in Egypt*. London: Macmillan, in press.

Karam, Azza M., et al. *Islam in een ontzuilde Samenleving*. Amsterdam: Royal Tropical Institute Press, 1996.

Karshenas, Massoud. "Economic Liberalization, Competitiveness and Women's Employment in the Middle East and North Africa." Paper presented at the Seminar on Economic Liberalization and Women's Emloyment in the Middle East and North Africa, Nicosia, Cyprus, 10 Nov. 1995.

Keddie, Nikki. "Afghani, Jamal al-Din." In *The Oxford Encyclopedia of the Modern Islamic World*, vol. 1, edited by John S. Esposito, 23–27. New York: Oxford Univ. Press, 1995.

Kuttab, Eileen. "Palestinian Women and the Intifada: Fighting on Two Fronts." *Journal of Arab Studies Quarterly* 14, no. 2 (1993): 69–85.

Lahham, Hanan. *Min hadi al-Quran*. Riyadh: Dar al-Huda, 1989.

"Lawsuits Filed Against Health Minister over Ban on Female Circumcisions," *Agence France Presse*, 2 Oct. 1996.

Lawyers Committee for Human Rights. *Beset by Contradictions: Islamization, Legal Reform and Human Rights in Sudan*. New York: Lawyers Committee for Human Rights, 1996.

Lazreg, Marnia. *The Eloquence of Silence: Algerian Women in Question*. New York: Routledge, 1994.

Lorfing, I. "Women Workers in the Lebanese Industry." In *Women and Work in the Third World*, edited by Najat M. Sanbary. Berkeley and Los Angeles: Univ. of California Press, 1983.

Lorfing, I., and M. Khalaf. *Economic Contribution of Women and Its Effect on the Dynamics of the Family in Two Lebanese Villages*. Geneva: International Labor Organization, 1985.

"Love Marriage Sparks Legal Battle over Islam, Human Rights," *Agence France Presse*, 23 May 1996.

Makdisi, Jean Said. *Beirut Fragments*. Oxford: Pergamon Press, 1991.

Marty, Martin E., and R. Scott Appleby, eds. *Fundamentalisms Observed*. Chicago: Univ. of Chicago Press, 1991.

Mayer, Ann Elizabeth. "Reflections on the Proposed United States Reservations to CEDAW: Should the Constitution Be an Obstacle to Human Rights?" *Hastings Constitutional Law Quarterly* 23 (1996): 756–65.

———. "Rhetorical Strategies and Official Policies on Women's Rights: The Merits and Drawbacks of the New World Hypocrisy." In *Faith and Freedom: Women's Human Rights in the Muslim World*, edited by Mahnaz Afkhami, 104–32. London: I. B. Tauris, 1995.

Mehdi, Rubya. *The Islamization of the Law in Pakistan*, 95–108. Chippenham: Nordic Institute of Asian Studies, 1994.

Mernissi, Fatima. *Beyond the Veil: Male-Female Dynamics in Modern Muslim Society*. London: al-Saqi, 1985; Bloomington: Indiana Univ. Press, 1987.

———. "Femininity as Subversion: Reflections on the Muslim Concept of Nushuz." In *Speaking of Faith: Cross-Cultural Perspectives on Women, Religion and Social Change*, edited by Diana Eck and Devaka Jain, 95–108. New Delhi: Kali for Women, 1986.

———. *Islam and Democracy: Fear of the Modern World*. London: Virago, 1993.

Mies, Maria. *Fighting on Two Fronts: Women's Struggles and Research*. The Hague: Institute of Social Studies, 1982.

Mitchell, Richard. *The Society of the Muslim Brothers*. Oxford: Oxford Univ. Press, 1993.

Moghadam, Valentine M. *Modernizing Women: Gender and Social Change in the Middle East*. Boulder, Colo.: Lynne Rienner, 1993.

Mohanty, Chandra T. "Cartographies of Struggle: Third World Women and the Politics of Feminism." In *Third World Women and the Politics of Feminism*, edited by Chandra T. Mohanty, Alice Russo, and Lourdes Torres, 1–50. Bloomington: Indiana Univ. Press, 1991.

———. "Under Western Eyes: Feminist Scholarship and Colonial Discourse." In *Third World Women and the Politics of Feminism*, edited by Chandra T. Mohanty, Alice Russo, and Lourdes Torres, 51–80. Bloomington: Indiana Univ. Press, 1991.

Mumtaz, Khawar, and Farida Shaheed. *Women of Pakistan: Two Steps Forward, One Step Back*. London: ZED Books, 1987.

Nasr, Seyyed Hossein. "Comments on a Few Theological Issues in the Islamic-Christian Dialogue." In *Christian-Muslim Encounters*, edited by Yvonne Yazbeck Haddad and Wadi Zaidan Haddad, 457–67. Gainesville: Univ. of Florida Press, 1995.

Nicholson, Linda J., and Nancy Fraser. "Social Criticism Without Philosophy: An Encounter Between Feminism and Postmodernism." In *Feminism/Postmodernism*, edited by Linda J. Nicholson. London: Routledge, 1990.

Paidar, Parvin. "Feminism and Islam in Iran." In *Gendering the Middle East: Emerging Perspectives*, edited by Deniz Kandiyoti. London: I. B. Tauris, 1996.

"Pakistan-Human Rights: Can a Muslim Woman Choose Her Partner?" Inter-Press Service, 16 Oct. 1996.

"Pakistani Woman Fights to Keep Husband," Reuters World Service, 20 May 1996.

"Pakistani Women Fight to Choose Husbands," United Press International, BC cycle, 7 May 1996.

*People's Rights, Women's Rights*, no. 2. Cairo: Legal Research and Resource Center for Human Rights in Cairo, 1996.

Rahman, Fazlur. *Islam and Modernity*. Chicago: Univ. of Chicago Press, 1982.

———. *Major Themes of the Quran*. Minneapolis, Minn.: Bibliotheca Islamica, 1980.

Renard, John. "Islam, the One and the Many: Unity and Diversity in a Global Tradition." In *Islam: A Challenge for Christianity*, edited by Hans Küng and Jürgen Moltmann, *Concilium*, special issue, 31–38. London: SCM Press, 1994.

Rouse, Shahnaz J. "Gender(ed) Struggles: The State, Religion and Civil Society." In *Against All Odds: Essays on Women, Religion and Development from India and Pakistan*, edited by Kamla Bhasin, 16–35. New Delhi: Kali for Women, 1994.

Rugh, Andrea. "Reshaping Personal Relations in Egypt." In *Fundamentalism and Society*, edited by Martin E. Marty and R. Scott Appleby. Chicago: Univ. of Chicago Press, 1993.

Rutenberg, Taly. "Learning Women Studies." In *Theories of Women Studies*, edited by Gloria Bowles and Renate Klein, 72–78. London: Routledge, 1983.

Sadik, Nafis. "The UNFPA Contribution: Theory to Action Programmes." *Development* 1 (1990): 7–12.

Sadowski, Yahya. "The New Orientalism and the Democracy Debate." *Middle East Report* 183 (1993): 14–26.

Sarehane, Fatna. "Legislation comparée: Maroc, le statut personnel: Droit commun, capacité, mariage, filiation." Pt. 2–1. N.p.: Editions Techniques-Juris-Classeurs, 1993.

el-Sayed, Moustapha K. "The Islamic Movement in Egypt: Social and Political Implications." In *The Political Economy of Contemporary Egypt*, edited by Ibrahim M. Oweiss, 222–39. Washington, D.C.: Georgetown Univ. Press, 1990.

Schimmel, Annemarie. *Deciphering the Signs of God: A Phenomenological Approach to Islam*. New York: State Univ. of New York Press, 1994.

Sha'ban, Bouthaina. "The Muslim Woman in Syria." Al Nahj, Center for Socialist Research and Studies in the Arab World, no. 5 (1995): 87–99.

Shaheed, Farida. "Controlled or Autonomous: Identity and the Experience of the Network Women Living under Muslim Laws." *Signs* 19, no. 4 (1994): 997–1019.

———. "Linking Dreams: Network of Women Living under Muslim Laws." In *From Basic Needs to Basic Rights*, edited by Margaret A. Schuler. Washington, D.C.: Women, Law and Development International, 1995.

Shahin, Emad Eldin. "Under the Shadow of Islam: Morocco's Diverse Islamic Movements." *Middle East Insight* 11, no. 2 (1995).

"Shari'a or Civil Code? Egypt's Parallel Legal Systems. An Interview with Ahmad Sayf al-Islam." *Middle East Report* 197 (1995): 25–27.

Siddiqi, Muhammad Zubayr. *Hadith Literature: Its Origin, Development, and Special Features*. Cambridge: Islamic Text Society, 1993.

Sims, Holly. "Western Models, Indian Women: The Legacy of Foreign Aid." In

*Bridging Worlds: Studies on Women in South Asia,* edited by Sally J. M. Sutherland, 225–39. Berkeley and Los Angeles: Univ. of California Press, 1991.

Singerman, Diane. *Avenues of Participation: Family, Politics, and Networks in Urban Quarters of Cairo.* Princeton, N.J.: Princeton Univ. Press, 1955.

Slyomovics, Susan. "Hasiba Ben Bouali, If You Could See Our Algeria: Women and Public Space in Algeria," *Middle East Report* 192 (Jan.–Feb. 1995): 8–13.

Smith, Jane I., and Yvonne Y. Haddad. "Eve: Islamic Image of Women." In *Women and Islam,* edited by al-Hibri. Special issue of *Women's Studies International Forum,* vol. 5, no. 2 (1982): 135–44.

Spark, Muriel. *Loitering with Intent.* New York: Coward, McCann and Geoghegan, 1981.

Stewart, Philip J. *Unfolding Islam.* Reading, United Kingdom: Ithaca Press, 1994.

"Sudan's Capital Bans Mixing of Sexes in Public," *New York Times,* 27 Oct. 1996: 6.

"Sudan Defends Sexual Segregation Laws," United Press International, 24 Oct. 1996.

Taraki, Liza. "The Development of Political Consciousness among Palestinians in the Occupied Territories, 1967–1987." In *Intifada, Palestine at the Crossroads,* edited by Jamal R. Nassar and Roger Heacock, 53–71. New York: Praeger, 1990.

*Tasks of Women in Industry.* Beirut: Institute for Women's Studies in the Arab World, 1985.

Yuval-Davis, Nira, and Foya Anthias, eds. *Woman, Nation, State.* London: Macmillan, 1989.

Women Living Under Muslim Laws (WLUML), *Dossier 1,* Feb. 1986.

———. *Dossier 2,* Apr., 1986.

———. *Dossier 3,* July 1988.

———. *Plan of Action,* unpublished document, Aramon, 1986.

———. *Women and Law Country Project,* Shirkatgah, Lahore, 1992.

———. *Women Laws Initiatives in the Muslim World,* Shirkatgah, Lahore, 1995.

Zipes, Jack D. *Arabian Nights.* New York: Signet Classic, 1991.

## United Nations Documents

*Beijing Declaration and the Platform for Action: Action for Equality, Development and Peace.* Advance Unedited Draft. Geneva: United Nations, Department of Public Information, 1995.

*Convention on the Elimination of All Forms of Discrimination Against Women (CEDAW).* New York: United Nations, Department of Public Information, 1993.

*Covenant for the New Millenium: The Beijing Declaration and Platform for Action.* Santa Rosa: Free Hands Books, 1996.

*Declaration of the Elimination of Violence Against Women.* Vienna, 1993.

*From Nairobi to Beijing: Second Review and Appraisal of the Implementation of the*

*Nairobi Forward-Looking Strategies for the Advancement of Women.* Report of the secretary-general. New York: United Nations, 1995.

*Human Development Report 1995.* New York: Oxford Univ. Press for the United Nations Development Programme, 1995.

*Human Development Report 1996.* New York: Oxford Univ. Press for the United Nations Development Programme, 1996.

*International Covenant on Civil and Political Rights.* New York: United Nations Office of Public Information, 1966.

*International Covenant on Economic, Social and Cultural Rights.* New York: United Nations Office of Public Information, 1966.

*Report of the Fourth World Conference on Women.* New York: United Nations, 1995.

*Universal Declaration of Human Rights.* N.p.: United Nations Department of Public Information, 1948.

*Vienna Declaration and Programme of Action.* New York: United Nations, 1993.

*Women: Looking Beyond 2000.* New York: United Nations, 1995. *World's Women, 1995: Trends and Statistics.* New York: United Nations, 1995.

# Index

Abdel Razik, Mostafa, 134
Abduh, Muhammad, 13, 134
Abu Dhabi, 142
Abu Nasr, Julinda, 103, 105
Abu Zaid, Nasr Hamid, 33–34, 35, 36, 169nn. 16, 17
Academic research, 98–99
Action Committee of Women Living under Muslim Laws, 142
Adam (Biblical character), 49, 52
'Adl (justice), 44, 53, 57
Advocacy, 92
Affirmative action, 132. *See also* Quotas
al-Afghani, Jamal ad-Din, 13
Afghanistan, 9, 29, 37–38, 159
Africa, 11, 36, 134, 135–36. *See also* North Africa
Agarwal, Bina, 4
Aisha (wife of Muhammad), 55, 88
Algeria, xvii; fundamentalist Islam in, 14, 15, 81; human rights violations in, 142; personal status code in, xviii–xix, 16–17, 72–73; structural adjustment in, 149
Algerian Constitution, 15, 166n. 2
Algerian Council of Ministers, 78
Algerian Family Code (Qanun al-usra), 15, 74, 78–79, 81
Algerian National Assembly, 15
Ali Pasha, Mohamed, 134
American University of Beirut, 102, 174n. 9b
Amin, Kassem, 134
Amnesty International (organization), xix, xx, 124–25
Androcracy. *See* Patriarchy
Ansar women, 55

Arab countries: cultural differences among, 137; *HDR* on, 158; IWSAW and, 106, 108; MB and, 168n. 19; national machineries in, 159; socioeconomic progress in, 103
Arabic language, 47, 97
Arab-Islamic Renaissance, 13, 17
Arabism, 166n. 8
Arab League, 161
Arab Regional Conference (1996), 161
Arab women: Badre on, 103; at Beijing conference, 159; *HDR* on, 158; IWSAW and, 101, 102, 105, 108; scholarly, 107; Western professionals and, 104
Arranged marriages, 75
Asia: al-Azhar graduates in, 134; Beijing conference and, 124; Cairo conference and, x; feminism in, 20; national machineries in, 131; Shari'a in, 135; veiling in, 143. *See also* South Asia; Western Asia
Asian-Pacific Resource Centre for Women, 90
Asian Women's Institute, 103
Astin, Helen S., 84, 87
Atheism, 14
Austen, Jane, 59
Awakening movement, 13–14, 17
al-Azhar al-Sharif, 26; female graduates of, 50; FGM and, 36; reformist ideology at, 134; scriptural compilation by, 136; state control of, 168n. 21

al-Baahithat (Women Researchers), 107
Badran, Margot, 55